Charles Williams. (Line drawing by Anne Spalding; reproduced by permission.)

The Pattern in the Web
The Mythical Poetry of Charles Williams

Roma A. King, Jr.

The Kent State University Press
Kent, Ohio, and London, England

© 1990 by The Kent State University Press, Kent, Ohio 44242
Library of Congress Catalog Card Number 90–33588
ISBN 0–87338–412–1
Manufactured in the United States of America

Library of Congress Cataloging-in-Publication Data

King, Roma A. (Roma Alvah), 1914–
    The pattern in the web : the mythical poetry of Charles Williams /
Roma A. King, Jr.
        p.   cm.
    Includes bibliographical references.
    ISBN 0–87338–412–1 (alk. paper) ∞
    1. Williams, Charles, 1886–1945 – Knowledge – Folklore, mythology.
2. Williams, Charles, 1886–1945. Region of the summer stars.
3. Williams, Charles, 1886–1945. Taliessin through Logres.
4. Arthurian romances – Adaptations – History and criticism. 5. Myth
in literature. I. Title.
PR6045.I5Z8   1990
821′.912 – dc20   90–33588
                                                                    CIP

British Library Cataloging-in-Publication data are available

To Thelma Shuttleworth

Till death,
and so long as the whole creation has any being,
the derivation is certain, and the doom accomplished.

—"The Queen's Servant," 123–25

Contents

Acknowledgments

I am indebted to a number of institutions and many individuals for assistance in researching and preparing this manuscript for publication. To the staff of the Marion E. Wade Center, Wheaton College—the late former curator, Clyde S. Kilby; the present director, Lyle W. Dorsett; and the associate director, Marjorie Lamp Mead—I am grateful for both personal assistance and for the privilege of researching their vast resource of materials. They have graciously granted permission for me to quote information essential to this study, and have honored me with the Clyde S. Kilby Award. I owe thanks also to the British Library, London, and to the Harry Ransom Research Center at the University of Texas at Austin. I have received encouragement from the members of the Charles Williams Society, London, who have generously shared with me their remembrances of C. W. and their insights into his poetry. I am grateful to the society and especially to Molly Switek for permission to quote from *The Charles Williams Society Newsletter.*

I was first introduced to works of Charles Williams many years ago when I was a graduate student at the University of Michigan by the Reverend Robert Whitaker, who was then on the staff of St. Andrew's Church, Ann Arbor, and chaplain and director of the Canterbury House on the campus. The enthusiasm sparked by that initial introduction has persisted and culminates now some thirty years later in the present study.

I want to express special thanks to Thelma Shuttleworth whose contribution to this work would be hard to estimate. I remember how her eyes lighted up and her voice became vibrant with excitement when I told her I was writing a book about C. W.'s poetry. Before we parted we had discovered a commonality of interests and enthusiasm that made us old, old friends. Since that day we have exchanged many words, personally and by correspondence, on matters of which this book is composed. Her deep love for Williams, her belief in his poetry, and her keen critical sense have made her an invaluable critic. She has generously given information that I could have obtained from no other source. She has read the manuscript, and, in addition to many suggestions that she made to me personally, I have a file of letters from her that contain some of the best criticism that any writer could hope to have. I am deeply in her debt.

Joe McClatchey, Wheaton College, also read the manuscript and was the source of much valuable help and encouragement.

Robert A. Gilbert of Bristol, England, an authority on the life and work of A. E. Waite, with generosity admirable in a scholar, provided materials on Williams's relation with Waite and the Golden Dawn Society, which at the time remained unpublished. Anne Spalding and Anne Ridler, both of Oxford, provided information, and Miss Spalding graciously granted permission for me to reproduce her line drawing of Williams for the frontispiece of this volume. Preston and Susan Wiles in a sense launched the actual writing of this book by organizing a little group of readers who met regularly at their home in Dallas for a period of time to read and discuss the Taliessin poems. It was during those sessions that I decided the time had at last come to write this work. To them, my affectionate thanks.

Gerald Near, Dixon and Betsy Wiles, Russell and Frances Smith, and the Reverend Canon Uriel Osnaya provided technical assistance that made my task much easier and my compositional frustrations fewer. To them a most enthusiastic thanks!

Lucille King, my wife, who shares my love for Williams, and Betty Wells, my friend, both read the manuscript and saved me from embarrassing errors.

I am grateful to David Higham Associates for permitting me on behalf of Michael Williams (to whom I owe other thanks) to quote from both published and unpublished works of Charles Williams.

I gratefully acknowledge my indebtedness to the following publishing houses:

Oxford University Press for quotations from *The Image of the City and Other Essays,* edited and with an Introduction by Anne Ridler, for quotations from *Defending Ancient Springs* by Kathleen Raine.

Harcourt Brace Jovanovich and Faber and Faber for a quotation from *Selected Essays, 1917–1932* by T. S. Eliot.

Farrar, Straus and Giroux and Faber and Faber for a quotation from *On Poetry and Poets* by T. S. Eliot.

Bookmakers Guild, Inc. for permission to quote from an article printed in *VII: An Anglo-American Literary Review,* vol. 2, 1981.

I express special thanks to the Right Reverend John M. Krumm and the Episcopal Diocese of Southern Ohio for a generous grant of money that made it possible for me to do research in England for a period of time.

Introduction
Patterns in the Web

M y purpose in this book is to examine critically the poetry of Charles Williams and the claims it makes on us as a significant literary achievement. My primary interest is in the poetry as poetry. I will focus on *Taliessin through Logres* and *The Region of the Summer Stars* as representing the culmination of Williams's achievement both intellectually and artistically. I shall necessarily refer to other works: the early poetry, particularly that treating the Arthurian myth; the fiction; and the prose, particularly the literary and theological works that illuminate my concerns. My conviction, however, is that the two volumes under discussion are for the most part self-contained, the poetic creation of a coherent mythical vision of man and his place in the larger creation of which he is part. This is not to deny that the individual poems are complex and have relevancies outside their restricted limits. Complexity and a certain difficulty are the nature of all good poetry. Robert Browning, in response to critics who charged that his poetry was obscure, said that he never intended his poems to serve as a substitute for an after-dinner cigar. Nor did Williams. There is a difference, however, between difficulty and obscurity. Williams's aim was certainly to include in his two major works, if not in each poem separately, all that was necessary to their being understood by a perceptive and patient reader. He wrote:

> It has sometimes been said that it is necessary to know Malory's *Morte D'Arthur* in order to follow Taliessin. I very much hope that this is not so, both because I should think it improper in principle for any poet to require from his readers the knowledge of another work and also because the chance of any interest in *Taliessin* would thereby be considerably decreased. (Essays 179)

The inner dust jacket for the first edition of *Taliessin through Logres* carries a statement of which, according to Anne Ridler, Williams wrote the first draft that serves as the perspective from which I approach these poems. It reads:

1

These poems are the product of Mr. Williams's maturity. The progress which he has been following through his prose and verse up to "Cranmer," "Seed of Adam," and "He Came Down From Heaven" is in these new poems at once summed up and mapped out ahead. The matter and the style require and reward attention. The poems do not so much tell a story or describe a process as express states or principles of experience. The names and incidents of the Arthurian myth are taken as starting-points for investigation and statement on common and profound experience. Different poems are thus applicable in each man as occasion arises. They need to be all read before any individual one is pronounced obscure, and it is unlikely that to the widening public who read and study Mr. Williams's other work any of these poems will remain finally obscure. (lxiv)

Myth, not theology, provides the initial context of *Taliessin through Logres* and *The Region of the Summer Stars*. For Williams, myth is not a fictional tale but a serious intuitively apprehended pattern of cosmic relationships imaginatively embodied in a structure that points beyond itself to an illuminating reality about the nature of man and his place in the cosmos. The myth itself is universal and constant; its structures, diverse and evolving. Myth arises from what Carl Jung called "an *a priori* factor in all human activity, namely the inborn, preconscious and unconscious structure of the psyche" (11). Man's behavior, delineated in myth, Jung continues, "results from patterns of functioning" that he calls "images," images that are primordial in that they are peculiar to the whole species, and, if they ever "originated," their origin must have coincided at least in part with the beginning of the species. They are the "'human qualities' of the human being, the specifically human form his activities take" (12). Man carries within himself his unconscious, the prototype of which myths are the conscious expression, each shaped in its outward form by the internal diagram of which the outer is an attempted map. Myth, then, is rooted in the universal psyche, and the specific form that it takes varies among diverse cultures. Kathleen Raine has written:

> Myth is more than a mere element in events; above all it is the context of events. In the absence of myth, events have no context, and poetry becomes a thing of parts, not wholes. One might, on another level, define myth as symbol in movement and transformation, for myths are essentially, like dreams, dynamic; they express transformation and metamorphosis; they express processes, progressions of the imaginative life. (133)

The important words in this statement are *context, movement, transformation, metamorphosis, processes, progressions*. They suggest the dynamics of the imaginative life as a continuous activity of creating images of the ultimately imageless.

Joseph Campbell, a humanist, further defines the origin and scope of myth by saying that when we consider the human species from a psychological rather than a physical point of view we discover that its distinguishing characteristic is to order life according to the mythic. He identifies three prevailing themes found in all great myths: "the recognition of mortality and the requirement to transcend it"; confrontation of the individual with "the necessity to adapt himself to whatever order of life may happen to be that of the community into which he has been born"; and an awareness of the universe and the "enigma of its relation to his own existence: its magnitude, its changing forms, and yet, through these, an appearance of regularity" (16–17). Neither a Jungian nor a secularist, Williams was, nevertheless, a great mythmaker, and he would have understood what Jung and Campbell were saying. His materials are that body of literature called the "matter of Britain," the story of King Athur and the Holy Grail. His orientation is Christian, but all the elements outlined by Campbell are present as major themes in his poetry. The Taliessin poems reveal their full richness only when they are approached as myth. In the poems, as they evolve, myth takes precedence over theology. Williams responds to all myths and to the universally recurring images in which they are embodied. He saw all as part of one web emanating from a common center, each filament distinct and yet each fully itself only in relation to the whole–an effort to image the imageless that the insatiable spirit of man continues to pursue. Of the earlier chapters of the Old Testament, for example, he wrote:

> It may be said, roughly, that certain patterns in the web are already discernible: the recognition of the good, everywhere and always, as good, the reflection of power, the exercise of intellect, the importance of interchange, and a deliberate relation to the Centre. (*HCD* 39)

The word *patterns* occurs repeatedly in Williams's writing and signifies essentially that which Jung meant when he spoke of "patterns of function." Williams found patterns not only in the Judeo-Christian tradition but in seemingly alien myths (Greek, Roman, Egyptian, Celtic, occult) that he considered different modes of the one archetypal Myth from which all, in some degree, emanated, and to which all aspired to return. His thinking is inclusive and synthesizing. He lauded Voltaire, for example, for having courageously written "across the brain of Christendom: *'Ecrasez l'Infame'*"; yet he also says:

> Voltaire seems actually to have thought on a low level; he did suppose that the fact that there were a thousand reputed Saviours of the world proved that there was no Saviour of the world, and that the different circumstances and natures of many mothers of many gods disproved the Virginity of the Mother of God. We know that neither affirmation nor denial are as simple as that. (*DD* 202)

In short, Williams complains that Voltaire, great as he was, nevertheless was captive of his age, an eighteenth-century rationalist to whom all myth was either a vestige of an unenlightened past or the deliberate perpetuation of a pious fraud. His criticism is aimed primarily at Voltaire's manner of thinking, which led him to a false conclusion.

In turning to the matter of Britain, Williams took as his subject more than a narrative account of a series of events, a chronicle that would stand or fall on its historical accuracy. He embraced a mythic vision of man and of his relationships to ultimate reality. Clyde Kilby recalls that Jung speaks of "the slender threads of the knowable" and the need to find mythic means of bringing those hints together in some meaningful pattern. He writes:

> Systemizing drives essentiality away, but successful creativity attracts it. While the basic requirement of systemizing is abstraction, myth is concerned not with parts but with wholes. Myth is necessary because reality is so much larger than rationality (not that myth is irrational but that it easily accommodates the rational while rising above it). (28)

He quotes R. J. Reilly who, in a review of Owen Barfield's *Orpheus,* wrote that the drama

> proceeds on the assumption that myth is an imaginative depiction of meaning, not by a single mind but rather by the imagination of a race . . . the imagination of man brooding on the world, dreaming of events and relationships occurring between the natural and the supernatural, between the human and the divine, when meaning may only crudely be reduced to rational statement. (28–29)

There is in all myth something that does not depend on the factual accuracy of its images, the events or relationships, but rather accepts the images as pointers beyond the literal meaning to the imageless of which they are cyphers. Williams offers the great Jewish myths of the Creation and the Fall as examples. He is dogmatic only as a poet, demanding always that his myth be true not in any narrow literal sense, but that it be consistent with experience, self-contained, poetically coherent, that all the images be related intellectually, emotionally, and sensuously about a center, that, in short, it have organic unity. He said of the ancient shapers of the Arthurian myth that they did not have to be especially pious; they had only to be good poets capable of developing and relating important images. The Sacred Spear, the Dolorous Blow, the Holy Grail, the three hierarchical Lords came in time, he said, to be identified with the Body of Christ and thus to become "a part of the tale." At first, he writes,

> It is not . . . much more; there are hardly any theological attributions. But poetically there is now a union and a centre – not so much a Christian centre as an artistic. From this poetic point of view, the whole development of the myth is a kind of working out of a theme which is eventually discovered to be the Christian theme. (FA 66–67)

Precisely for this reason, Williams considered the discovery of Galahad as the artistic center of the myth one of the greatest triumphs of the imagination in all literature.

There is in the cycle a sense of that dynamic process of working out and discovery. Williams's perspective is Christian, but the reader is never made to feel that the development of the myth is controlled by an externally imposed system of thought, rather that the system emerges naturally and inevitably from the life of the myth itself. The myth comes first, and the theology is subsequently "discovered." Thus the poems live, claiming our attention more as imaginative patterns of reality than as theological argument. The term *religious poetry* is in a real sense misleading. There is only poetry, Williams argues, some of which takes the religious experience as its subject:

> Poetry, one way or another, is "about" human experience; there is nothing else that it can be about. But to whatever particular human experience it alludes, it is not that experience. Love poetry is poetry, not love; patriotic poetry is poetry, not patriotism; religious poetry is poetry, not religion. But good poetry does something more than allude to its subject; it is related to it, and it relates us to it. (*EPM* 3)

Poetry corresponds with the experience in its own way, however. Imaginative, not rational, it brings disparate facts together in a whole that is greater than the sum of its parts, by a process beyond rationalization. "For what poetry says *is* the poetry," Williams writes. He continues:

> It is not and cannot be concerned with anything but itself. Nor shall we, reading those lines, expect this poetry to fulfill its own desire after any style

but its own. We shall not expect intellectual justification – though our intellects must not be offended. Nor moral, though whatever scheme of morality be implied, whether our own or not, must be of a high and enduring sort. We shall, in fact, require only . . . that the poem shall justify itself. (*EPM* 117–18)

If, then, the purpose of poetry is not to make us more religious, or more patriotic, or more rational, or more whatever, how can it be said to relate meaningfully to experience? Poetry does, indeed, tell us something, since, as Williams admitted, in this life, given what man is, something must be said. The significance of poetry, however, lies in something more than the mere saying. In the presence of great poetry, he writes,

We are told of a thing; we are made to feel as if that thing were possible to us; and we are so made to feel it – whatever the thing may be . . . [and] that our knowledge is an intense satisfaction to us; and this knowledge and this satisfaction are for some period of time complete and final; . . . [and this] through the medium of words, the concord of which is itself a delight to the senses. (*EPM* 3)

That statement assumes man's insatiable capacity for all kinds of experience and his delight in knowing them in concord – that is, intellectually, emotionally, and sensuously, as experience or possible experience rather than as detached historical fact or abstract thought. How specifically, then, does poetry treating a religious subject, as the Taliessin poems do, relate us to the experience? In this way. It can, in the hands of a master, make us feel at least temporarily that such an experience is possible for us (though it may not be) and feel it so pervasively that the knowledge is satisfying and seemingly complete and final, capable of making us suspend disbelief and enter into the world that the poet has created. There must be something in all good poetry treating religious experience that transcends narrow sectarian bounds. The capacity to increase our imaginative range, to relate ourselves actually or potentially to new experiences, justifies poetry regardless of its subject because, as Williams remarks, "The chief business of man is at any moment to be realizing his powers of intellectual apprehension – to understand, to the utmost of his capacity, things as they are" (*Beatrice* 91). Things as they *are*. Whether Williams is talking about poetry or religion, accuracy is the prime requirement. Hell, he says, is inaccuracy. So are all man's frustrations. Adam's inaccurate relation to the Center was his fall. There are, of course, degrees approaching accuracy. Williams accepted all myths as images of "the inborn, preconscious and unconscious structure of the human psyche," of the brooding of the universal mind on the mystery of human existence and of man's destiny. A sense of transcendent mystery, the recognition of a coherent pattern in creation, the feeling in man of alienation and the need for reconciliation with the whole are in some form and to some degree recurring themes in all myth. All are inspired attempts, to use Williams's words, "to measure the angle of creation" and to discover the mystic "diagram of glory." The word *measure* is important in Williams's vocabulary. It denotes, above all, accuracy. Williams wrote to Raymond Hunt on 1 March 1940:

> I dimly remember once thinking that the interrelation of words did in some sense measure the poets, and now I think it might be related to the Co-inherence; the measure of the Co-inherence in us is the measure of us–in Christ or in others; that of course, in Christ either way. So that our lives are wholly measured when they wholly co-inhere; they are wholly known when they wholly co-inhere. (Hunt)

So might we say of myths. Each is valid to the extent that it touches accurately upon those intuited patterns of reality and to the degree that it embodies them in an imaginative structure that is compelling. That does not mean that Williams is a relativist and considers all myths equally meaningful. He thought some more comprehensive than others, and, therefore, more nearly universal, a better representation of the eternal diagram that all myths attempt to map. Indeed, he claimed for the Christian version the consummation, the distillation of truth so far as man is capable of receiving it. His achievement as a poet, however, rests not on his theological beliefs but on his ability to illuminate the web and so to relate all the connecting images of which it is composed to communicate a sense of wholeness and to make us feel "as if that thing were possible to us and . . . to feel . . . that this knowledge, satisfaction, and finality are all conveyed through the medium of words, the concord of which is itself a delight to the senses" (*EPM* 3). T. S. Eliot spoke to the same point when he wrote: "For it is ultimately the function of art, in imposing a credible order upon ordinary reality, and thereby eliciting some perception of an order *in* reality, to bring us to a condition of serenity, stillness, and reconciliation; and then leave us, as Virgil left Dante, to proceed toward a region where that guide can avail us no farther" (*On Poetry and Poets* 87).

The context and major thrust of Williams's mature poetry, then, is mythic. The structure, it might seem, if it were to follow traditional patterns, would be traditionally classical narrative epic. Williams's initial intention, indeed, was to write an epic, according to Anne Ridler, a plan that, however, he abandoned early (lx). In the 1920s, he composed over fifty short poems on Arthurian subjects of which a number were published in *Three Plays* (1931), *Heroes and Kings* (1939), and in an anthology edited by Lascelles Abercrombie, *New English Poetry*. Ridler, who has brilliantly traced the transformation of the projected epic into the cycle we have, writes of these:

> There are some successful things, in the old pastiche style. . . . The poems are diffuse, and make free use of exclamations to eke out the rhythm; the reader is inclined to echo the words of Kenneth Mornington in *War in Heaven:* "a little minor, but rather beautiful. . . . Better be modern than minor." So Williams himself came to think, and he began experimenting with new versions of some of the poems. (lx)

These early poems are interesting as illustrations of Williams's transition from his early to his later style. They are not, however, sufficiently significant to assure his literary reputation. None is essential to an understanding and appreciation of the cycle as it eventually emerged. Into two mature volumes Williams put all of value that he had at the time to say about the Arthurian myth. I maintain that *Taliessin through Logres* is complete in itself and that it, with *The Region of the Summer Stars,* rounds out the myth as he conceived it. More poems might have enriched the mythic pattern but would not have expanded it essentially. We do know that he considered *The Region of the Summer Stars* a work in progress toward a volume to be called *Jupiter Over Carbonek*. Moreover, in a letter to Raymond Hunt he speaks of a possible third volume whose subject Williams vaguely defines as the grail, but this projection remains a shadowy possibility, and never, I believe, even in Williams's own mind, was it a real probability (Wade Collection). What we have composes an imaginative working out of a consistent myth in a memorable structure.

What motivated Williams to think that he had to become modern? It was clearly no desire to be faddish, for no other twentieth-century writer remained more aloof from the merely trendy. It was, I think, his increasing compulsion as an artist to be accurate and a growing feeling that, if he were to be honest within the limits of his own inescapably modern sensibility, he had to cultivate a poetic structure appropriate to the vision he wished to communicate. His concerns, I think, were less to be contemporary in a narrow exclusive sense than to utilize available sources to get beyond all periods to that which is continuous in the human spirit. He wished to be prisoner of neither past nor present. We might go so far as to call Williams a reluctant modern and say of him what Eliot said of all poets in his essay on Baudelaire: "If he is sincere, he must express with individual differences the general state of mind—not as a *duty,* but simply because he cannot help participating in it" (Eliot, *Essays* 340). His early poetry was derivative, full of Shakespearian and Miltonic echoes that even to him must have begun to sound a bit off-key. In a commonplace book that he kept during the 1920s for notes on the Arthurian myth and his projected epic, we find, for example, this questioning statement:

> the "romantic," meaning the use of all sorts of common things and words for images and expressions—as distinguished from the classical remoteness of, say, Milton. It would be possible to mould this to what restraint or swiftness or lucidity was desired. The very stuff of mingled light and darkness should show in the poem . . . ? Is this what Dante did. Cf. also the A. V. ". . . ? Abercrombie's suggestion (*The Epic*) of great Odes." And: "The whole point of plainsong is to decorate the unimportant syllables." ?is this a principle of Art? . . . ? Turn into "Never decorate except in unimportant parts." (Ridler lix)

The reference to Abercrombie's *The Epic* is especially suggestive. In that book, Abercrombie expressed the need for a modern poetic form that would "give us immense and shapely symbols of the spirit of man, conscious not only of the sense of his own destined being, but also some sense of that which destines" (94). Such had been the aim of the classical epic. Abercrombie was skeptical, however, that the old structures were adequate to the task in the twentieth century. He wrote:

> If we are to have, as we must have, direct symbolism of the way man is conscious of his being nowadays, . . . it is hard to see how any story can be adequate to such symbolic requirements, unless it is a story which moves in some large region of imagined supernaturalism. And it seems questionable whether we have enough *formal* "belief" nowadays to allow of such a story appearing as solid and as vividly credible as epic poetry needs. (93)

Beginning with the romantic movement in the late eighteenth century, Western man underwent a radical shift of sensibility: a loss of "formal belief" in an order of values imposed from without and a conviction that he possessed the inner power to shape his own values and the responsibility of imposing them on an otherwise meaningless existence. In the arts, specifically, it has meant (to use M. H. Abrams's image) that art is no longer considered a mirror reflecting values but rather a lamp, illumination from within, that imposes values on the external world. The transition is from an objective to a subjective point of view.

After Milton, Abercrombie held, nothing more could be done with the so-called objective myth. In such works as Goethe's *Faust* and Hardy's *The Dynasts,* however, he saw a new potentially epic form, more episodic than narrative, which he called subjective. It might seem initially to have its origins from within a character but, upon closer observation, would be seen to expand quickly as a result of the character's consciousness of himself as being an interrelated, interdependent part of a larger pattern to embrace the whole of creation, not only the destined but that which destines. The movement would, nevertheless, be from within and therefore subjective rather than objective.

Williams himself experienced the difficulty of belief for contemporary man. Indeed, he might have been describing himself when he characterized Kierkegaard as "a realist and unbeliever–both in this world and in the other; and his life of skepticism was rooted in God" (*DD* 213). He distinguished between the medieval and the modern mind, saying that the former assumed that it had both the questions and the answers and found its excitement in pointing out how an opponent's argument, if prolonged, would lead to a denial of the correct answer; the latter, in contrast, has the questions but not the answers until it discovers them, if it does, and even then it has no way of checking them. He was sufficiently imbued with the modern sensibility to write sympathetically of what he called the "quality of disbelief" of which he said:

> It is entirely accurate; it comes straight from the Creed. It covers all the doctrines. It is entirely consistent with sanctity. Yet undoubtedly it also involves as much disbelief as possible; it allows for, it encourages, the sense of agnosticism and the possibility of error. It hints ambiguity–nicely balancing belief and disbelief, qualifying each by the other, and allowing belief only its necessary right proportion of decisiveness. (*DD* 190)

Williams pursues one possible path for the modern mind, although perhaps not that most often associated with contemporary thought.

What, then, did Abercrombie propose that caught Williams's attention? In a pluralistic society in which there is no single system of belief, the general purpose of the epic is to abandon a structure that is in itself symbolic of a rationality and a kind of unity incompatible with contemporary diversity and skepticism and resort to a "sequence of odes expressing in the image of some fortunate and lofty mind, as much of the spiritual significance which the epic purpose must continue from Milton, *as is possible . . . for subjective symbolism*" (95–96; my emphasis).

Williams, who was sympathetic to the aims of the epic, indeed wished to project a vision of a unified and meaningful cosmos from which the individual derives meaning. It was a vision more imaginative than rational, closer in structure to the myth than to dogmatic argument, more modern than classical or medieval, more readily expressed through the episodic short poem than sequential narrative. "The whole content of a long series of poems," he writes,

> may not be clear at once, nor indeed can be. But enough is clear to purify the rash tendency to take *anything;* . . . it is necessary to what Shakespeare in the *Dream* referred to as the growth of "something of great constancy." I have observed that to be true which I had before suspected – that, in any such series, the Images have continually to be re-imagined; everything is given and yet nothing is permanently given. The poet who, in his own mind, mistakes his own word for the thing imagined is lost. (Essays 182–83)

Williams wanted to recover the scope of the myth that Malory, he felt, had intuited in outline but failed fully to develop and that subsequent writers, particularly the Victorians, had grossly misconstrued. "It was clear," he wrote, "that the great and awful myth of the Grail had not been treated adequately in English verse" (Essays 180). The failure was to be explained, he said, not "by dragging in religion," but by saying that "none of these poets had the full capacity of the mythical imagination" (Essays 187). He came to feel that his culminating poetic work demanded that "full capacity of the mythical imagination" and a corresponding structure, tentative, fluid, associational rather than rational, appealing to the intuitive and imaginative rather than the merely logical. The result is a cycle of shorter poems of which in each "everything is given and yet nothing is permanently given"; of which each is in its limited way a complete and functioning whole and yet dependent for its ultimate meaning upon a larger pattern of which it is part. The result for the reader is a sense of dynamic search and discovery that opens upon a continually widening and ultimately comprehensive vista.

In an essay on William Butler Yeats, Williams said that, prior to the publication of Yeats's poetry, English literature drew upon three great traditions: Greek, Norse, and Christian. To those, he said, Yeats added the Celtic. Williams contributed another, I think, which requires some explanation. He took a body of materials generally considered of doubtful respectability and an unlikely subject for serious poetry and made it an important part of his writing. I refer to what he loosely called the "occult." It embraces a wide range of arcane knowledge and practice, including, for example, astrology, alchemy, divination, conjuration, theosophy, Cabalism, the Sephirotic Tree, and the tarot cards. Although they can hardly be said to form a myth, these practices certainly contain much material that is mythic. What, we ask, was his interest in the occult and in what ways did he consider its use organic to his poetic purpose? That interest was serious and continuing; it cannot be ignored. From 1917 to 1927 or 1928 Williams was an active member of the Fellowship of the Rosy Cross, the mystical order founded by A. E. Waite, poet, metaphysician, and mystic. This order, always referred to by Williams, according to Anne Ridler, as the Golden Dawn, had its roots in Theosophical, Rosicrucian, and Masonic traditions. Waite called his group Christian and stressed mysticism rather than magic, thus distinguishing it from other similar groups then active in London. Williams was first attracted to Waite as early perhaps as 1915 when he read his book *The Hidden Church of the Holy Grail.* In his enthusiasm, particularly for Waite's treatment of the grail myth, Williams wrote Waite and received in return an invitation to visit him in his home in Ealing. Thus began an association that was to continue for several years. Waite and his order undoubtedly influenced Williams at a crucial stage in his poetic development, an influence that continued beyond the years of their personal association.

We can now speak with certainty about Williams's association with Waite and of his branch of the Golden Dawn. Robert Gilbert of Bristol, England, has recently come into possession of invaluable materials including minutes of the meetings of the order and a diary that Waite kept during the years of his active acquaintance with Williams. The diary shows that on several occasions between 1915 and 1927 Williams visited Waite. One such visit came on 23 October 1917, just before he was initiated into the order as a neophyte. That he took membership seriously cannot be questioned. He attended meetings regularly, conscientiously mastered the readings, participated in the rituals, proceeded through various grades of membership, and becoming finally a member of the Outer Order, the highest achievement possible. More than once he held high office. According to the minutes, Williams attended his last meeting in June 1927. His only other recorded contact with Waite came on 26 September 1928 when Waite, according to his diary, called on him in his office in Amen House. What occurred at that meeting we do not know, but apparently it terminated Williams's active association with Waite and the Golden Dawn, although both remained influences on his subsequent writing (Gilbert 147–48).

What attracted Williams to the Golden Dawn and, for a period of ten years, absorbed much of his thought and time? That he did not put the same credence in magic and occultism as did his contemporaries MacGregor Matthews, Aleister Crowley, or even William Butler Yeats (all members of a different branch of the order) is apparent. He clearly expressed his own views in an essay "The Index of the Body," written in 1942, years after he left the order. What he says in that essay about astrology is equally applicable to all other aspects of the occult to which he was attracted:

> The word "occult" has come into general use, and is convenient, if no moral sense is given it simply as itself. It deals with hidden things, and their investigation. But in this case we are concerned not so much with the pretended operations of those occult schools as with a certain imagination of relation in the universe, and that only to pass beyond it. The signs of the Zodiac were, according to some students, related to the parts of the physical body. The particular attributions varied, and all were in many respects arbitrary. But some of them were extremely suggestive; they may be allowed at least a kind of authentic poetic vision. (Essays 83)

The most suggestive phrases here are "a certain imagination of relation in the universe" and "a kind of authentic poetic vision." Occultism is the continuing search for a hidden spiritual world that Williams considered equally as important as the visible. Its basic premise is that God created both man and the cosmos to co-inhere around a single Center, forming an interrelated, interdependent web, a tradition expressed in the often repeated dictum "As above; so below." The concept found expression among the Theosophists as the doctrine of correspondence, which perhaps dates back to Cornelius Agrippa, who held that all terrestial things owe their power to a celestial pattern and that by a proper understanding of their correspondence one could use the earthly images to induce spiritual powers. The theme of the coherent universe is found alike in Greek, Norse, and Celtic myth, in Jewish mysticism, Moslem monotheism, and in Christianity.

Clearly, Williams was not attracted by the magical rites in themselves, by what he calls "the pretended operations of those occult schools," but by the vision of unity they affirm. That vision, in each case, he maintained, was the expression of a spiritual reality inherent in the universal psyche and a mirror, in varying degrees of accuracy and completeness, of things as they really are. "The predisposition towards the idea of magic," he wrote,

> might be said to begin with a moment which seems to be of fairly common experience—the moment when it seems that anything might turn into anything else. . . . A room, a street, a field, becomes unsure. The edge of a possibility of utter alteration intrudes. A door, untouched, might close; a picture might walk; a tree might speak; an animal might not be an animal; a man might not be a man. One may be with a friend, and a terror will take one even while his admirable voice is speaking; one will be with a lover and the hand will become a different and terrifying thing, moving in one's own like a malicious intruder, too real for anything but

fear. All this may be due to racial memories or to any other cause; the point is that it exists. It exists and can be communicated; it can even be shared. There is, in our human centre, a heart-gripping fear of irrational change, of perilous and malevolent change.

Secondly, there is the human body, and the movements of the human body. Even now, when, as a general rule, the human body is not supposed to mean anything, there are moments when it seems, in spite of ourselves, packed with significance. This sensation is almost exactly the opposite of the last. There, one was aware that any phenomenon might alter into another and truer self. Here, one is aware that a phenomenon, being wholly itself, is laden with universal meaning. (*Witchcraft* 77–78)

For Williams, then, the occult was part of the data with which the poet, "the imagination of this world," worked. He recognized the authenticity of the occultist's poetic vision and of the evocative power of his images but, at the same time, was aware of a danger. The vision could be perverted and the images distorted if they were seen not as reflectors of a higher spiritual power but as instruments in themselves to create and control. The occultists in his novels—Giles Tumulty, Gregory Persimmons, Considine, Simon— and in his poetry—the Headless Emperor—are symbols of evil. Their prototype is Simon Magus, the nefarious charlatan denounced in the New Testament by Saint Peter. They are black magicians who reenact the defiant act of Adam. In the poems their natural realm is P'o-lu, that nonkingdom situated at the antipodes; they have existential existence but not substantive reality, for they possess no independent being apart from that of which they are shadows. Like the succubus, the male demon in occult lore, they are sterile, lacking power to impregnate. Merlin, the white magician, whose native habitat is Broceliande, the place of making, in contrast, desires neither power to create nor to direct and is content to be the selfless instrument of a power beyond his own.

One aspect of occult lore must be given special attention because of its pervasive influence in shaping Williams's imagination and its continuing presence, directly or indirectly, in the poems. Williams drew heavily upon a strain of mysticism that had its origin in the medieval Jewish community and existed only as oral tradition, a closely guarded secret by the initiate few, until around 1280 when it was written down perhaps by Moses de Leon and came to be known as the Cabala, or, as it is also spelled, Kabbalah. Members of the Order of the Golden Dawn, including Williams, however, drew their information directly from the so-called Christian Cabalists of the sixteenth and seventeenth centuries. Such writers as Pico della Mirandola, Reuchlin, Cornelius Agrippa, and Henry Moore, borrowing from the original sources, adapted its message to conform outwardly at least to their Christian beliefs.

A basic concept of Cabalism consistent with Christian thought is that everything in the cosmos is in constant interplay with everything else and that all things cohere around and are sustained by an irreducible power, the Center. The primary image is the Sephirotic Tree, which presents diagrammatically the interrelations between man, the cosmos, and God. Its suggested dynamics depicts man's spiritual quest for union with the whole of which he is part. Above the Tree, the source of all below, abides the Infinite, the Vast, the hidden and incomprehensible godhead. At the base of the tree lies the region of Malkuth, the material Earth, sometimes called the "Shekinah," representing the divine presence in creation. Malkuth is the feminine counterpart of the male God, the emanation, that went out from him at the time of creation and is now, as it were, an exile from his presence. Malkuth is the tenth of the Sephiroth, or stages of spiritual growth through which man must pass on his spiritual ascent. Those nine form a triad of triads, arranged in a triad of columns. The column on the right, "The Pillar of Mercy," is masculine; that on the left, "The Pillar of Judgment," is feminine. Together they represent the two opposing forces in God, and, consequently, in his creation, the love that creates and the wrath that destroys. The middle pillar, asexual, as is God in his fullest manifestation, represents the balancing and reconciling forces.

Psychologically, the first triad represents the unconscious, or unawakened spirit of man awaiting spiritual ascent into awareness; the second, the conscious, or the highest state of awareness to which man can in a normal state attain. The third represents the superconscious and is separated from the lower two by an abyss that distinguishes between the ideal and the reality, the imageless and the image. It is not necessary to know the intricate details about all the Sephiroth, but some knowledge of the first four will throw light on Williams's poetry. They are Malkuth (earth), Ysod (air), Hod (water), Netzach (fire). Earth is feminine; air is masculine. Ysod, standing just above Malkuth, is also called the funnel or the genitals through which divine energy flows downward impregnating the Earth. Hod, feminine, lies to the left of the tree; Netzach, masculine, lies to the right. Standing in opposition, they represent fragmented and opposing elements of the godhead awaiting reconciliation. As Williams tells us in a note to "The Death of Palomides," the achievement of Netzach marks man's victory over the elements and is the last stage through which he passes into the second triad, the highest state normally available to man. Beyond the abyss between the second and third triad lies union with God, a state of superconsciousness. And, finally, transcending all is the impenetrable mystery, the unknown,

often in mystical circles called the "Nothing" or the "Zero," since "He" possesses no qualities and yet encompasses all qualities, the Supreme Unity of all things past, present, and to come. He is no-thing; the *Ein Sof.* To use Williams's own language, which in this study is pervasive, He is the "simultaneity of time" and the "accumulation of distance."

The Sephirotic Tree is a diagram of man's nature and place in the universe and of his ultimate spiritual destination. For Williams, it, along with other occult elements, was never more than "an authentic poetic vision," "a certain imagination of relation in the universe" – but it was that. He found it a valid source of vivid imagery.

1

The King Stood Crowned

The king stood crowned; around in the gate,
midnight striking, torches and fires
massing the colour, casting the metal,
furnace of jubilee, through time and town,
Logres heraldically flaunted the king's state.
— "The Crowning of Arthur," 1–5

The establishment of the kingdom is the subject of *Taliessin through
Logres*. Although there is a skeletal thread of a story, the poetic sequence is less a retelling of the traditional myth than an interpretation of
it. Taliessin, the poet, whom Williams calls "the imagination of this world,"
is spokesman, but Williams's concern is less for the individual, the single
great man, poet or king, than for the society as an organic unit. Williams
prefaces the work with a quotation from Dante's *De Monarchia,* which in
his translation reads: "The essence is created for the sake of the function
and not the function for the sake of the essence." That is, man exists for
a designated work and not necessarily for the work that he may choose for
himself. Behind this statement lies Williams's concept not merely of a Christian society but of all meaningful societies. "The Coming of the Kingdom,"
he writes, "in myth, in legend, in law, in history, in morals and meta-
physics, has been the coming of a thing at once exclusive of all things and
inclusive of everything. All the threads of the pattern have that nature, and
the whole pattern is of the same nature" (*HCD* 134).

The word he uses to describe the pattern is co-inherence. He assumes
that the whole cosmos is an organism in which all parts are interrelated, interdependent, co-inhering, matter and spirit, body and soul. His primary
image is a web of intricate filaments all emanating from one creating and
empowering Center. The parts are so related that the slightest vibration in
one is felt throughout the whole, and a break in one is a break in the

organism. Each filament exists for the web and not the web for the filament. In Williams's version of the Arthurian myth, the web has been torn, material creation has been separated from its spiritual context—Logres from Carbonek, Arthur from Pelles, and both from the empire and Sarras, the archetypal City of which all earthly cities are images. The central theme is that wholeness can be restored only through the coming of the Holy Grail, in Williams's Christian version, an image of Christ's sacramental presence and power operative in creation; the healing of the Grail King, Pelles of the Grail Castle in Carbonek, who suffers from a "Dolorous Blow" (an image of man's Fall); and the reunion of Arthur with Pelles, the reconciliation of matter with spirit. The action is a working out of that theme in Logres under King Arthur. The initial steps toward that end, a reassertion of the incarnational principle as the basis of all reality, are traced in the first five poems following the introductory "Prelude."

Joe McClatchey, in a perceptive article, has called the "Prelude" a "lyric virtually informing all those to follow." He continues: "With its three numbered sections of three stanzas of three lines each, it mathematically recalls the Trinity. Each section suggests one Person of the Trinity; the first the Father, the second the Son, and the third the Spirit" (VII 102).

The third section is especially interesting. The reference is actually to the spirit in a state of perversion. What might at first seem mere absence, the emphasis on monotheistic morality and incoherence, is precisely the point. The rejection of the co-inhering spirit and the intrusion of dualism have undermined the Christian empire and dissipated the "glory of substantial being." There are echoes in the first stanza also of the first chapter of John's gospel: "In the beginning was the Word . . . and the Word was made flesh." In the poem, the word of the emperor establishes the kingdom, and the "double-fledged Logos" becomes the intermediator of light. This would seem to identify the emperor with God, but Williams rejects that interpretation. The emperor is, literally, the historical figure; figuratively, he is an image of the earthly king, "God-in-operation, God-as-known-by man" (Notes). It is central to Williams's understanding of the incarnational nature of creation that God manifest himself through his works. The empire is the earthly type of the Holy City, Sarras. Williams describes it as "(a) all Creation— with Logothetes and whatnot. . . , (b) Unfallen Man, (c) a proper social order, (d) the true physical body" (Notes). In short, it is a microcosm of the co-inherent web of all being. Sophia, its central city, is both a place and a quality, a center of worship and a spirit of holy wisdom. The word *immaculate* describes both the origin and the measure of Sophia's song, which, conceived independently of man, remains a mystery of grace. Her wisdom, however, is mediated through various "gates" and "containers," specifically Carbonek, the place of the Holy Grail; Camelot, the geographical location of King Arthur's court; and Caucasia, the whole of natural creation. The gates and containers function much as the Sephiroth do in Cabalistic lore. The pirates are men in their state of incoherency after the Fall and before the pattern of Logres is imposed on them.

There follows a highly suggestive phrase: "geography breathing geometry." Geography is the study of the physical surfaces of the world. Its aim is to map in realistic detail the outward appearance of things. It is concerned with the concrete and specific, not the abstract and general. Geometry, on the other hand, is precisely concerned with the abstract and general. Its purpose is to discover and depict diagrammatically constant identifying relationships between points, lines, and squares. Geography describes outward appearances; geometry seeks designs and patterns by which objects may be related on the basis of corresponding internal structures. The diagram, unlike the map, does not describe, say, a particular triangle, but diagrams that system of relationships among its parts by which all triangles may be identified. All triangles regardless of size or kind, for example, have three angles and three sides. A map will direct one to a known place. Geometry, and, particularly trigonometry, enables one to perceive from and within the known that which was previously unknown. The word *breathing* associated with the creation and the impartation of the Holy Spirit, suggests the organic relation, the identity of matter and spirit. "God," Williams quotes Plato as saying, "always geometrizes." That is, he works with correspondences, relationships, organic systems. Williams assumes that, on the basis of what man knows, he can reasonably infer that he is part of a larger system and that by geometrizing can discover the relation between the human below and the unknown above. It is the intent of all imaginative activity to discern that pattern of relationships: for the individuals with Logres; for Logres with Byzantium; for Byzantium with Sarras; and for all with God. Religion proposes to bring all men into a co-inhering relationship within the web. God geometrizes — and, says Williams, so did the Hebrew prophets: "The wheels and the eyes, and the spirit in the wheels, and their lifting up, have been subject to a good deal of gay humour, but they are a myth of a vital pattern of organisms" (*HCD* 40).

In the early days of Logres the "vital patterns" between macrocosm and microcosm were apparent: "The organic body sang together" ("The Vision of the Empire" 1). In the second section of the "Prelude," however, "The blind rulers" prefer the "fallacy of rational virtue," the wisdom of men, to the divine wisdom of Sophia. "The seals . . . were broken," an obvious reference to chapters five through eight of the Book of Revelation in which the seven seals are opened and dire prophesies of war, pestilence, famine, earthquakes, death, and finally, apocalyptic judgment are foretold. The forces of evil are loosed in the aftermath, "the chairs of the Table reeled." That is, the chairs—the knights who occupied them—are diverted from their intended function. Here, as in the Book of Revelation, judgment is tempered, however. In the midst of the seeming chaos, "Galahad quickened in the Mercy." Galahad, according to Williams, is not Christ but that "in the human soul which finds Christ" (Essays 190); or, as he states in another place, he is man's capacity for divine things. From the beginning, there was an empty chair, the Perilous Sell, which remained vacant at the table. It represented the place left empty by Judas at the time of his betrayal. It was, by divine edict, to remain unoccupied until one designated "in the Mercy," the high prince Galahad, appeared to claim it. The plan for the redemption is simultaneous with the Fall, the two actions, at one in eternity, are necessarily experienced sequentially in time. "History began," Williams says. Time is out of synchrony with eternity. Williams elaborates: "the Empire of the poem exists as the substance of the actual Empire, and (like Logres) is half withdrawn and half becomes history, because Logres has fallen, and our understanding has diminished" (Notes).

Both language and action of the last three lines of the second section have literary antecedents. The language is borrowed from the sixth chapter of Revelation; after the opening of the sixth seal, we are told, terrified men, from kings to bondsmen, "hid themselves in the dens and in the rocks of the mountains, And said to the mountains and rocks, Fall on us, and hide us from the face of him that sitteth on the throne, and from the wrath of the Lamb." The action also parallels that of Adam and Eve who, after discovering they were naked, hid behind fig leaves and among trees.

Terror of the wrath is understandable, but in the "Prelude," it is the "lord of charity" before whom men quail. Paradoxically as it may seem, the psychology is sound and the action consistent with Williams's recognition of "vital patterns of organisms": "the recognition of the good, everywhere and always, as good, . . . the importance of interchange, and a deliberate relation to the Centre" (HCD 39). Williams is speaking, of course, about good as a principle and not about good acts as distinguished from bad ones. Indeed, the men of Logres retained a residual desire for the good and an intuitive yearning for a relation with the Center, but in their fallen state they had lost the "good of intellect" and confused the good with its perversion. Their orientation is so awry that flashes of the emperor riding in the sky challenge their misconceptions and make disturbing demands on them. Even the lord of charity seems an ogre to them—their sense of goodness, and not wrath, invoking their worst terror. In the final section, Williams further develops a theme introduced earlier, "The Moslems stormed Byzantium."

This is at once a historical event (although chronologically inaccurate) and a symbol of a spiritual reality in the kingdom. When Williams speaks of Moslems (or of Jews or Greeks or any other racial group) he refers not to a country and a people, but to a system of belief, a way of apprehending reality. Here he has in mind both a non-Trinitarian monotheism and a gnostic heresy that spread from the East through the early Christian church. The Persians posited two antagonistic creative forces—Ormus, the evil, and Ahriaman, the good—that were in continuous conflict. Creation of earth and man (a mistake it was thought) had meant a plunge of spirit into matter, a condition that could be relieved only by freeing spirit once again of material contamination. Moslems, Williams observed, rejected the Incarnation and the potential redemption of matter, referring both to the Persian dualism and to Manichaeanism, a kindred Christian heresy that taught that evil resided in matter and flesh. The threat to the co-inherence of such belief knows no national barriers. The Moslem conquest of the empire was, therefore, both a military and a spiritual victory, spearheaded both from without and from within. The mamelukes (slaves) seized the countryside; the imams (spiritual leaders) captured Sophia. The inner life of the empire was undermined and the vision of organic unity eroded: "lost is the light on the hills of Caucasia, / glory of the Emperor, glory of substantial being" (26–27). The word *lost* is precise: lost and not extinguished. The map of the land had been altered, but the diagram remained. Geography, however, no longer openly breathed geometry.

One turns to the "Prelude" from the earlier poetry, even the relatively late *Heroes and Kings* (1930), with a sense of shock. The change is not only radical but has come swiftly. *Taliessin through Logres* appeared in 1938, but Ridler, whose introduction to *The Image of the City* is invaluable both for its information about the composition of the poems and for its critical insights, thinks that Williams was working on "Prelude" before September, 1934 (lxiii). It is not certain when he finished the poem, but clearly he revised it many times. At one time between 1933 and 1938, he wrote, "Pretty soon I shall abolish the Prelude altogether. Or else leave any odd stanzas I like with no care for any intellectual co-ordination" (Ridler lxiii).

As early as 1934, then, the great change in Williams's style was already underway. His early book *Poetry at Present* (1930) is, in view of his later work, undistinguished and interesting primarily as an indication of the milieu out of which his new poetry emerged. *The English Poetic Mind* (1932) and *Reason and Beauty in the Poetic Mind* (1933) are seminal critical statements. Further, in 1932, Williams wrote an important essay on Hopkins as an introduction to the second edition of Hopkins's poems. It is significant not only for its insight into Hopkins but also for what it tells us about

Williams's own concerns at the time. His emphases are more technical than ideological. He dwells perceptively on prosody, diction, rhythm, alliteration, and interior rhyme. Williams's intense study of Hopkins, following his reading of Abercrombie's *The Epic* and his essay on Yeats (in *Poetry at Present*) helped him identify some of his own problems. He was influenced by both Yeats and Hopkins, but it cannot be said that he came to imitate either poet. There are very few echoes, and those perhaps incidental, of either in the Taliessin poems. Ridler, for example, says, "He took from Hopkins, for one thing, a habit of rhythm, of breaking up a statement into short segments linked by rhyme and by paired stresses, which Hopkins had adapted from early English poetry" (lxi). She concludes, however, "I do not mean to suggest more than that Hopkins gave him a key to unlock resources which he already had. But something was needed to break the too-facile cadence of his earlier verse" (lxii).

Williams said that he was beginning to work out his new style in *Windows of Night* (1924) (which is obvious, for example, in a poem like "On Meeting Shakespeare") and that he continued in *Heroes and Kings*. The real break came, however, in *Thomas Cranmer of Canterbury* (1936), the play which he wrote for the Canterbury Festival. Perhaps the realization that he was writing lines to be spoken on stage to a live audience was an additional incentive to pursue his developing style and to achieve a rhythmic pattern and a colloquial diction consistent with his evolving objectives in the new poems. Whatever the stimulus, the results were little short of amazing. The new style was to be seen in all his subsequent poetry.

The nature of that change is suggested more specifically by comparing two passages from "Prelude," one an earlier version (for which I am indebted to Ridler, lxiv) and the other from the poem finally published:

> I have called to the dark to hide,
>   to the hills to cover me,
> lest I should see in the starlight ride
>   the lord of charity:

> Call on the hills to hide us
> lest, men said in the City, the lord of charity
> ride in the starlight, sole flash of the Emperor's glory. (16–18)

Has Williams, as he threatened, abandoned care for intellectual coordination? I think not. Precisely the opposite has happened. The first version is personal and lyrical; the second, dramatic, a fact that not only objectifies and universalizes but intensifies the thought and emotion. In the first, the will seems to be doing the work of the imagination; the language is merely rhetorical. In the second, Williams has passionately apprehended the subject in relation to its poetic structure. In the passage there are syntactical groupings governed by thought and emotion rather than by an externally imposed prosody. By skillfully manipulating the rhythm, in the later version, the poet focuses attention on each unit separately without, at the same time, losing the sense of overall pattern that makes the part one with the whole. The monotonous rhythm, the obtrusive rhyme, the awkward syntax, and the rhetorical repetition are gone.

Williams had abandoned the traditional clichés, verbal and technical, to permit meaning in all its dimensions—intellectual, emotional, and sensuous—to emerge more precisely. Structure as something apart from meaning no longer predominates. The closely woven, dense texture of the lines, which demands the reader's total concentration, signals the style that characterizes the Taliessin poems that were to follow.

The next five poems, composing the first stage in the building of Logres, recount the conquest of the land and the crowning of the king. There are one long and four shorter ones, in two of which Taliessin and two in which Arthur is the central figure. Vocation—the man for the work or the work for the man?—the theme of all five, is brought to focus in the last poem, "The Crowning of Arthur." "The Return of Taliessin" comes first; "The Vision of the Empire" is second; and "The Calling of Arthur" follows. Events falling between the king's calling and his crowning—the numerous encounters between Christian Briton and pagan enemy—are condensed into the single siege of Mount Badon. With the triumph of Mount Badon, the outlines of the vision take hold on unmade Logres, and the kingdom with the king's crowning begins to be built.

One's first impression of "Taliessin's Return to Logres" is of speed and action. Taliessin "lightly" comes to land in the harbor of Logres "under a roaring wind" that strains the golden sails and causes the galley to creak. With equal urgency he rides off to the hills of Wales. The impression of speed is supported by the rapidly moving three stressed lines, which are linked tightly by an almost obtrusive rhythm. Initially, the intense speed seems out of control, the overpowering mechanics of the lines threatening to obscure meaning. Counterbalancing this, however, the rigid stanzaic structure restrains and directs the rhythm so the effect is that of seeing the emerging energy of Broceliande being ordered by the shaping power of Byzantium. Taliessin goes among the great oaks—that strain and creak (but do not break) under the wind—protected by the emperor, who rides above him in a "train of golden cars." Although he has been impaired by the Fall, Williams says, man can still on occasions "see the Emperor riding in the skies and see the flung stars—flashes of perfection" (Notes). Taliessin sees seven such stars shoot (a strong action verb) across the sky, matching force with force. Seven is a mystic number. According to Genesis, God created the world in seven days; the Jewish menorah has seven branches; the Book of Revelation is addressed to the seven churches; there are seven gifts of the Holy Spirit. Seven is the number of wholeness, cosmic harmony, spiritual power, and wisdom. The seven stars may be the Big Dipper (a pattern of stars); symbolically, however, they correspond to shaping spiritual forces that direct and drive Taliessin toward wholeness in Logres.

With the emperor and the stars, Christian symbols, Williams includes the pagan symbol of the golden sickle, which flashes seven times in the Druid wood. The Druids, he said, represent a kind of natural poetry, and their reaching with the sickle after the sacred mistletoe signifies the universal aspiration of man for spiritual truth. According to Pliny the Elder, Druids worshiped the mistletoe, performing sacred rites by gathering its growth with a golden sickle and making a drink from its berries that was held to assure fertility. The harp, which had hung silent on Taliessin's back, "sprung to sound," as, released and fulfilled, he makes his way along the "road that runs from tales," rumors, which after Byzantium have become facts. He approaches again the mysterious Broceliande on which the best commentary is written by Williams himself in *The Figure of Beatrice:*

> The image of a wood . . . has become a great forest where, with long leagues of changing green between them, strange episodes of high poetry have place . . . and there are other inhabitants, belonging even more closely to the wood, dryads, fairies, and enchanter's rout. The forest itself has different names in different tongues—Westermain, Arden, Birnam, Broceliande; and in places there are separate trees named. . . . So that indeed the whole earth seems to become this one enormous forest, and our longest and most stable civilizations are only clearings in the midst of it. (107)

Here Williams heightens the sense of mystery and foreboding by invoking memories and emotion of Milton's "Comus," Keats's "Ode to a Nightingale," Wordsworth's *Prelude,* and Dante's *Divine Comedy.* Line twenty-six is an adaptation of a passage from the *Inferno* in which Virgil and Dante, arriving at the gate of hell, read on its lintel the dread inscription warning those who enter therein to abandon all hope. In terror, Dante cries out against the severity of that sentence, but Virgil urges him to forgo all fear and cowardice, saying that they have arrived at that point in their spiritual journey when Dante of necessity may see those who have lost "the good of intellect." They will be for Dante both a warning and an incentive.

Broceliande, too, is an ambivalent place, capable indeed of inspiring in all men the fear that Dante experienced, but it is a positive as well as a negative force. "Mystically," Williams writes, "it is the 'making' of things. Nimue is the Nature of Creation as the mother of Merlin (Time) and Brisen (Space); she is the source of movement and of distance. . . . She is almost the same state represented by the Emperor's Court, but more vast, dim, and aboriginal. The huge shapes emerge from B.; and the whole matter of the form of the Empire" (Notes). She is the great cauldron of raw, amorphorous matter waiting to be given form by the creating and shaping mind and hands of man. All good things have their potential in Broceliande. She is a force to be feared only when man loses "the good of intellect" and becomes victim rather than master of her great powers. Druid sprung and Byzantium trained, Taliessin calls "on the Mercy" and is reassured when he sees:

> a diagram played in the night,
> where either the golden sickle
> flashed, or a signaling hand. (38–40)

Here the implication of line 12 is made explicit: the seven stars do form a diagram. Williams brings the pagan sickle and the Christian hand into relation with their heavenly correspondent. In merging the two traditions, Taliessin acknowledges in both a pattern of glory, the one the fulfillment of the other.

In stanza 6 the golden sickle and the signaling hand become a single image, the golden arm, the culmination of all mythic visions, in which man, reaching to gather fate in the forest, catches in his outstretched palm the Christian hallows. With the creaking ship and the falling wood behind him, and the newly received hallows in his hand, Taliessin comes to the King's camp. The sound of the harp "syllabled the signal [directing, confirming] word [Word] to the sound of running flames, a Pentecostal outpouring." The seemingly uncontrolled speed and action of the initial stanzas have been caught and given shape and direction by a myriad of shaping hands.

Taliessin's arrival in Logres marks his passing by way of Byzantium from imprecise paganism to an ordered kingdom-in-the-making. Logres is part of the empire, a society in which knowledge from the throne has transformed the old magic into a new spiritual power: "T. has been in Byzantium and seen the whole pattern of the body and the order. . . . he has gone out of the direct presence of the Emperor into the outer world, which is precisely a place of images; from the Sacred Palace to the waters of the Golden Horn, from 'God in Himself' to 'God in His creatures'" (Notes). The empire is pictured in the form of a female human body. Williams drew

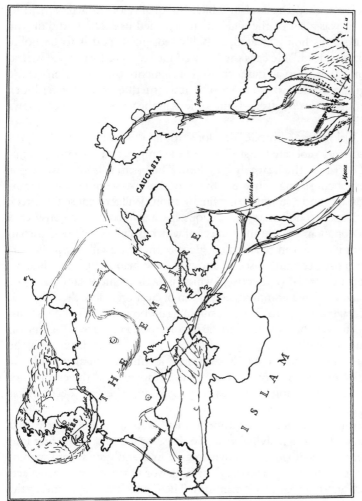

The Empire as a body. This drawing originally appeared as the endpapers to the first edition of Charles Williams's *Taliessin through Logres* (Oxford University Press, 1938; reproduced by permission).

this image from astrology in which he saw an imaginative system of relation-ships between the body and cosmic phenomena. He, no doubt, also had in mind Saint Paul's description of the church as the Body of Christ. "It [the body]," he wrote, "is, in fact, for all our difficulties with it, less fallen, merely in itself, than the soul in which the quality of the will is held to reside; for it was a sin of the will which degraded us." The body, on the other hand, "was holily created, is holily redeemed, and is to be holily raised from the dead." He calls the body an index. So to treat it, he writes, "is to assume that, as in an index the verbal element – the *word* given – is the same as in the whole text, so in the physical structure of the greater index the element – the *quality* given – is the same as in the whole structure" (Essays 82, 84–85).

"The Vision of the Empire" develops around this basic image. The pro-vinces or themes replicate the structure of the empire and the empire repli-cates that of Sarras, the heavenly kingdom. The poem falls into two major parts, the first consisting of five and the second of two sections, a brief tran-sitional passage, and a summarizing final section. Williams chose the Greek numerals 1 to 9 to designate the sections, perhaps because he considered them appropriate in a poem the subject of which is a vision of the Christian empire with its center in Byzantium. He uses the minuscule script (lower-case), that most frequently used in ancient Greek manuscripts (see line 6), rather than the uncial (uppercase), which is perhaps more familiar.

The first section communicates a vision of creation before the Fall, and, as in the imagination of the poet, it might again become (1–5). In sections 2–5 the themes of the empire are made to correspond to parts of the human body: Caucasia with the buttocks, Logres with the head, Gaul with the breasts, and Italy with the hands. Section 7 identifies Jerusalem with the reproductive organs. Section 8 describes the emperor and the empire not as they appear in section 1, but as they exist after the Fall. Section 6 is transitional.

An organic body, universe or poem, then, is composed of diverse parts that co-inhere as a single living structure. It is, we are told in the first four lines, harmonious – it sings; it is dynamic – it lives and grows from within. The image is reinforced by a series of rhyming words: the body *sang*, dialects *sprang* from and *rang* back to Byzantium. The *streets repeat* the sound of the throne. Between the throne and the repeating streets, the *logethete* pass con-tinually down and up (down first because the initiative is from above) the porphyry stair bearing "missives through the area of the empire." Literally, a logothete is a letter or a sign used to replace an entire word ($ for dollar). The logothete here speaks for the emperor. In Williams's imaginative vi-sion, the porphyry stair links the themes with the throne and provides the means of concourse between the two. It is a complex image that recalls Jacob's ladder and Dante's golden stair in paradise. Williams's stair, however, is porphyry, the color of blood, inspired, Williams suggests, by the fact that in the Palace a porphyry stair led from the hall up to the throne room, and also because the birthing room in the emperor's palace was called the porphyry room. The stair symbolizes the descent of God to man so that man might ascend to God, the archetypal shedding of blood by which man is redeemed, and, also, the dying unto self that is demanded of all who pursue the Way. The missives that the logothetes carry are "The Acts," "the identities of creation," all the phenomena through which God reveals himself to man. It is as though the "Greek minuscula" were being translated into the language of the masses.

The first section suggests a continuous movement of creative activity. The presence here of dynamic images and their absence later become a unifying element. In the first five sections, we find: "The Acts issue" (5), "the logothetes run" (10), "the nuntii loosened" (17), "Chariots and galleys sprang" (20), "the roads resounded with the galloping lords" (59), "the fleet took me, distances of the sea" (78), "a single sudden flash" (96). In sections 8 and 9, in contrast, we see the images in reversal: "feet of creation walk backward" (131), "galley hardly moves" (132), "flagging hands" (135), "distance drags at the sailor's hearts" (136), "on the stagnant level" (146), "dragging octopus bodies" (153), "walks on the sinking floor" (155).

One of the most dramatic effects comes from one image seen from two perspectives, the first in section 1 and the other in section 9:

> . . . in the mechanism of motion,
> rowers' arms jointed to the imperial oars. (18–19)

> the stiffening mechanic of arms and oars fails. (133)

In the first, there is organic motion, creative activity. Human arms and imperial oars are not merely joined but jointed. In the second, the movement "stiffens" and fails; the arms and the oars become immobile. The arms no longer function as arms nor oars as oars.

Williams begins to construct his expository map in section 2 with a description first of Caucasia, the material creation identified with the buttocks. He writes, "I can never see why the buttocks are funnier than any other part of the body; they support us when we sit, they are balance and (in that sense) justice" (Essays 181). Referring to the buttocks as the "fundamentals," he first discusses Caucasia. Man's response to the emperor begins on Earth and actualizes through earthly means. Byzantium, Williams said, is the whole concentration of body and soul rather than any special member of the body. Thus, Caucasia is understood substantively as that element that in union with spirit composed the whole of creation before the Fall.

Taliessin looks anew at creation in the afterglow of Byzantium and sees, as if on a sea of sapphire, the shapes of the "identities," all created objects, as images of the divine glory. Sinai, where Moses received the commandments, represents law and judgment; Ararat, where the Ark came to rest, represents mercy and grace; the polarities between the two generate a continuing creative tension. On Ararat God confirmed the goodness of his creation and covenanted never again to destroy it, giving as his pledge the sign of the rainbow, of which the flash of light and color in the lines following is suggestive.

Beyond Ararat stands Elburz, a mountain in the Caucasus that Williams described as "the grand type of the mingled lowness and height, fertility and chastity, verdure and snow, of the visible body" (Notes). Elburz represents the true glory of the material creation and of the natural instincts of men. Beginning with line 30, we are treated to a kind of fertility rite, a celebration of the oneness and goodness of creation before "the Adam" (the term used by Williams to indicate mankind, inclusive of both Adam and Eve) knew the acts in contention. Here on Elburz the light of the emperor's "sun shone on each roundmound / double fortalices defending dales of fertility" (33–34). Literally, the "round mounds" refer to the mountain peaks and, figuratively, to the rounded mounds of the emperor's buttocks. The buttocks are erotic, but, Williams says, "they are plainly and naturally so" (Essays 181).

Here the sexual implications are clear. The "blades" refer literally to the weapons of war that protect the province. On another level, they indicate the dashing young men who bear them. They engage in a "dancing" contest with the "stripped maids" who both invite and repel their conquest. Blades also suggest piercing, penetrating. The rhyming of *blades* and *maids* suggests the coming together of opposites in a life-creating relation, a reflection in the holy flesh of male and female, the fructifying union of Sun (male) with Malkuth, which is feminine. The maidens joyfully bear the diagram of the emperor's glory in their fecund bodies. In summary:

> Spines were strengthened, loves settled;
> tossed through aerial gulfs of empire
> the lost name, the fool's shame,
> fame and frame of lovers in lowlands of Caucasia,
> rang round snowy Elburz.
> The organic body sang together. (40–45)

Recognizing the "lost name" (seeing the imprint of God on all creation) and rejecting the "fool's shame" (of human sexuality) is an essential step toward recovering man's lost wholeness of body and spirit.

Over against Ararat stands Elburz and over against Caucasia stands Logres, less as opposite than counterpart. In section 3, consequently, Taliessin turns from Caucasia to Logres, from buttocks to head, from matter and flesh and natural instincts to the ordering and disciplining mind. In Thule, the "skull-stone," anciently thought to be the northernmost point of the world, Logres rises "in balance and weight, freight of government with glory" (50). From her emanates order and law. She is a magic creation, an embodiment of the ideal within the actual. Logres is to be established through the united efforts of Merlin ("time's metre") and Brisen (space), Taliessin, and Percivale. Percivale, the imagination of this world, is associated with the star Phosphor and shines over both Camelot and Carbonek, foreseeing the reunion of Arthur and Pelles and the coming of the grail. Lancelot, ambiguous figure of chastity and adultery, is symbolized by a lion, representing majesty and strength. He responds to Guinevere's majesty, but paradoxically. He smells as any wild beast, and, yet, at the same time, he "adores" and is bewildered. The good in him cries for possession, but to possess is also to destroy. In this brief reference we see for the first time one of those apparently unsolvable cruxes that will prevent the coming of the grail.

Merlin defines the various tasks, and the men of Logres drive the pirates from the land. Thus, a way is made for the establishment of the Round Table. It stands "rigid" in contrast to that time when, as we have been told in the "Prelude," the chairs of the table will reel. The table is a symbol of the co-inherent relation of the knights who sit around it, a relation that will be broken.

Perhaps the most important word in section 4 is *trigonometrical*. It recalls the phrase "geography breathing geometry" that Williams used in the "Prelude" to suggest the difference between a map and a diagram. Here its purpose is to differentiate between dogma and experience and to confirm the importance of both. "Gaul," he wrote, "is 'fruitfulness' (a) the breasts, (b) traditional organization, (c) scholastic debates and doctrines, (d) theology" (Notes). Man is nourished by the milk of *intelligo* and *credo*, echo of St. Anselm's *credo ut intelligam*, and of Abelard, with whose lectures Williams writes, "the University of Paris may be said to have begun" (*DD* 109). That milk, however, is merely trigonometrical, a diagrammatic system by which one is able to infer the unknown from the known. Theology, like poetry, is a pointer, not itself religion.

Taliessin, born a Druid and natively imbued with a spirit of mystery and awe, had studied in Gaul; we are not told when. There he heard "the chariots on the road" without necessarily having seen also the "golden cars" of the emperor above ("Taliessin's Return to Logres" 9–10). His enlightenment came fully only after he went the "distance of the sea" and discovered from the throne itself that the manifestation of glory in Logres was another and lesser replication of the arch-glory of Byzantium. There he witnessed the transformation of the iron chariots into golden cars, theology into lived experience. The experience enabled him to return to Logres and direct his imaginative vision toward the building of the kingdom as an integral part of the empire.

Section 5 unifies and focuses the poem up to this point. The material creation, the mind and will of man, the capacity for abstracting and formulating, are futher shaped by the hands of Rome, repeating, in their degree, the hands of Byzantium. Back of both, however, are the hands of God for whom the emperor is operative. The hands of the pope point back toward the "signaling hand" that guided Taliessin on his return from Byzantium and forward to the perversion in the "indecent hands" of the Headless Emperor, which have been rendered incapable of indicating direction and dispensing grace (150). All hands remind us of Michelangelo's fresco of the *Creation of Man* in which the hand of God reaches from above toward the upstretched hand of Adam below in the act of completing the crowning of creation by infusing the inert body of the created with the living soul of the creator.

Williams suggests that there is in the poem an evolutionary movement. The section begins with "a mist," obviously an echo of the second chapter of Genesis: "But there went up a mist from the earth, and watered the whole face of the ground. And the Lord God formed man of the dust of the ground." The passage not only illuminates this particular line, but it also reminds us in passing that the ground to till precedes the man to till it. A primordial creation is suggested where the now extinct elephant and bear prowled on the broad ledges of the shoulders, that part of the human body that falls below the head, representing life before the appearance of man. The image recurs in "The Crowning of Arthur" where the "shouldering shapes" are recognized and transformed and emblazoned on the knights' coats of arms as the virtues (41–45). Here, one step forward, strength is articulated with arms, joints, wrists, and, especially, hands, into which strength flows and is concentrated. The hands are distinctively human instruments, "love's means to love." In *The Greater Trumps,* a terrified Nancy faces an angered cat poised to spring on her. Helpless, she thinks, "'It's got no hands,' and this seemed to her so horrible that she nearly lost control. It had no hands, it had no spiritual instruments of intention, only paws that patted or scratched, soft padded cushions or tearing iron nails—all four, all four, and no hands" (231).

The image that follows is that of "hid cones," hidden because they are a mystery; they represent the means of the unseen power of the greater being transmitted to the lesser. Williams provides his own interpretation:

> The cones are more difficult to explain. The delicate and sensitive palms are conceived as full of points from which cones flowed down into the *substance* of our being. The mass of the points makes up the activities and passivities of the hands, for which Rome stands; which is an image of Byzantium as the hands of the whole being. The nails are (i) evolutionary and agricultural (ii) amorous (iii) architectural. The "circle" at the bottom of our substance is Christ; "seed-springing surrender," the Fructiferous Passion. The nails then are the actual nails. (Notes)

The fingernails represent man's efforts, which the nails of the cross complete. Rome is the spiritual center of the West, the pontifex (bridge builder) between the empire and Rome and between Rome and the provinces. Rome passively receives and actively gives the pattern imposed upon her by the emperor. In "a single sudden flash" we see the mystery of reconciliation of human and divine, as the pope breaks the bread and blesses the wine, an act that once broke the heart of God and now that of man and opens him to the inpouring of saving grace. Our hands of incantation, all our efforts to seize and control, are changed into hands of adoration. The mass becomes a continuing symbol of the organic unity.

But why, the question arises, must the unity be mediated, the gold of the empire pale to the white vesture of Rome, God himself become flesh to expiate—what? What crossed the will of the emperor? Section 7 explains. The central image is of something twisted: a thought (103), an act (110), creation (114), man (118–19). Jerusalem is identified with the reproductive system. It is the "hollow," the place where life begins and the physical means through which it is perpetuated. In Williams's scheme, however, sex itself is not what crossed the emperor's will, although the sexual along with every other bodily function was impaired when man fell. The fact that the offence occurred in Jerusalem, that Pelles was wounded in the thigh, suggests that the blow fell where the Adam was most vulnerable, leaving both them and their progeny maimed at the source of life. The sin, however, was aberration of the will, not the body.

Williams calls what happened in the hollow of Jerusalem an alteration in the Adams's way of knowing. They were not destroyed for wanting to know but for wanting to know in a manner reserved to God alone. In a chapter in *He Came Down From Heaven*, "The Myth of the Alternation in Knowledge," he says that, although there was nothing in creation but good,

God did allow the contingency that man, if he chose, could know the good in perversion:

> It [the Fall] was merely to wish to know an antagonism in the good, to find out what the good would be like if a contradiction were introduced into it. . . . It was a knowledge reserved to God; man had been warned that he could not bear it. . . . A serpentine subtlety overwhelmed that statement with a grander promise—"Ye shall be as gods, knowing good and evil." Unfortunately to be as gods meant, for the Adam, to die, for to know evil, for them, was to know it not by pure intelligence but by experience. It was, precisely, to experience the opposite of good, that is the depriva- tion of the good, the slow destruction of the good, and of themselves with the good. (18)

Dissatisfied with "Joy's single dimension," the Adam wished to know both good and its privation, evil—"the principles at war." He chose. Williams alters the details of the Genesis story. Instead of eating an apple—the act itself, he says, might have been anything, something as silly as eating an apple—they climbed the tree in search of the broader perspective, the God- like view. The result was a disaster that was felt through the whole creation because, as men, they could know that knowledge only as experienced knowledge. The withering and dying of the tree in wake of their ascent pre- cisely images the privation—the drying up—of the life-giving substance that sustains the natural world. The Adam, themselves, became contorted with- out and within "a double entity / spewed and struggled, good against good" (118–19). They hung from the dead tree "wrying," an anticipation of the Second Adam, who for their misdeed would hang too on another tree. The word *wrying* brings into focus a number of related images: *turning, twisting, contorting, perverting*.

Ironically, the Adam had their wish: "they saw the mind of the Em- peror as they could," as the Adam and not as God, as actualized expe- rience and not as unexperienced possibility (120). Up to this point Wil- liams has spoken of the Adam, male and female, as one, but now they become a "double entity," two figures, alone. "He walked . . . in the night of himself" (22–23). Byzantium, from which he was now exiled, insen- sitively sleeps. He is pursued by "a white pulsing shape," an astral body, the self without himself that he has rejected and ejected. Ironically, the shadowing shape is at once a token of the salvation lost and of the salva- tion to be regained—contingent, that is, upon Another's wrying upon an- other tree.

In the last stanza Williams returns to the sexual image with which he began: "Conception without control had the Adam of the error" (126). They gave birth to life's perversion, death. Their offspring Cain was soon to slay his brother Abel in an act that would signify the ever spreading disintegration of the social structure. The last sentence, characteristic of Williams's style under certain constraints, contains three short sentences, each followed by a complete break in thought and rhythm so that each is given ponderous weight: "They had their will; they saw; they were torn in the terror" (129). The opening explosive consonants and the alliteration give the words *torn* and *terror* special emphasis and support, as no amount of rhetoric could—the full sense of fragmentation of the unity described in the first five sections.

Few passages in Williams would be more difficult to paraphrase than section 8. It is an integrally related kaleidoscope of images so tightly interwoven that it is almost impossible to extricate one without destroying the whole. It stands, a depiction of fragmentation, in startling contrast to section 2, and the visionary section with which the poem concludes: "The morn rose on the Golden Horn" (23); "Elburz sinks through the Golden Horn" (130); "The organic body sang together" (165). The sinking Elburz may be linked also with line 155: it "walks on the sinking floor of antipodean Byzantium." In section 2, in light of the morning, Elburz, symbol of the rosy flesh, is reflected in the water of the Golden Horn (fecundity awaiting impregnation). In this section, however, the image of reflecting and impregnating light disappears. There is no mention of the sun and only a single reference to the moon, where it is said to be obscured behind volcanic dust, image of dryness and sterility in contrast to the water and the "mist" that accompanied the first creation (148, 81). The second line of the section goes beyond mere absence and suggests perversity: "the feet of creation walk backward through the waters," a reversal of the creative process, the loss of the good of reason in P'o-lu (131). These two qualities—loss and perversity—are themes of this section. In the second stanza, the hardly moving galley, the stiffening arms, and the "sea's unaccumulated [endless, unmeasurable] distance [that] drags at the sailor's heart" suggest that vitality has departed. The purple sails, torn so that they no longer serve their original purpose, have been patched with undyed canvas by man himself, an allusion to the ineffectuality of man's unredeemed, "undyed," efforts (a pun?) to repair the loss. We see the result. The single galley, no longer an inner-supporting fleet but an isolated ship, hardly moves. The gold oar of Caucasia is no longer brought to Byzantium to be fashioned into shapes of glory. The visionary spirit no longer shines (the sun has disappeared and the moon is obscured). Fructifying exchange is lost. Instead, there is sterility and violence:

On the brazen deck blasts of hot ashes
fall from unseen volcanoes; harsh birds,
stabbing at sea-broods, grating their mating calls,
cover it; down their flight gusts drove once the galley. (143–45)

Nature devours itself and sex becomes mere sensation. Love is lost. Instead of the voice of the turtle we hear only the harsh and grating voice of mating birds.

There follows the ultimate perversion: the Headless Emperor. He dwells in P'o-lu, Williams's name for hell, which lies geographically and spiritually at antipodean Byzantium. Williams noted that P'o-lu "is the Chinese name, of about the period, for the point of Java – the extreme point (Nobody knew New Zealand then)" (Notes). The word *Po* may derive from the same word in Taoism, which stands for the earthly or negative part of the soul. Williams, perhaps, would have been familiar with the word through his activities in the Fellowship of the Rosy Cross. Both the Headless Emperor and his empire are more illusion than substance, an obverse parody of the real emperor enthroned in Byzantium: "The Empire is – to man, or to some men – lost; the antipodes are the vision reversed, 'the ejection to the creature.' . . . The 'headless figure' is the sight of the Emperor *there* (the 'Ape of God'); the image is taken from the tale about Justinian. Everything is parodied, and holy intellect is lost" (Notes).

In mock religious ceremony, the "Ape of God" walks on a sinking floor dressed in a crimson cape, "lifted from his body" by two attendants to expose his nakedness. The sinking floor is a recurring image in Williams's work, signifying the final void or abyss. It is his poetic expression of the bottomless pit and more effective for his purpose because its impact is at once intellectual and kinetic. In *Descent into Hell,* for example, Wentworth at the near end of his descent into the void, is described as "standing on the bottom of the abyss; there remained but a short distance in any method of mortal reckoning for him to take before he came to a more secret pit where there is no measurement because there is no floor" (218). Perhaps nowhere does Williams express more poignantly the meaning that the phrase had for him than in a letter to his wife, 27 May 1940. The war had begun, he had been "exiled" to Oxford with the Press, and Mrs. Williams had remained behind in London. After she had returned home following a weekend visit with him in Oxford, he wrote, recalling an earlier time when he was in a hospital and she visited him:

[I recall] evenings in the hospital when you had been to see me – for the first week – and disappeared round about eight o'clock – or half-past, was it? Something of the same substance disappeared with your bus, & I looked at Oxford as I looked at the ward. You will know that odd sensation: it is not "missing anyone"; it is disappearance of a solid, almost of the floors. One does not "miss" the floor; one misses a chair or a dish or a table, but not the solid existence. When that goes, one is left dancing in the air— uncertain, heavy, lost. That is how I felt in the hospital and that is how I felt today. (Wade)

Perhaps the most suggestive word in the section is *phosphorescent*. It is a word that Williams uses ambiguously. He associates Percivale, for example, with Phosphor, the morning star, and makes him a medium through which the reflected light of Venus, the Third Heaven, is transmitted to Earth. In "The Coming of Galahad," Gareth reports that, when Galahad had washed his hands, the water became phosphorescent, and, in response, Taliessin says that he has seen the princess Blanchefleur walk dropping light as "all our beloved do." All these references are positive. As a description of the Headless Emperor, however, the word has another possible meaning, that of the mere appearance of light rather than of light itself. It can mean the emission of a false light from an object, often decaying debris, shining without combustion or sensible light. All these characteristics are accurately descriptive of the Headless Emperor, whose relation to the true light has been severed. Williams returns to the word in "The Prayers of the Pope" (*The Region of the Summer Stars*) when describing the Headless Emperor, calling him "a formless colour, the foul image of the rose-garden" and says that there was "none to know what was real and what unreal / or what of sense stayed in the vagrant phosphorescence." Williams has chosen the precise word to communicate his meaning. P'o-lu and its sham emperor have no substantial being.

He calls special attention to the Headless Emperor's hands and penis. The hands are not "spiritual instruments of intention" but rather indecent hands hidden under his cope in an act of self-stimulation that "disallows" (perverts) the flush on the mounds of Caucasia. Caucasia—the rose garden— becomes P'o-lu.

The phosphorescent penis and the preoccupation with self present a perversion of the source of life and a rejection of a co-inherent community, love as self-indulgence rather than life-giving exchange. Williams explains: "all capacities are reduced to a kind of sensational preoccupation with one thing, and that is why the crimson cope obscenely resembles the first high flush of Caucasian love. If one gets fixed in Caucasia—" (Notes).

Finally, the Headless Emperor rules inarticulately over an inarticulate sea. It is terrifying to be without hands and speech. The Ape of God can no longer speak the Word nor actualize its meaning without hands. Having lost the power of communicating, he is alone. Significantly, there is nothing else in P'o-lu that approximates a human being. His companions are headless, speechless octopuses.

The last section falls, it would seem, outside the sequence and refers to neither country nor individual; it is addressed to the Infinite. The first three lines are a condensation of the four with which the poem began. There follows a song in praise of the unity that was before the alteration of knowledge when the organic body, flesh and spirit, sang together, and of the unity that shall again come to be when time is once again subsumed into eternity. The view remains uncompromisingly incarnational, however. In an essay entitled "Sensuality and Substance," Williams begins by quoting Julian of Norwich:

> "For I saw full assuredly," wrote the Lady Julian, "that our Substance is in God, and also I saw that in our sensualite God is; for in the self point that our Soul is made sensual, in the self point is the City of God ordained to Him from without beginning; into which seat He cometh and never shall remove it . . . and as anent our substance and sensualite it may rightly be cleped our soul: and that is because of the oneing that they have in God." (Essays 68)

This *Te Deum* speaks of all parts of the body, which, as an organic unit, has become the "substantial instrument of being"; the strength of the shoulders mediated through the arms into the hands; the legs and ankles; the hips, the thighs, the spine (including the genitals and the buttocks) – all that is Logres. And beyond that? If there be wit, regimen, measurement, even in the marshes beyond P'o-lu or among the headless places, they too shall ultimately "bless him, praise him, magnify him for ever." Such is the vision of the coming Logres.

The next three poems, "The Calling of Arthur," "Mount Badon," and "The Crowning of Arthur," can be considered as a unit.

"The Calling of Arthur" is more about Merlin and Cradlemass than about Arthur. Cradlemass represents the mordant remains of the old Roman kingdom in Britain, the failure of one civilization, now a pagan wasteland, the ruins out of which a new Christian society is to be built. Merlin represents the vision of the new kingdom: "Now I am Camelot," he says, "now am I to be built." Arthur is the instrument through which the building is to be accomplished.

Merlin is introduced, however, through the eyes of the yet unschooled Arthur, not necessarily as he is but as he is imperfectly perceived to be. To

Arthur, Merlin appears primarily the embodiment of the savage wasteland and, perhaps, as the spirit of awesome Broceliande. His wizardry, in the somber aspect of black magic, is suggested here more strongly than anywhere else in the series:

> Wolfish, the wizard stared, coming from the wild,
> black with hair, bleak with hunger, defiled
> from a bed in the dung of cattle, inhuman his eyes. (2–4)

The wolf as a symbol of savagery and barbarism appears frequently in Williams's poetry, an ambivalent figure signaling great strength that may be used for either good or evil. The wolf (*lupus*) gives his name to the fertility festival, the *lupercalia,* celebrated by old Rome on 15 February. In "The Son of Lancelot," Williams associates this pagan celebration with the birth of Galahad (and, by extension, the birth of Jesus). In that poem Merlin is magically transformed into a wolf, a white one. As young Arthur sees him, however, he is "black with hair." Williams distinguishes between black and white magic. Black magic, *goetia,* is self-seeking and harmful; white magic, *theurgy,* is selfless and benevolent. A power exists that can be used for good or perversely for evil. To Arthur, Merlin comes from the wild, whether from savagery or Broceliande, and is associated with black magic. His presence produces a hypnotic effect. Merlin "stared . . . inhuman his eyes." That last phrase is ambiguous. It could refer to the appearance of Merlin in Arthur's eyes or to a look more than human, perhaps demonic, in Merlin's eyes – or to both. It remains, at any rate, for Arthur to discover whether Merlin will be for him a black or a white wolf.

In his reconstruction of the myth, Williams took great liberty with the traditional presentation of Merlin. In the older accounts he appeared primarily as a wizard, with little distinction being made between black and white magic. Williams omits, for example, the incredible events connected with Merlin's birth as it is told in Malory, choosing rather to say simply that he is the parthenogenetical child of Nimue. He rejected altogether Tennyson's account of his inglorious demise as inconsistent with the myth. Among his predecessors, he regarded Swinburne's interpretation as perhaps the most acceptable. "Merlin had been saved by Swinburne," he wrote,

> in the new force with which in *Tristram of Lyonesse* he charged the Merlin-Nimue relationship, from the weakness of the older tales, and when the prophetic wizard of Malory was considered free from this, he took on all the qualities of Time. But he remained a white magician, a theurgic power, and the rod of a magician is not a toy. It is energy and direction. (Essays 182)

Clearly, in the first meeting, Arthur sensed Merlin's power but not its true direction. That awareness remains to come.

Arthur, the king-to-be, is brought into immediate contrast with the king-that-was, Cradlemass. The most obvious difference is that Cradlemass is old and Arthur is young. The basic differences are more profound, however. Cradlemass represents a failed pagan society and Arthur the new Christian kingdom that is to replace it. The word *eye(s)* appears four times in the poem, catching attention less for its frequency than for the context in which it is used. It occurs first in line 4, where it refers, perhaps, both to Arthur's and to Merlin's eyes. Merlin, however, is the vision that Arthur is yet to grasp. The other references are specifically to Cradlemass. He wears a mask that obscures "all but one eye" of his face (8); he peers with "one short-sighted eye" through Nero's emerald (10); and, finally, the mask is pulled from the "one-eyed face" (34–35). The eye is a symbol of vision and perspective. In Merlin it is "inhuman," or better, more than human, enabling him to see Logres in the context of eternity. In Cradlemass the eye is single, inwardly directed, capable of encompassing only the most immediate, his own needs and comforts. Merlin's vision embraces more than the human, Cradlemass's less. Arthur will in time see at least briefly through the eyes of Merlin, the builder; Cradlemass sees through the eyes of Nero, perverter and destroyer.

Cradlemass wears a mask that "o'ergilds" his wrinkled, desiccated face. Beneath the gaily painted surface is a dried-up body, itself a wasteland comparable to the one described in stanza 6, where the word *waste* appears three times, used ambivalently. It means, on the one hand, in line 21, that in itself the snow is excessive and uncomfortable, a genuine waste; moreover, it is frozen water and incapable of relieving the drought conditions symbolic of the spiritual decay of the land—an image central in the original myth. On the other hand, it is itself a controller and a director, holding the people, as it were, prisoners in its frozen grip. Under the waste the "hovels" lie, and all human life languishes. This snow covers everything, unlike that on Elburz where the snowy peaks are counterbalanced by verdurous vales ("The Vision of the Empire" 29). The mask suggests both Cradlemass's false outward appearance and his essential unreality. It is intended to obscure his wrinkled face and his callous lack of concern for people: "he polished his emerald, misty with tears for the poor" (20). Moreover, like all evil, like the emperor of P'o-lu, he is more illusion than reality. In contrast to Arthur's boldness, he is maidenly; unlike "the rounded bottoms of the Emperor's glory," his rump is cold and small. In contrast to Merlin, who appears wolfish to the young Arthur, Cradlemass is a little animal that squeaks with "callous comfort"—not just an animal but a diminutive one, perhaps a rat, without the power of human speech. His end is to die in his litter. He is also

> a sea-snail's shell
> fragile, fragilely carved, cast out by the swell
> on to the mud. (14–16)

Fragility suggests insubstantiality. Moreover, in an old myth, familiar to all who know the lore of the Sephirotic Tree, shells were the symbol of the impurities of existence to be discarded after the Fall of Man. Cradlemass is just such a castoff.

One of the most disturbing aspects of the old kingdom is that "mallet [hammer] and scythe are silent" (22). We remember that nearing P'o-lu "[t]he single galley hardly moves, / the stiffening mechanic of arms and oars fails" ("Vision" 132–33). Here all is fixed in snow and ice (reminiscent of the nethermost part of Dante's hell). The hammer and the scythe are universal symbols of the unity of the common people, the hammer signifying the worker, and the scythe the peasant. Instead of being the king for the kingdom and leading his people in creative building, Cradlemass has in his "one-eyed" way possessed the kingdom for himself, a signal of what the new king should not do, and, at the same time, a foreshadowing of precisely what he will do.

In stanza 7, however, there comes a radical turn, a transition from the winter of old Rome to the spring of envisioned Logres. With the appearing of the spring moon and the drawing tide, "the people ebb," emerge, that is, from beneath the winter snow and ice, and, like all water, flow back toward the center from whence they came—to the sea, the source of all life. Bors is a type of hammer and scythe (sickle), the potential builder of the kingdom. His banner "is abroad," and he requires only to be led. Where is the leader, the king? The stage is set and awaits his coming. Bors and Elayne "mend the farms, get food from Gaul." The south is up with hammer and sickle. With Bors and Elayne the people hold "Thames mouth," the port of entry, to the breasts of Gaul from which sustenance comes. There is here, as elsewhere in the poem, a sense of urgency: "Lancelot hastens. . . ." The verb is active, the tense present. Only the king awaits.

Stanza 9 is Arthur's charge to unmask Cradlemass, to dispel the illusion, and to turn the vision into reality. The last stanza is broken into short rhetorical units separated by full stops, which, contrary to expectations, give each line a sense of great speed. It is as though the urgency of what is under way could tolerate no embellishment. The poem ends as it began:

> I am Camelot; Arthur, raise me. (36)
> Enlightened, or partially enlightened, Arthur acts:
> Arthur ran; . . . Camelot grew. (37–39)

Called, Arthur takes up his task of first clearing the country of pirates. Williams condenses the eleven battles in Arthur's conquest of Britain into one, the final encounter at Mount Badon. That victory is the subject of the poem, "Mount Badon," the transition between the calling and the crowning. It makes a statement about the poet and his function in a Christian society. Poetry is not disembodied vision but, rather, vision made concrete, strictly speaking in words but, on a larger scale, in action. Taliessin was a soldier as well as a poet—or better, as the poem illustrates, he was a good soldier because he was first a poet. Both Logres and Rome were built on a song, the product of an imaginative vision.

Taliessin, the king's "captain of horse," is poised with his household on a ridge overlooking the battle that is already under way. He sees the king, the dragon, and his troops in the center of the field: Lancelot and Gawaine with their men are on his left and right, respectively. Back of them is Bors with his supporters, the masses, hammer and sickle. The forces of Logres confront the "indiscriminate" (undisciplined, barbarous) host that "roared at the City's wall." Taliessin waits in a "passion of patience" for the moment when he and those under him will engage in battle. Taliessin goes unnoticed: "none stopped; they cropped and lopped Logres." The rhyme and the alliteration suggest something of the rough but undisciplined brutality of their attack—"their luck held." For all their strength they were less than a unified army, lacking as they did a "civilized command." Nevertheless, they made disturbing progress.

Both stanzas 2 and 3 begin with the same line: "Staring, motionless, he sat." The implication is that of preoccupied sloth. To many of his men it seemed that he "dreams or makes verse," assuming that poetic vision and successful warfare are unrelated (20). The poet knows otherwise. His waiting, charged with passionate activity of another order, is not mere loitering. "In the silence of a distance" time and space gave way to a vision that places the isolated present into relation with the universally recurring. He finds himself alone with Virgil, another time, another poet, feeling with him "the deep breath dragging the depth of all dimension" for a word, a thought, an invention that will bring into actuality the city of his vision, uniting both creative word and inventive act (34). He sees Virgil's stylus strike the wax as though it were a sword (Augustus's or Arthur's) flashing on the field of battle (Roman or British); the "beaked lines" of the *Aeneid* swoop as though they were the metal-tipped prow of the galleys attacking Actium. Virgil's poetry, he realizes, provided the diagram upon which Rome was built, and his, that upon which Logres will be established. Virgil's was a noble vision. "The firm modesty, the rich measurement, which are Virgil's had in their union Virgil's secret of power; and all tenderness went with it. He imagined a moral world," Williams writes (Essays 126). Through that vision and Augustus's strength Rome came into glorious being. "The Calling of Arthur" contrasted two civilizations in the figures of Cradlemass and Arthur; "Mount Badon" brings them together in the vision of two poets.

Virgil represented the highest intellectual, moral, and spiritual reach of which man is capable, and Rome was its actualization. There is in Taliessin's scope, however, a dimension lacking in Virgil's, a recognition of the need for "grace" in addition to intellect and vision and moral will. Virgil's lofty vision, high morality, and awesome power built but could not permanently sustain an enduring city. Cradlemass witnesses the last relic of that supreme effort in its inevitable decay. "The hero of the Roman epic was 'Aeneas the true,'" Williams writes;

> the Divine Hero [in contrast] asserted himself to be as true as truth, true to another origin as well as to his earthly *patria*. The *pietas* of Virgil was a part of and an image of a greater. The poem presented a city; the Maid-Mother's son was the foundation of all cities, . . . Virgil's rod, the hexameter, the *virga virginis,* could pierce and measure much, but not the deep apostasy of man's heart, or only with the magical sound of exposition and not with mystical fact. (Essays 126)

His revery ended, Taliessin stirred and surveyed the field, searching for the spot where the "pirate chaos" would most likely yield to the "law of grace." At his word the household swung into battle as "hierarchs of freedom." The word *hierarchs* here means the human instruments of divine power used to free men from chaos by a proper ordering of events and relationships toward the establishment of a co-inherent society. There follows in lines 55–57 and 62–64 a complex image based on a passage from the Book of Revelation. The "golden candles of the solstices" are reminders of the old pagan festival that was transformed to become a celebration of the birth of Jesus, the new overcoming the old. The "golden-girded Logos" of the poem stands "as a son of Man" amidst seven golden lamps with seven golden stars ("starry-handed") in his right hand. The lamps stand for the churches, and the stars are the seven planets signifying the cosmic reign of the new king, a mystery all the more impressive when we recall that to the ancients the stars were not inert matter but concentrations of mysterious spiritual power. The old Rome is being rebuilt on the fields of Badon; a new Christian Camelot is emerging.

On the day of Badon all warriors were "banded," amulet fashion, with the Name, protected by a stronger than mere armor. The "mere stress of glory" is more than man alone can bear. The soldiers' hair was drawn as though it were threads of light upward through the air to become conduits of a heavenly grace to the battle below. The Tower of Badon, the Tower of Babel, the Falling Tower of the tarot cards—all symbols of man's pride—heard the "analytical [revealing, exposing] word, and the grand art," poetry and something beyond poetry, which "mastered the thundering hammer of Thor" (66). The new city was born. Taliessin, who in his "heart . . . determined the war," kneeled, deferring in an act of obedient exchange to the king.

"The Crowning of Arthur" is the climax of the first five poems. It falls into two parts in which Logres is first seen as it might be in organic relation with Byzantium and then as it actually is to become in the aftermath of the Dolorous Blow. The poem begins in a blaze of light and color and festive celebration. Midnight is striking and a new day is beginning. Arthur, crowned, stands with his friend Lancelot to receive the adulation of his people. Between the two there are unity and exchange, the king holding in his mind a vision of the kingdom that is to work its way through the blood of Lancelot. Over them wave heraldic banners, symbols of virtues and capacities of those who are to build the kingdom. In all their rich variety and scope, they "heraldically flaunted the king's state" (5).

On the king's banner, ramping, towering above all others, is the figure of a dragon, a beast variously interpreted imagistically as being both good and evil. It is, however, universally acknowledged to personify primeval force, a supernatural and cosmic power that demands respect. On Lancelot's banner is a lion, a figure in Williams's myth denoting majesty, strength, and beauty. Perhaps we could say, using Williams's terminology, that Arthur's station on the hierarchical ladder is one of function—he is the acknowledged king; Lancelot's is one of merit—he is the best and bravest and, Malory says, the purest of the knights. Lancelot's lion, we are told,

> had roared in the pattern the king's mind cherished,
> in charges completing the strategy of Arthur;
> the king's brain working in Lancelot's blood. (13–15)

And in lines 56–59:

> . . . the king's friend kneeled,
> the king's organic motion, the king's mind's blood,
> the lion in the blood roaring through the mouth of creation
> as the lions roar that stand in the Byzantine glory.

Lancelot's role in the kingdom is at least twofold. He is to act for the king, and he is, as it were, to be the king's judge and conscience. When Williams speaks of the lions roaring, he is thinking, no doubt, of the figures that are said to have stood at the base of King Solomon's throne and roared approval when the wise king rendered a just sentence. In "Lilith" (*Heroes and Kings*) the lions are described: "Beneath, low crouched the lions – material strength / leashed to the will of the Lord." The lions on Lancelot's banner represent one of the "shouldering shapes" from Broceliande that have been brought under control and made a functioning part of the co-inherent society. Along with this image of controlled strength, however, comes a contingency. We recall that in "The Vision of the Empire" Lancelot's lion "bewildered by the smell of adoration / roars around Guinevere's body." The bewilderment results from the conflict within Lancelot, a lover and a man of honor, between his love for Guinevere and his loyalty to Arthur to whom he feels honor-bound.

Merlin, "presaging intelligence of time" and not blind chance, climbs the tower of Saint Stephen's cathedral church in Camelot and surveys the scene from the perspective of Saint Sophia, discovering concord between the imaged and the image: "The kingdom and the power and the glory chimed" (20). He sees the blaze of fires, the tributaried light of candles, and the blaze of torches whose light reflects on the mail of the knights and transforms them into one "aureole flame" that envelops the whole scene with a halo of glory. The flame is a pervasive symbol throughout the poem. It may, as it does here, signify an outpouring of Pentecostal spirit or, as in the case of Morgause and Lamorack, uncontrolled sensuality, and between Lancelot and Arthur, destructive anger. Fire may either purify or consume.

Merlin comments on four banners. There is first the Lord Percivale's deep blue shield pointed with stars. The color is that of purity, and the stars are symbols of aspiration. Percivale is identified with Phosphor, the morning star, Venus, as she appears just before dawn. Elsewhere, Percivale is called "the imagination of the other world" and paired with Taliessin as "twin brothers of the grand art." In spiritual matters he ranks second to Galahad alone; Williams also calls him the "young romantic" in contrast to Dinadan, "the young rationalist."

Lamorack's banner is black with an "argent fess" on which rides a red moon. Williams uses the moon, on one level, to suggest the visionary and imaginative and, on another, to suggest the regenerative powers of grace. In all instances the moon is considered a powerful, mysterious force, but Lamorack's moon is red, not silver, because its powers have turned violent. The banner has become indistinguishable from Morgause's face just as his life has been tragically and destructively linked with hers. Her forehead, seen from a casement, in the glow of the flames (burning wood or passion), appears to have "swallowed the fire." Morgause, Arthur's sister, wife of King Lot, Lamorack's mistress, is amidst the glory, a portent of coming disaster.

Dinadan's band displays a silver dolphin swimming on a crimson background in "bloody waters." The dolphin, a frequent symbol in early Christian art, usually signifies diligence or swiftness. In *The Place of the Lion,* Williams speaks of four archetypal powers ("mighty Splendours"): strength (lion), subtlety (snake), beauty (butterfly), and speed (eagle). Speed enables one to respond positively and unhesitatingly to an offer of grace. He writes, "One and indivisible, those three mighty Splendours yet offered themselves each to other—and had a fourth property also, and that was speed" (184). Behind Dinadan's mockery, referred to twice in the same line, lies a near tragic seriousness. He possesses a quality of mind that Williams calls "defeated irony," the ability to pursue life's paradoxes to their furthest limits and beyond to discover that the seeming contradictions—mockery—are but different aspects of a single truth. The intended taunt often proves merely true. Williams's best example is that taunt flung at Jesus on the cross: "Others he saved; himself he cannot save." Percivale intuits what Dinadan arrives at more arduously. In *The Forgiveness of Sins,* Williams describes what he means by "defeated irony":

> The fear is in making statements about God. There both the possibility of truth and the possibility of communication fail. Neither rhetoric nor meiosis will serve; the kingdom of heaven will not be defined by inexact terms, and exact terms. . . . Exact terms! It is not altogether surprising that we are driven back sometimes on irony, even on a certain bitterness. At least, so, we acknowledge the impossibility of the task; besides, we may find that our ironies are merely true. (2)

Perhaps "a bloody fish under bloody water" refers to the blood-red water by which salvation comes and also to Dinadan's own tortuous death to come at the hands of Gawaine and Agravaine.

Finally, Merlin's eyes fall on Bors's banner on which appears a golden pelican, the fabulous bird that feeds its young with blood drawn from a self-inflicted wound. Williams puns on his name: "the shield of Bors / bore . . ." (39–40). Bors bears others' burdens. He is a man of the people, a husband, a father, and a worker with his hands, a contrast to both Percivale and Dinadan. He, man of action in a workaday world, and Percivale, the man of contemplation, will go with Galahad, the High Prince, to Sarras, although Galahad alone will achieve the grail. Bors will return to continue his work, a witness to the power of the grail in the kingdom after Logres has diminished to mere Britain.

Merlin sees the beasts and birds on the banners as the "shouldering shapes" from Broceliande after they have been caught and fixed by man into the "hierarchic, republican" order that is also the intended pattern of Logres. From his view below with the people, Taliessin sees the beasts also as powers, mighty Splendours, in which all parts of creation exist for serving the kingdom in the cosmic web of glory, both affirming and celebrating the vision of unity: "Over the mob's noise rose gushing the sounds of the flutes" (50). This marks a turning point in the poem and, indeed, in the entire sequence. Never again will Logres seem so near to achieving the vision of the kingdom. The uncertain relation between Arthur and Lancelot and the disturbing presence of Morgause and Lamorack are portents of disaster.

There is also the matter of Guinevere whom Williams treats honestly, even sympathetically. He felt that she had been presented unfairly by early writers, saying that "the queen seems to have been, as it were, doomed to infidelity. Her husband was not to love, in that kind, at all, and she was to love too much. In a literary sense, indeed, the later Lancelot was to be her salvation, for it was he by whom she was to endure a great passion and to come to some penitence, whereas otherwise she might have remained linked with a score of unknown names" (FA 230). Williams recognizes the part that the illicit love for Lancelot played in the downfall of Logres, but nevertheless contends that "The fault of Logres is rather in A. than in L." (Notes). And, indeed, Malory reports the king as saying, after Guinevere's adultery has been exposed: "I am sorrier for my good knights' loss than for the loss of my fair Queen; for queens I might have enow, but such a fellowship of good knights shall never be brought together in no company" (II, 35). Guinevere appears in an atmosphere of romance, a potential Beatrice:

> Through the magical sound of the fire-strewn air,
> spirit, burning to sweetness of body,
> exposed in the midst of its bloom the young queen Guinevere. (53–55)

Her chalice, we are told, "flew red on an argent field" (60). She is in a very real sense the chalice, the Jerusalem, intended to become but never to be mother of the kingdom.

Williams uses the word *exposed* as a verb describing Guinevere's presentation to the court. It is the same word that he uses later in "Taliessin at Lancelot's Mass": "we exposed, we exalted the Unity" (37). In that poem the action is the elevation of the Host, but here it is Guinevere whom Lancelot brings "into the king's mind" (62). She will never occupy Arthur's heart, but her hand will be entwined in an ambiguous relation with Lancelot. Arthur could see Guinevere only as an object to round out the picture of him-

2

The Marble of Exchange

Virgil was fathered of his friends.
He lived in their ends.
He was set on the marble of exchange.
— "Taliessin on the Death of Virgil," 39–41

Money is the medium of exchange,
. . . Money is a medium of exchange.
— "Bors to Elayne: on the King's Coins," 64, 89

The kingdom is established. The king is crowned. What happens next? This would seem the logical question. In a sense, however, nothing happens between the crowning of Arthur and the birth of Galahad. The Dolorous Blow, however, has already been struck, and portents of disaster have marred the festivity of the crowning: "the king made for the kingdom, or the kingdom made for the king?" ("Crowning" 63).

Identification of the Dolorous Blow with the Fall might seem to present a problem. The Fall occurred in the mythical past, and Balin, who was to wound the Grail King, has not left the court at the time of the crowning. The chronology appears wrong. The Fall, however, which, on the temporal level, must be considered an event, becomes, on the mythical or eternal level, a recurring reality, a summation in a simultaneity of time and accumulation of distance of every rebellious assertion of the ego, every human effort to destroy co-inherence. The Fall happened. It is *happening*. The actual wounding of the Grail King is the vivid and concrete reassertion in historical time of that which is said to have happened once when man chose to know God in antagonism.

We may assume that, during those years preceding Galahad's birth, the necessary business of the kingdom was conducted and that, if pursued, it might prove interesting. Williams, however, is not interested in narrative

49

and includes no more of "story" than is necessary for his purpose. He is concerned about the establishment of the co-inherent kingdom, flawed from its inception by the Dolorous Blow, and about the coming of the grail and its achievement throughout the kingdom.

"What, then, is the achievement of the Grail?" Williams asks, and he replies:

> Dante, in a later century, was to put the height of human beatitude in the understanding of the Incarnation; in a lesser, but related, method Angela of Foligno was to speak of knowing "how God comes into the sacrament." To know these things is to be native to them; to live in the world where the Incarnation and the Sacrament (single or multiple) happen. It is more; it is, in some sense, to live beyond them, or rather (since that might sound profane) to be conscious of them as one is conscious of oneself, Christ-conscious instead of self-conscious. The achievement of the Grail is the perfect fulfillment of this, the thing happening. (FA 78–79)

For Williams the grail was more than a symbol pointing to a reality; it partook of the reality itself. "The word sacramental," he wrote, "has perhaps served us less than well; it has in popular usage suggested rather the spiritual *using* the physical than a common—say, a single—operation" (Essays 85). One needs, Williams believed, to look deep within rather than beyond material things. The imagination assists one in discovering in the Incarnation and the Sacraments the will of the divine to reveal himself in and through matter. "Christ-consciousness" and "Sacrament" are other ways of speaking of the co-inherence, of substitution and exchange, and of the power by which it is made effectual in creation. "[T]he thing happening" means the coming now as a transcendent reality of the kingdom in Logres as it already is in Sarras.

The ten poems discussed in this chapter emphasize romantic love and imagination (poetry) as means of its achievement. In the first six poems, Taliessin, the "imagination of this world," is the chief spokesman. The emphasis is on the personal and on romantic love and creative imagination as means by which co-inhering relations are discovered and pursued. "Taliessin's Song of the Unicorn" explores the conflict between romantic love and creativity. "Bors to Elayne: On the Fish of Broceliande" presents Elayne as a Beatrician figure, a God-bearer, to her lover Bors. The next two poems, "Taliessin in the School of the Poets" and "Taliessin on the Death of Virgil," seek to define the limits of poetic imagination. The last two poems, "The Coming of Palomides" and "Lamorack and the Queen Morgause of Orkney," are examples of love perverted, a source of fragmentation rather than salvation, a contingent allowed from the time of creation. In the last four poems, Percivale, "the imagination of the other world," is the central figure. Emphasis shifts from the small unit to the larger social unit, the kingdom. The first, "Bors to Elayne: on the King's Coins," reaffirms romantic love on the personal level but questions whether that relation can be achieved in the kingdom. The next three poems, "The Star of Percivale," "The Ascent of the Spear," and "The Sister of Percivale," become cosmic in scope and explore relations beyond those between individuals and within the kingdom—the relation of the kingdom to the divine archetype.

"Taliessin's Song of the Unicorn" is about vocation and romantic love, specifically, about Taliessin, the poet, and his relation with the woman to whom he offers love. It is a probing psychological inquiry into the nature of the poet and the seemingly all-absorbing demands of his art. It begins with the "shouldering-shapes" of Broceliande, including the unicorn, the centaur, and the gryphon, "in myth scanned [recorded]" (3). They are great primordial forms, the archetypal images, that emerge from Broceliande, or what Carl Jung would call the racial consciousness, of powers not only different from but often seemingly contradictory to the rational faculties. They come, Jung thought, often as images in dreams; more often, Williams believed, through the intuitive imagination. They remain, however they come, a rumor until given embodiment in action. The centaur, part horse and part man is a wild, lawless creature, often depicted as drawing Dionysus's car or being ridden by Eros, an image of animal passion. The fabled unicorn, with a horse's body, an antelope's hind legs, and a single long, twisted horn in the center of its forehead is a beast of great speed and beauty. Christians turned the creature into an allegory of the risen Christ and its horn into "the horn of salvation." It was said that the unicorn successfully evaded all hunters but could be trapped by a pure maiden to whom he was attracted because of her chastity. He became, therefore, a Christian symbol of purity and meekness. The centaur and the unicorn stand as opposites, the one representing sensuality and the other chastity. The gryphon, a creature with a lion's legs and body and an eagle's head and wings, was said to be the largest of the birds; its wingspread, it was claimed, could hide the sun. It was the sun's guardian, sacred to Apollo, and it was associated with fertility.

The imagery of the poem is religious and sexual, a fact in which Williams saw no contradiction since he maintained that body and soul were merely different modes of the same substance. The "gay hunter" and his "spear flesh-hued" are explicitly physical; the possible transformation of the fleshly woman of the first part of the poem into the Virgin Mother in the latter, and the final identification of the unicorn's [found] voice with the Word ("O twy-fount, crystal in crimson of the Word's side") is bold, bordering on blasphemy (26). The fierce strength of all three "shouldering-shapes" and the intensity of the conflict they generate are suggested by recurring verbs expressing violent action and of nouns and modifiers suggesting savagery: *raid, quick, strum, riot, quell, threat, spoiled, point, twisting, thrust, pinned, plied, throes, horn-sharp, blood-deep, lightning-wide.*

The poem falls into two parts. The first twenty lines describe the poet as unicorn, implying that he is predestined to fail in romantic love. The second, beginning with line 21, amplifies the first. The poet, the speaker, presumably Taliessin, maintains that the poet is set apart, a kind of Nazirite, whose vocation demands total dedication. His impulse, therefore, is to reject human relations that seem to disperse his creative energies. It is not that he lacks interest or capacity; he is the "quick-panting unicorn" who will come "to a girl's crooked finger or the sharp smell of her clear [chaste] flesh" (6). The poet in him, however attracted, nevertheless fears a normal sexual relation as a threat to his vocation. Williams's fullest explanation comes in his discourse on the relation between Aeneas and Dido in Virgil's poem:

> For we tend to think of Aeneas as betraying Dido by sailing away from Carthage, but Virgil thought of him as betraying Rome – or coming near it – by stopping in Carthage at all, once the storm had stopped. It is Rome which is important, not Aeneas' feelings or Dido's or in fact anyone's; there was never a poet with less care for the individual than Virgil. It is true he has also an intense care for the individual; the death of Dido, like the death of Pallas later, is an agonizing business, and Aeneas feels it so. But he has no doubt what he ought to do – what in fact he *must* do: morality in this sense is one with that Necessity which is another name for Destiny or his Fate. (*Story* xiii)

The poet can no more betray his vocation than Aeneas could desert Rome – not even for love. In both cases the way lies in renunciation, not, however, in mere negation. The woman asks more than the poet is able to give. She feels in her flesh the strong "shouldering shapes," the latent natural forces, "direct sex" among them, which demand expression: they "raid the west." To her the unicorn with his pirouetting horn seems an alien creature, "snorting" a love she neither understands nor fancies. He is unable to speak the words she wants to hear, nor can he use his "horn" in other than a "ghostly" (unembodied) manner. Pirouetting is a form of dancing, and for Williams that means poise, balance, speed, beauty, an image of artistic wholeness. To the woman, however, the horn is "gruesome."

Even if the unicorn were to conquer her ("quell" in the obsolete sense "to kill" and also in the Elizabethan sense of sexual consummation) her blood would be neither stimulated nor satiated. The seemingly sterile horn is good only to be polished for rifling "between her breasts." The word *rifling,* suggested by the twisted horn, can also imply plundering, stealing. It can take but not give. In contrast, a "true man," gay hunter, would possess her, and together they would hang over their bed the "spoiled" (given two horns and made less a unicorn) head of the unicorn. By an ironical reversal, he would be made more nearly human, a cuckold, if not a true lover. Sensuous without being sensual, even the cuckolding seems inevitable and right. Yet it is incomplete—both for the poet and the gay hunter—less than either might rightly ask.

The reference to the poet Catullus and his torment at the hands of the faithless Lesbia introduces a note of pathos that anticipates the second part of the poem. If there were a woman, Taliessin muses, who could understand the unicorn's strange love, she might complete the poet, and, with him, give birth to a new voice in which the demands of his poetry and their love might be reconciled. It would, indeed, require renunciation. Poetry is certainly a demanding master. The unicorn is "but a shade till it starts to run." Short of his vocation, the poet, as poet, has no identity. He is known only by his poetry. The statement might mean also that, by responding to a girl's love, he finds his real beginnings as a poet. On 16 November 1944 Williams wrote to his wife: "O I babble, but indeed we do grow to one thing in two modes; and indeed three—you, I, and we. The we being how much more the root of you and I than the other way around" (Mrs. Williams). Such a relationship would demand that a woman subordinate much in her that naturally demands expression, for the concentration of her energies toward that for which the new voice, the "we" existed. It would require that the poet subordinate himself, so far as consistent with his art, and that the "we" be given precedence by both. That such a process would be painful is clear:

> yet if any . . .
> should dare set palms on the point, twisting from the least
> to feel the sharper impress, for the thrust to stun
> her arteries into channels of tears beyond blood. . . . (21, 23–25)

Chastity, as Williams understood it, was not a technical matter negating one's sexuality, but it did mean its proper placement within the hierarchy of values. All the forces represented in the shouldering shapes might be concentrated into one huge tree to form the background of "dark [rough, abrasive] bark" against which their lives would be lived. The horn, while remaining a horn, would, like the spear that pierced Jesus' side, produce the flow of crystal, effecting the transformation that gives voice to the inarticulate unicorn whose song "enskied" the wild forces of Broceliande, uniting potential with actual so that it comes to be known among men for what it is. Each science, all forms of exact knowledge, are so defined and ordered that they become "horn-sharp [penetrating, impregnating], blood-deep [expressions of one's deepest nature], ocean and lightning-wide [universal]" (35). They become poetry.

The word *paramour* in the last line does not mean illicit lover, but retains an earlier meaning of "by or through love or lover." Romantic love points beyond itself to divine love, from the union of male and female to the Co-inhering City. In those states of "falling in love," Williams wrote, "the vision of the patterned universe is revealed to us." "Intellectual nuptials" means not merely intellect alone but rather the "good of intellect," the marriage of all man's powers in an indissoluble union. All the shouldering shapes, Taliessin says, might be brought by the voice of the "we" poet into co-inherence and made a structuring force toward building the city.

This poem about order, control, and balance, about vocation, romantic love, and the organic city, is written in a single sentence of thirty-six lines in which the thought, though complex, is nevertheless rigidly directed toward a clearly conceived, clearly communicated end. As a counterpoint to the free-flowing lines that move with something of the steady, repetitive motion of an incoming tide, a sense of form is maintained by a rigidly controlled rhyme scheme, which is effective without being obtrusive. It works because it emphasizes the steady forward movement, and, at the same time, reminds us that within the stanzas there are also restraints, control, pattern, organic unity.

In "Bors to Elayne: The Fish of Broceliande," the perspective shifts. Bors, husband and father, man of affairs, speaks of his beloved Elayne, not as she ideally might be but as he has experienced her. The change in view is noticeable not only in the matter of the poem but, particularly, in the structure. Bors's speech is less elevated than Taliessin's; his diction is more concrete, composed primarily of common nouns, descriptive adjectives, and action verbs, and the syntax is more colloquial. His method is tentative, questioning rather than declaratory, searching rather than visionary. We follow his thoughts in the process of forming. His questions in the first part remain only partially answered or not answered at all. Often his thoughts break off and his speech becomes incoherent or stops altogether. In contrast to the one long sentence in "Taliessin's Song," Bors's are broken into smaller units, many of them mere fragments, suggesting suspension of thought, not yet fully developed or incapable of further explication. The impression is of a pragmatic mind confronting a metaphysical mystery and deciding that, beyond a certain point, speculation must give way to action.

When the poem begins, the kingdom had been won, the king crowned, and Bors sent south to catch and control the emerging shapes from Broceliande, giving them form, that is, mapping them, turning geometry into geography—in short, to get on with the business of building Logres. This poem, however, is not exclusively about his workaday life. He recalls that Taliessin sang of the "sea-rooted western wood" (8). "A forest of creatures . . . monstrous beasts in the trees, birds flying in the flood" (10–11). These are the more practical man's version of the visionary's centaur, unicorn, and gryphon. Bors recognizes in the images powers corresponding to those which he feels awakening within himself. Taliessin's song speaks of universal things in a language that each man must translate into images that lie latent in his unconscious or arise from common experiences. To Bors it speaks supremely of his wife Elayne and of the love they share.

His immediate subject is the fish, which, Williams says, "is the strange quality of R.[omantic] Love, which comes from B.[roceliande] originally and seems to flash through the beloved; here the beloved is seen so and not as the Empire" (Notes). That is, Elayne's body itself becomes the image, a little empire itself, of that from which it derives and to which, in its degree, it corresponds without ceasing to be the human body of a woman. That body becomes the whole "forest of creatures," but, as Bors realizes, it is itself not the origin and the source of the fish that comes rather from the mysterious depth from which life originally emerged and in which it is perpetually being renewed. Moreover, he knows that Elayne, herself, cannot summon the fish at will. It must come as a gift from him, and one that is not his own to give but only to transmit: "I plucked a fish from a stream that flowed to that sea" (12). It is manifested in the union of man and woman, a twy-nature, a "you" and an "I" that becomes a "we." Although its ultimate origins remain a mystery, its appearance is substantial. It emerges from Broceliande and flashes through Elayne's entire body, up her arms (she must, it is implied, reach to take it), around her shoulders, and down her back, where, no matter how "lordly at home is set the dish," it defies being caught by net or hook or gaff (man's reason or skill) (17). It illuminates and transforms the flesh before sweeping "back to its haunts in a fathomless bottomless pool" (25). At that moment of illumination, what Williams elsewhere calls the "Beatrician moment," Bors sees Elayne as Dante saw Beatrice: "as she is 'in heaven'—that is, as God chose her, unfallen, original; or (if better) redeemed; but at least, either way, celestial" (*Beatrice* 27)—a God-bearer.

Elayne becomes the transfigured "holy and glorious flesh"—a process in which Bors had participated and one that provides a foretaste of the salvation they both share. It is a mystery. Through line 27 Bors has questioned:

"was it you?" "from you?" "shall I?" "is there a name then, an anagram of spirit and sense, / that Nimue the mistress of the wood could call it by?" (26–27). He can only acknowledge the mystery. No one but a fool or a zany, he says, would claim to know or dare to name that which has happened: "(what? [is the name] how? [is it made operative]) to bring it from the stirred stream, / and if–[this were done and it came]" (31–32).

Words fail. If what Bors has experienced by some magic could be made visible to the human eye, one would see it as "inhumanly flashing . . . / aboriginally shaking the aboriginal main" (32–33). Like the unicorn it is only a shadow until it becomes operational between a man and a woman. The only response to that aboriginal power from without comes from the aboriginal within, experienced although not understood. One triumph of the poem is its communicated sensuousness, the kinetic response it evokes in the reader, through highly charged action verbs and visually evocative adjectives. Only gradually does the fuller meaning of the image of the fish emerge clearly. "The fish," Williams says, "is not exactly Christ, but the early Church symbolized Christ by a Fish; so the light of R[omantic] Love is of Christ" (Notes). The twy-nature, then, refers both to human lovers and to Christ, the Word made flesh. Christ's love, archetype of human love, is both joy and pain, affirmation and renunciation, as the diagram of the fish on the catacomb walls signifies. Even so, Bors says, "Will you open your hand now to catch your own *nova creatura?* . . . / Take; I have seen the branches of Broceliande" (40–43). Broceliande is itself a twy-nature, both a sea and a forest, a sea-wood. The word *branches* might refer to the great growth of limbs and leafage from the nurturing roots of Broceliande, as the lines following seem to suggest. It might also refer to the many little tributaries that flow out from the "fathomless bottomless pool" to carry streams of transforming glory through the bodies of the lovers, from one of which Bors plucked his particular fish. In either case, it suggests the organic relation between sea and tributary, trunk and limb, reminiscent of Jesus' statement "I am the vine; you are the branches."

Bors accepted the possible pain as a price for the glory, knowing that although Camelot is built, it is not yet the end of making. Broceliande has riches still to bestow, a foretaste which he experiences in the transfigured body of his beloved: "Everywhere the light through the great leaves is blown / on your substantial flesh, and everywhere your glory frames" (47–48). Two words in that last line are especially significant. The "holy flesh" is also *substantial*, not as a medium for conveying spirit but actually as that of which spirit and flesh are only differing modes of the same thing. The light blown through the leaves *frames*, shows and illuminates, Elayne's body, revealing her, at least to Bors, in her true glory. It might also be said that her substantial flesh frames and makes manifest the light. She is at once the container and the contained.

The next two poems, "Taliessin in the School of the Poets" and "Taliessin on the Death of Virgil," explore the limits of poetry and the function of the poet. The first describes the far ranges of the poet, and the second, the reaches beyond which he cannot go. Vocation and exchange are main concerns.

In the first Taliessin passes through Paul's and Arthur's door to the school of poets. The reference is to Saint Paul's Cathedral and the Old Bailey, the sacred and secular arm of the social order. In "The Two Domes," an early poem in *Windows of Night*, Williams speaks of the domes visible from his office at Amen Corner:

> Justice is perched on one, with her sword and scales,
> And over her shoulders the ancient commentary,
> The cross, in huge silence that neither hopes nor rails,
> Peeps,—all judgement's ironical overthrow. (5–8)

Their juxtaposition questions the relation of the one to the other and of both to poetry. We recall Wallace Stevens's statement that for contemporary society, for whom religious belief has become impossible, poetry must perform the function once served by religion. Williams, however, saw the scales and the cross as complements, not contradictions, and each as something in its own right. Poetry, he argued, has its own existence, *sui generis,* and could never fulfill the void left if religion were lost. It might be substituted for religion, but it would never replace it in kind and would continue to function as poetry and not as religion. Williams's passion for accuracy demanded more precise definitions and clearer distinctions than Stevens's statement provides. The exposition of this poem is the relation of the secular and the sacred in poetry with emphasis on both their interrelation and their ultimate separateness.

Taliessin steps onto the floor into which the figure of Apollo, the Latin god of the sun and of poetry, has been worked. In him the distinction between sacred and secular was blurred. He treds upon a "mud-born python," a legendary serpent born of the slime left by the floodwaters. The serpent is generally connected with the Earth oracle that presided at Delphi before the advent of Apollo. According to tradition, he had power to possess individuals and, unknown to them, prophesy through their mouths, their speech becoming a kind of divine madness both feared and respected. Apollo slew the python and became, in his stead, god of poetry.

In the floor design, rays of light emanate from the figure and enmesh the entire world in their glow—London, Rome, and the underseas—symbolic of Apollo's association with the sun and a witness to the power of poetry and its role in founding earthly societies. Rome, it is said, was built on a song. But, as Taliessin stands in the doorway with his back to the sun, a darkness falls over the room, and the outline of his shadow "lapped the edge of the god," suggesting that Apollo, in his turn, is being replaced by a greater Power, just as he had earlier replaced the python (2). A new sun and a new God is rising over an old, dead civilization. The old poetry was concerned largely with rituals and prophecies, Virgil himself having enjoyed a reputation as a white magician. Taliessin, however, diverts the attention from "skins of runes and vellums of verse," from otherworldly poetry to a worldly activity related to the human body that overshadows that of the old god (15). Poetry is the "imagination of this world." For Taliessin it is less that the shadow blots out than that it gives the old a new dimension. The human body, encompassing in its flesh the divine pattern of the universe, becomes, for him, the proper study for young poets.

In stanza 4 Taliessin addresses the unfulfilled aspirations of the neophyte poets while the king's doves coo in the courtyard. The doves are first bird, but they might also image the beauty of this world, counterpart of the falcons, birds of prey, in lines 71–72. Poetry is not mere inspiration, divine madness, spoken by captives of a god, but a discipline. That delicate control demanded by poetry, he speculates, would be destroyed by the slightest alteration in the carefully weighted gold that extravagantly overlays the butterflies' wings. The making of such creatures requires craftsmanship. In line 29 Williams introduces a recurring image in his poetry, the hazel, cut and uncut. The uncut and the hazelnuts, he says, are the "actuality of 'natural grace' so to call it" (Notes); the cut includes all means of measurement of that power—doctrine in the church and morality (discipline and codes of behavior) in human society. For the poet the uncut hazel stands as a kind of natural imaginative energy, and the cut stands for the means by which that energy is turned into an expressive structure. The fruit comes on the uncut plant; it is harvested by the cut.

The key word for stanza 5 is *accuracy,* the accuracy of the weighted gold on the butterflies' wings, or the precise measurement of the "swaying [uncut] hazel's shade" and the light on the back of a neck. In both poetry and religion, Williams considers accuracy essential. "Accuracy, accuracy, and again accuracy!" he wrote—"accuracy of mind and accuracy of emotion" (Essays 157). It is the poet's task to see clearly and to get things right. One pattern of accurate measurement is found in the human body. Taliessin describes man standing upright with arms outstretched, and he sees underneath the "creamed-with-crimson" flesh an implied diagram of intersecting lines pointing in the four directions of the compass, head to heels, radial arms point to point. The figure reveals the pattern in which the poetic mind perceives "at least a kind of authentic vision" by which he experiences "physically, in its proper mode, the Kingdom of God: the imperial structure of the body carries its own high doctrines – of vision, of digestion of mysteries, of balance, of movement, of operation" (Essays 83, 87). In "The Vision of the Empire," we recall, Williams speaks of the body as an index, a means of establishing the correspondence between that which is above and that which is below.

Discipline for the poet is both internal and external. It begins within. The poet must exercise control over his emotions. In the study of the human body, the "field" (a term from heraldry), the "thighs and shoulders bare," are "grace-pricked to gules [redness] / by the intinctured heart's steel" (39–40). The last three words comprise an oxymoron. The heart, although blood-suffused, must remain steel-hard if it is to prick to gules. That is, the poet, as a man, must have broad-ranging sympathies to enter into the suffering of mankind, but, as a poet, he must also retain his objectivity and his accuracy as a craftsman. It is Virgil's *pietas* that Williams finds admirable in the *Aeneid*. "They [the poets]," he said, "will break our hearts with the agony of this or that man or woman, but their own hearts are always steeled" (*Story* xv).

Nevertheless, in lines 41–42 Taliessin concludes that great poetry is more than discipline. It is also scope and depth of vision. Those qualities have direct relation to the poet's mythical grasp of creation. For Williams Christianity, without being exclusive, encompasses most comprehensively and accurately the pattern of the intended kingdom. The poet, he writes, "best . . . fathom[s] the blossom / who fly the porphyry stair" (41–42). The posts, the right and left newels, may not seem greatly significant, as Williams suggested to C. S. Lewis, but they are in the poem and either do or do not have meaning, either should or should not be there (50). Their meaning emerges clearly in context of line 62, "the willows of the brook sway," the willows being, Williams says, the "name given to the lower parts of the Sephirotic Tree but here they are the shaking natural growths" (Notes). How Williams came, consciously or unconsciously, to include newels in the poem, is clear. He is recalling imagery suggested by the Sephirotic Tree, which, as we have seen, represents opposing forces in creation, masculine and feminine, active and passive, mercy and judgment. They are further related to the two domes with which the poem begins. They are, in mystic tradition, the two opposing forces in God: the love that creates and the wrath that destroys to create anew; being complements not contradictions, they eventually find reconciliation by way of the path that reaches from lowest Earth to highest heaven. The imagery of the pillars played an important role in the initiation rite of the Golden Dawn.

That which began in separateness culminates at the head of the stair (at the top of the tree) in unity. Around the throne the seeming contradictions and tensions find release; every joining of every disparate line becomes a center, reminiscent of the definition Williams was fond of quoting: "God is a circle whose center is everywhere and whose circumference is nowhere." The two words *tangle* and *compensations* in line 52, first seemingly contradictory, actually describe precisely the balance of the hierarchical order in which merit is judged by the way each part functions in relation to the whole. At the top of the stairs, every impulse is a gift of grace and every wondrous possibility is a will to possess. There to love is to merit and to see is to pursue. The resolution of the many into the One, the ingathering of all creation unto God, is suggested by the elliptical structure of the lines in which every unnecessary word is omitted, leaving primarily substantives – for example, "impulse a grace and wonder a will." Such precision is part of Williams's strength and, perhaps, one source of his alleged obscurity. Byzantium provides the diagram of which Logres is the intended but unrealized enfleshment. That which is there gathered to the "Nth" (ultimate) remains separate and often contradictory.

That contrast reminds Taliessin again of human suffering and of man's frustrated hopes. He recalls the *Aeneid*. Palinurus, the courageous steersman of Aeneas's ship, was thrown overboard and drowned by an avenging god just before the ship reached port, and he was permitted only a glimpse of Rome "seen from a wave" (69). This incident becomes even more meaningful in context of the poem that follows, when we recall that Palinurus's life was a sacrifice demanded by an angered Neptune in return for the safe arrival of Aeneas and the rest of his men. Even among pagans the idea of substitution is present, but here it is for man to appease the god, not God for man. Taliessin remembers also the specters of the unburied dead who in Hades vainly reached out hands (*"Tendebantque manus"*) in longing for the shore on the farther side of the impassable river. Such failures and unrequited aspirations define the all-pervasive state of P'o-lu, just as union around the throne defines Sarras.

Even the poem, Taliessin laments, is limited. Williams never forgets that Dante denied Virgil entrance into paradise. As Taliessin sang of the "stemming and stalling of great verse," his voice sharpened and even the king's falcons, blindfolded birds of pursuit, stirred uneasily. The poet's cry stirs a confirmation in all nature of the "Acts in contention" (81).

As the young poets, moved by the universal sigh, search for direction in the pattern on the floor – god or man? – the dark glamour of the old god takes on new color, and the patterns of multilinear red spread and shape into a single design. Indeed, Taliessin, the form of "anatomized man [man stripped to the bones and revealed in his basic design]," type of the Sacred Body, knows that the answer to the mystery lies neither in the old gods nor in the new man-poet, but rather in the Word made flesh. He watches as the young poets, breathless with enthusiasm, explore the newly discovered body to which he has directed them and recognizes a new danger, another dichotomy. The poem that began with an emphasis on the body ends with a prayer that the new Christian poetry embrace wholeness, a unity of vision, body and soul, that poetry become as accurate in portraying wholeness as that exemplified in the wings of the butterfly. The butterfly in Christian symbolism signifies not only earthly beauty but immortality. Taliessin prays, "Be thou a Savior, O Lord."

The poem has all the features of a traditional lyric. It is written in regular stanzaic form with alternating four-five beat lines. With one exception each stanza ends with a complete sentence, and only one contains more than a single sentence. There is an obscure but regular end-rhyme scheme, lines 2 and 6 of each stanza rhyming. There is considerable alliteration and repetition but only one example of internal rhyme: "and the nuts of the uncut hazel fall / down the cut hazel's way" (65–66). Here the rhyming of *nuts* and *uncut* and *cut* suggests the interrelation between intuition and effort, grace and law. The result is a highly ordered lyrical structure in which each element is handled so subtly that no one calls attention to itself but forms part of an organic whole. It is a masterful example of the nuts of the uncut hazel falling along the cut hazel's way.

In "Taliessin on the Death of Virgil" the theme is less the limits of poetry than the limitlessness of divine grace operating through the laws of substitution and exchange. Virgil, Augustus, and the founding of Rome provide a parallel–and a difference–to the building of Logres. Virgil himself represented the highest intellectual and cultural achievement of which man is capable, and Rome was a great secular city, structured "on moral and civil decencies." Taliessin and Arthur shared Virgil's dream of a city, but differently. The basic spiritual law of Logres was to be substitution and exchange. The taunt flung at the dying Jesus, "Others he saved; himself he cannot save," Williams called a precise definition of the City. Up to a point, he admits, this seems to demand no more than had been recognized as necessary in the old Roman empire. Actually, the statement means more than Virgil could possibly have grasped. In "What the Cross Means to Me," Williams distinguishes between "Love-in-substitution" and mere substitution: "By that central substitution, which was the thing added by the Cross to the Incarnation, He became everywhere the centre of, and everywhere He energized and reaffirmed, all our substitutions and exchanges" (Essays 137). Virgil's pieties, though great, operate in time, but those of the Cross partake of eternity, bridging the temporal lacuna between even pagan Virgil and his Christian admirers.

"Virgil fell. . . ." The poem begins with a line reminiscent of the conclusion of "The Coming of Arthur" in which Taliessin refers to the souls standing over the abyss awaiting the final judgment. The fact of human suffering and apparent incongruity between what Williams called the "finite choice" of the Adam and the "infinite distress" that followed is always just below the surface of all his thought. Virgil sees Augustus's great buttocks, symbol of the "experiences of good things," once so "infinitely large," which appear to the dying man "infinitely small" and gruesome, more like those of Cradlemass in "The Calling of Arthur" than those of the emperor in "The Vision of the Empire." The assumed foundation is not there. The word *fall* must be associated with Adam's fall, that downward plunge that carried in its wake the whole of Adam's seed. Into that void, against which both Rome and Virgil's poetry were impotent, Virgil drops. Others—family, friends and associates—came to the dying poet, but "none to save," because none could (14). Spoken about Virgil, the taunt is mere irony. The infinitely rushing downward plunge is suggested by the quick movement of the rhythmically irregular lines. The reader is pulled from one to the other by a recurring pattern of internal rhyme and repetition that scarcely permits breathing space as he is swept along with the action. The reference to Charon's ferrying recalls Aeneas's terror during his journey across the Styx on his visit to Hades, but with the difference that Virgil's ferrying is even more horrendous because his destination is no shore—not even that of Hades—but a timeless, spaceless void (17). The alliteration, rhyme, and repetition in the lines just quoted with their hissing sibilants and explosive consonants suggest the pull of the irresistible force from which "no man escapes," not even the great Virgil. The failure of art, Williams says, is the only tragedy possible for the Christian.

In the next section the perspective shifts from "that moment's infinity" to "the infinity of time" (20). The difference is between the reduction of eternity to a moment and the discovery that the moment is only a fragment of time. Thoughts about eternity, pious rhetoric for most, were for Williams matters of fact. Time was only a category of human thought. In *He Came Down from Heaven*, he points to the second clause in the Lord's prayer, which he interprets to read: "Thy kingdom come, thy will be done on earth as it [already] is in heaven." He also repeats with approval Boethius's quotation from Aquinas: heaven is "the perfect and simultaneous possession of everlasting life." This describes perfectly the view from the top of the porphyry stairs.

"Unborn pieties lived" (19). For Virgil, Williams says, the pieties were "honorable fulfillments of all moral duties–duties to the gods, duties to his country, duties to his family, duties to his friends" (*Story* xii). Virgil penetrated the mysteries of existence as deeply as man can without the Christian revelation, and his pieties were true pieties, living embryos, awaiting birth, as we would call it, through another. The Christian revelation, culminating in the supreme act of substitution and exchange on Calvary, gave Virgil's efforts a new dimension, turning human compassion and goodwill into actual acts of exchange.

This is not a poem about failure, not even about the failure of poetry. Though it is no bulwark against mortality, Virgil's poetry lives and yet does all that poetry can do, continuing into the Christian era to enliven and renew the human spirit. The poem is rather about the hierarchical ordering of values, of the proper relation between imagination and grace and between poetry and religion. It is a celebration of both the glories and the limits of man's creativity. Virgil's unborn pieties were to be given birth by others whom, pagan though Virgil was, he had helped to a grace beyond his own power to grasp. Those, his benefactors, "who had heard, for their own instruction, the sound of his calling," rushed with speed that exceeded that of his falling (29). They dived below him, caught him in "the net of their loves" (30). The web here suggests the Co-inherent City beyond his own reach. Those who had received from him all that a poet, even the greatest, can offer gave in return the one thing beyond poetry denied him, the one thing of eternal significance. Shyly, almost apologetically they offered:

> *deign to accept adoration, and what salvation*
> *may reign here by us, deign of goodwill to endure,*
> *in this net of obedient loves, doves of your cote and wings.* (35–37)

"The Coming of Palomides" and "Lamorack and the Queen Morgause of Orkney" further pursue the theme of romantic love and provide a counterpart to "Taliessin's Song of the Unicorn" and "Bors to Elayne: The Fish of Broceliande." In the earlier poems, the emphasis is on romantic love as redemption, either through renunciation or affirmation. Palomides sees momentarily a vision of Iseult not only as a beautiful woman but as an exhibition of unity and heavenly glory. The vision vanishes, however, and Palomides pursues not the glory but the blatant beast, physical sex. Lamorack, to whom apparently no heavenly vision comes, is entangled in an erotic relation with Morgause that destroys him and helps destroy the kingdom.

Palomides is an important figure in Williams's reconstruction of the Arthurian myth. He is the subject of two poems in *Heroes and Kings:*

Palomides' Song of Iseult" and "A Song of Palomides"; of three poems in *Taliessin through Logres:* "The Coming of Palomides," "Palomides Before his Christening," and "The Death of Palomides"; and of one planned but still unwritten at the time of Williams's death, the subject of which he described as "The Tournament of Lonazep: Palomides and Lancelot."

Perhaps part of Palomides' attraction for Williams lay precisely in the fact that he was a Moslem and so served an important purpose in the poem. Palomides' spiritual odyssey, traced in the three poems included in *Taliessin through Logres,* began in Ispahan, a Persian city of importance in its day. C. S. Lewis points out that it is an anachronism to make Islam contemporary with Arthur (*Arthurian Torso* 114). Williams was not thinking, however, specifically of a time or a race or a country when he introduced the Saracen knight, but of a point of view, a set of ideas and values. Mideastern religious thought rejected the Incarnation. On the map and diagram of the empire, Ispahan is identified with the place of ejection, literally, of body waste, and, figuratively, in the case of Islam, the rejection of the material creation. The Mohammedans rejected Persian dualism, without, however, allowing the Christian doctrine of creation and Incarnation. They too found evil to reside in matter and refused to believe that God had become man and lived for a time on Earth. Nor did they believe that flesh was subject to redemption and sanctification. Palomides had been taught to measure man after the pattern of the Greek rationalists and mathematicians, Archimedes and Euclid, for example, to whom the Christian gospel would have been repugnant.

Through the hazels (doctrinal teachings) of Lateran he had heard the gospel, which he explains in mathematical terms with which he is familiar: "trigonometrical," the same image that Williams used in the "Prelude." It refers to that diagram of constant relations by which the unknown can be inferred from the known, the greater intuited in the pattern of the lesser, the archetypal Holy Body in the human body. To Palomides' rational mind it seemed an anomaly that the spiritual center of Western Christianity should be located on the site where Coelius Vibenna had founded an Etruscan city that was later to be transformed into that Rome of which Virgil sang, and later still, into the city that "the Middle Ages supposed themselves to have received and sanctified as the 'Holy Roman Empire'" (*Story* ix). Behind all those cities, however, Williams discerned a basic pattern imperfectly followed in the earlier but fully revealed in the latter.

The word *prevent* could mean Etruscan magic halted the coming of the kingdom, or, used in its root sense, that it anticipated it (17). The spells of the sorcerers were a twisted parody of the restoration of creation and the union of flesh and spirit in the yet to come Incarnation. The Etruscans, who, without divine illumination, were unable to grasp that unity, gave way to the more enlightened Romans, and the Romans, in turn, gave way to a still greater Christ. The period between the old magic and the new mystery was one of preparation, however, during which Julius Caesar, undeterred by superstitions about the ghost-infested water surrounding Britain, opened the harbors of the north, making ready the coming of Logres. Palomides' dualism, however, is confined to no one time or place. The old gnosticism existed alongside Christian doctrine from the earliest days of the church. Palomides is an especially effective image because he represents the enemy both from without and within.

In the court of the Cornish King Mark, Palomides "saw an outstretched hand," just as Taliessin, on his return from Byzantium, had also seen a hand. It was the same hand but differently perceived. Taliessin saw it as pointing a way he should follow; Palomides saw it but was uncertain about its pointing. He saw Iseult's arm, lying on a table behind which she sat between Mark, her husband, and Tristram, her lover, and was gripped by one of those strange moments, which Williams explains in *Witchcraft,* when some phenomenon of the human body seems suddenly laden with universal meaning (77). Palomides sees a "ruddy" [fiery in function and bloody in substance] bolt run down her arm to fire the tinder [dry and flammable] of his brain. His emotions, perceptions, and sensations coalesce to give him, "uncrossed" though he was, a vision of Iseult not as she is seen by Mark and Tristram, consort and mistress, but as Dante saw Beatrice, "that is, as God chose her, unfallen, original, or (if better) redeemed; but at least, either way, celestial" (*Beatrice* 27). He "caught her arm in a mesh of chords" and, in turn, was himself caught and made to take anew his measurement of man (52). Though his speech, and, no doubt, his conscious thought, were still of Moslem Ispahan, he, by a kind of natural grace, "swung" and momentarily harvested the hazelnuts of Lateran. "Blessed (I sang) the Cornish queen" (55). In that light the queen's "Holy Flesh" seemed no longer waste for rejection but an inseparable component of all good, something to treasure and to rejoice in. So powerful is the spell that Palomides is convinced, as all young lovers are apt to think, that his experience is unique: "for till to-day no eyes have seen" (51). Williams, however, argues that falling in love is the most universal of experiences. In terms now familiar, Palomides sees in Iseult's arm the straightness of a perfect line, the diagram of glory. The arm, in short, becomes "geography breathing geometry," a vision of wholeness.

And then comes the inevitable question (the same that Bors asked): from where did this "new awakened sense" come? From himself? From the Greek mathematicians? Or, from some "greater Master"? The vision itself is the answer. Fiery circles seem to leap from Iseult's shoulders and finger points in arcs that form a perfect equilateral triangle:

> There flames my heart, there flames my thought,
> either to double points is caught;
> lo, on the arm's base for a sign,
> the single equilateral trine! (73–76)

His heart, his thoughts, and Iseult's arm. The influence of Dante is here especially apparent. Dante, in psychological and poetic idiom of his day, identified a lover's response to his beloved with three centers in the human body: the liver, the brain, and the heart. It is important to note that the body itself, in this case, specifically the arm, is the triangle's base. It is in the flesh that the manifestation occurs. The liver represents the physical, "the natural spirit"; the brain, "the animal spirit," or sense perceptions; and the heart, "the spirit of life," stands for compassion, for what Williams describes as "the union of man with his fellows, as in the blood" (*Beatrice* 14–20).

In this poem, the triple sides join to form "unions metaphysical," a "blessed" unity in which each element obeys and is obeyed by the other. It is a vision of wholeness, counter to all that the Saracen lord has been taught. "Through this perfect and equal relationship, realized at moments, we ought to be able to proceed," Williams writes; "the union of the three should push on through its own principle" (Notes). The vision might have meant salvation for Palomides as the fish had for Bors, if–if the situation had been different; if Iseult had been different; if Palomides himself had been different. As it was, they were not, and so it did not mean salvation. Iseult responds to Palomides' offered love by turning smilingly to Tristram; and Mark, insensitive to any spiritual nuances that the song might have, threw the Saracen lord a ring in payment for what to him had been a few moments of amusement. Palomides, resentful at being rebuffed and demeaned, is stirred by desire to possess the woman and by jealous hate for his rival. His sneering reference to "Tristram's plausible skill" is masterly understatement (128). The triangle becomes an isosceles, no longer the "single equilateral trine." It would be wrong to say that the experience became physical rather than spiritual. Rather, that which momentarily was both physical and spiritual became merely physical. The holy flesh became mere flesh. There, in the arm, the loss was manifest. The ruddy bolt quivered, darkened, and became angry fire, antithesis of the fiery circles that he had seen earlier. The lines connecting the three points of the triangle disappear, leaving only shoulder, finger points, and one star, the reconciling principle, hanging detached and alone in the cedar roof. The queen's arm lay "empty of glory."

For a moment Palomides had seen the queen as she is in God – complete woman, sensuously, emotionally, spiritually, an embodiment of the heavenly archetype, a transcient vision of the Unity. Now only the physical beauty remains, the unilluminated consort and mistress.

Palomides, seeing the lifeless form before him, recalls the foul chthonian spells that Coelius Vibenna cast over the dead, remembers the ghostly sea that marked the ports of Unity, and as the vision vanished, sees the pope diminished to the ghost of a man. The "glory of substantial being is lost."

Bitterly disillusioned, he reaches out for what is left. Flesh responds to flesh. Carnality replaces vision:

> I heard the squeak of the questing beast,
> where it scratched itself in the blank between
> the queen's substance and the queen. (140–42)

The first nine stanzas of "Lamorack and the Queen Morgause of Orkney" are built around a paradoxical image of unmovable rock and flying shapes summarized by the oxymoron "rigid tornado," perfectly embodied in the structure. The poem is composed of a series of quatrains, each containing two couplets. The number of stresses varies from line to line, and the movement is often clogged by a clustering of stressed syllables, the effect being that of a tremendous force encountering an equally strong resistance with resulting frustration and distortion. There are only two sets of internal rhyme, fewer than we expect in Williams's poetry, and those are used primarily to shade and point meaning. The verbs are mostly active, a contrast to the rigid rhyme scheme, but, at the same time, supportive of the uncontrolled fury and violence of the struggling and eventually released forms sculptured into the stone. We are reminded continually of the rushing wind and flying creatures, a contrast to the rock's hardness and immobility. The result is a tension between passivity and movement and the ponderous but inexorable progress of the action toward its dread end.

Lamorack was the brother of Percivale and Dindrane (Blanchefleur), the lover of Morgause, sister of Arthur, and wife of King Lot. She was also the mother of Mordred, born of her incestuous relation with Arthur. Williams does not tell us when Lamorack met Morgause or how he came to fall in love with her. It is not certain that the encounter related in this poem is their first meeting. Although Lamorack is irresistibly attracted, there is no evidence that he ever experienced of Morgause the vision that Palomides glimpsed of Iseult. The early poem, "Lamorack's Song to Morgause" (*Heroes and Kings*) is an unrestrained celebration of erotic love in which tenderness is overwhelmed by violence and selfless exchange by passionate possession. Apparently, Lamorack is simultaneously attracted and repelled by Morgause; he desires to possess her and, at the same time, knows that he is possessed by her. The joy he finds in the relationship is short-lived, and his awareness of its transience accounts perhaps for the passionate intensity of his attachment.

The affair is a contemporary version (in an ancient setting) of the Fall, less an event than a universal experience continually reenacted. Lamorack sees Morgause as she actually is, her face an image of the sculptured figures imprisoned in the "livid everlasting rock." The word *livid* can have many meanings. It is associated with bruises and redness, passion, or anger. Morgause's eyelids bruise Lamorack's bones, that is, disorder his body and inflame his passion; her Medusa-like face causes his eyes to "splinter." Like Adam, he sees double, the good as it is and the good in its contingent perversion; he is also splintered, rent apart, by that contingency. For man's protection, those forms were fixed in stone to insure against their becoming operative in human experience. Lamorack, nevertheless, chose to experience them in the only way he could: the "exorbitant flying nature round creation's flank burst" (4). They were *exorbitant* in the sense that, loosed from their mooring, they deviated from their intended role and became perverse realities. The full horror, both terror and fascination, of what had happened was epitomized by the bruising force of Morgause's face, which Lamorack saw as the "source of all stone," just as Palomides, in contrast, had seen Iseult's arm momentarily as "the source of all glory." Her face exemplified all contradiction, the triumph of mere physical passion and the perversion of romantic love. Like Taliessin and Palomides, he also saw a hand, but one that discharges catastrophe before which he is thrown.

The words "rigid tornado" suggest the paradox of human existence for which Williams found the perfect example in Shakespeare's *Troilus and Cressida*. The significant moment in that play comes, Williams says, when Troilus discovers Cressida's unfaithfulness and is unable to reconcile what he unquestionably sees with what he had believed to be the reality: her unswerving faithfulness. With the revelation of her perfidy his hitherto solid world is splintered, and what in his first agony he might have thought an isolated event becomes symbolic of all contradictions at life's center. Williams comments: "Troilus sways between two worlds. His reason, without ceasing to be reason, tells him that this appearance of Cressida is not true; yet his loss is reasonable and cannot protest because this is the nature of things. Entire union and absolute division are experienced at once" (*EPM* 60). The figures that could not be released have, indeed, been released. Palomides felt much the same, no doubt, when Iseult rejected his love, but also, like Troilus, he suffers as one who has believed while Lamorack savors the bitterness of one unable to believe.

The words with which stanza 3 ends, "Morgause Lot's wife," call to mind another wife who was turned to a pillar of salt, not stone, but equally inanimate and subhuman. Lamorack remembers that the archbishop had once preached about the carved figures, and he speculates that only "Coelius Vibenna and his loathly few" might actually have seen them, and then only as images of the twisted images in their own hearts (26). They have no substantial being. In this context, the first internal rhyme occurs:

> unless Coelius Vibenna and his loathly few,
> squat by their pot, by the twisted hazel art
> sought the image of that image within their heart. (26–28)

The harsh ugly sounds are appropriately descriptive of the magicians' appearance and of their rites, rites to which Palomides refers after the glory has disappeared from Iseult's arm. The sculptured figures lie sideways in the cleft, where they were intended to remain, impotent, known only to God. They remind us, in contrast, of the ancient Christian practice of burying the dead standing so they would be ready to respond quickly when Christ returned. Although intended never to be disturbed, they have nevertheless been summoned by–what? whom? the flying wings of the seamews? the mist? the mere "slant" of things? Is there indeed something twisted in creation itself for which God must bear at least a share of the blame? Their divinely permitted contingency was man's temptation. When Lamorack chose to see double, the impossible became possible; the stony figures split from their mooring and flew through the air. Chaos resulted. Nature turned against itself. Logres was convulsed (as the world quaked at the death of the second Adam) and man's wail was heard above the noise of the whirlwind. Terrified, man fled, pursued by those bruising creatures. The word *exorbitant,* to which we return, becomes even more suggestive when we recall that once it was used to describe the insane, those who had "lost the good of intellect." All this comes to focus in Morgause's face.

The poem breaks with stanza 10. Lamorack is back in Camelot where he sees Arthur sitting with Guinevere, his adulterous wife, on his right, and Morgause, his incestuous lover, on his left. Here we find the second set of internal rhymes: wife of *Lot,* / four sons *got* by him, and one *not*" (41–42). The obviously intentional doggerel serves to diminish any dignity or majesty that Morgause's position at the left of Arthur might give. Of the two women, both flawed, Morgause is the more terrible. Guinevere at least was capable of redemption, having loved someone other than herself.

There was between her and Lancelot a relation of some exchange, and that made a saving difference. The men of Sodom, Williams writes, were less sunken than those of Gomorrah, who, as he interpreted the story, were incapable of any love other than of self. Morgause's sin was not merely fornication and adultery, but incest, a form of self-love: "Balin had Balan's face, and Morgause her brother's" (47). She was a succubus, the image of Arthur, who was the image in turn of Morgause, each in love with himself. Incest is always destructive. Eventually, Morgause will be killed by her own sons, and Arthur will be slain by his bastard Mordred. The word *blow* in line 48 certainly refers to the Dolorous Blow, but it also refers to Mordred, the by-blow result of Arthur's "tossing" love with Morgause. The words *tossed* and *light feet* equate the casualness of their love with the irreverence of Balan's use of the Sacred Hollows as a weapon for self-protection (30, 62).

The "Crowned man" and the "crowned shape" are, of course, Arthur, crowned king by sacred rites and cuckolded by his friend Lancelot (58, 61). He came blindly, sight and reason distorted by lust, to a "carved tavern," which in his intoxication seemed no cell at all; to an "open grave," to which he remained blind, somewhere in the skirts of a blind wood (Broceliande's perversion), less the victim of fate, however, than of his own folly (58–59). Had he been chaste the incest would not have occurred. Over the couple hangs the cipher (the decree of the Great Ban), a reference to the ban placed by the pope on Arthur for his incest, but, more basically, to the divine ban on all forms of self-love, sexual or otherwise. Beneath them lay the blatant beast, his mouth open in a yelp and his feet wildly scratching— an image of that to which the couple has sunk.

Lamorack is a realist. He is aware of the mocking figures in the stone: of the ill-fated child that lies in Morgause's womb; he knows also that the cuckolder Arthur has been cuckolded. He has a foreboding of the "surreptitious" (stealthy, clandestine) swords, those that will slay him and Morgause and ultimately bring about the death of both Arthur and Mordred. Perhaps he foresees the splitting of the table, the departure of the grail, and the diminution of Logres into mere Britain. Nevertheless, fixed by the stone-hewn eyes and rendered incapable of action, he resigns himself to his fate: "I am the queen's servant" (77).

He has chosen and becomes one with Morgause in the gyrating rock. This is a more terrible version of Dante's image of Paolo and Francesca, because Lamorack and Morgause have gone to the nether realm beyond Sodom.

"Bors to Elayne: on the King's Coins" is a continuation of the poem on the fish of Broceliande. There the theme was romantic love between a man and a woman. Here Williams extends the scope to include the larger social order where the problems are more complex. With the smaller group, he says, the task is made easier because of the love and goodwill that naturally exists among members. When this condition does not exist and necessary exchange depends on the will, however, the difficulty is greater. Will alone cannot create love.

Bors is disturbed by the new monetary system that is being introduced as a medium of exchange, yet the idea of exchange is not the issue. Disturbed rather by the discussion among the king's council about a new proposed monetary system, Bors returns home to seek, at its source, a renewal of his own vision of the co-inherent nature of all social relations.

The first line of the poem, in its simplicity and directness, reminds us that Bors is an ordinary man, a soldier and a lover, a worker with his hands. Indeed, this is another poem about hands. "The hands," Williams commented, "always seem to me incredibly significant: and Bors feels that Elayne's hands have a power of doctrine in them more than the theological schools of Gaul" (Notes). The second line—"in your hand the bread of love, in your head lightness of law"—suggests the relation between love and law, a relation reinforced by the alliteration (*love, lightness, law*) and in the internal rhymes (*lightness, uprightness,* and *bread, head*). At the same time, Bors makes a distinction: love is concrete, contained in the hands; law is abstract, a thing of the mind. Williams, however, does not deny the usefulness of intellect, theological formulations, and social codes. Recalling Martin Luther's indictment, "Reason is the devil's whore," he retorts, "She may be, at least, the mistress of a passionate emotion, or she may indulge her own sensuality. But, to be fair to her, it is not only self-indulgence which drives her into controversies. Something has, in this world, to be *said*" (*DD* 169). Indeed, it has. The revelation of God in flesh was, after all, called the Word. Bors seeks the common ground between love and law and between the older means of exchange, labor, and the newer, money.

The first thirty-two lines of this poem explore the exchange rooted in love and expressed through labor, as we see it in the relation between Elayne and her household. "The uprightness of the multitude," confirmed in her body, becomes for Bors a diagram of the archetypal body. She looks at him and smiles, and he sees her warm love sweep across her face like wind over a field of corn. The phrase "wind's while" suggests something of the suddenness, the caressing sensuousness, and the transcending mystery of a harvesttime breeze. Someone had once said, Bors recalls, that Elayne's hair was like the color of corn, an image that does not satisfy him. It refers to externals, not substance, and the corn of Elayne's face is both corn and substance. Bors sees it in the flash of perfection that reveals a transcendent beauty. Corn, of which bread is made, gives life. Bread not only sustains the physical body, but in the Sacrament, as the Incarnate Body, it sustains the soul. Such images as that of corn, simple similes, may serve for adorning the margins of parchments in the schools of Gaul but are inadequately descriptive of what Bors has seen in Elayne. She is not marginalia but doctrine incarnate, and that is best communicated through the strength of her hands, "love's means to love."

Williams offers the following paraphrase of lines 15–17: "The power of man seems to me wound on your thumbs (which are like old heroes and saints to me) as on a winch" (Notes). As a critic, Williams avoided paraphrasing, insisting that the poem should be its own meaning. Even here he apologizes: "Sorry about this, but it *does* feel like it; this is just me being truthful" (Notes). Indeed, any good image must be truthful and accurate, and so this one is. The complexity of the syntax clarifies with careful reading. The association of Elayne's thumbs with his heroes is personal; that those heroes are ancient saints makes the thumbs also universal and gives them moral significance; thus the thumbs have powers beyond the normally human, the strength of which is accurately conveyed by the simile of the tightly wound winch. The ground is prepared, the seed sown, and the harvest reaped by those hands; from the corn of those hands comes the bread that feeds her women and his men. When each day is over and when the final harvest is reaped, there should be "none only to earn" and "none only to pay" (24–25). The importance of the idea is emphasized in a recurring pattern of alliteration, repetition, and internal rhyme in lines 24–25 and explicitly stated in lines 24–28:

> at the turn of the day, and none only to earn;
> in the day of the turn, and none only to pay;
> for the hall is raised to the power of exchange of all
> by the small spread organisms of your hands; O Fair,
> there are the altars of Christ the City extended.

The hall becomes a prototype of the City and Elayne's hands a paradigm of the altars of Christ the City from which bread, physical and spiritual, is dispensed to everyone.

From London, where the concern is to ration and rule, he returns to Elayne, "the sole figure of the organic salvation of our good," from "organization" to organicism (32). But can the figure that has governed Bors's household shape also the structure of the kingdom? Can the coins function for Logres as Elayne's hands for the household? Her hands transmitted a power beyond their own, but such is not so of the coins. In them Arthur releases a "creaturely brood" that assumes autonomy and proceeds to breed other little "crowns" (a unit of money as a symbol of sovereign rule) and small dragons (emblems of the Pendragon family and the universal symbol of power) (35). Competition replaces exchange; individualism replaces co-inherence. Like little animals, the coins forage through the countryside, carrying upon their backs little packs of values, little because they are incomplete. Nevertheless, within their limits they exercise tremendous power, replacing old values with new ones. Moral and social concerns are compromised. Arthur's own image authenticates the coins within secular limits, but, in the larger sense, the image of the king itself is not authenticated. Apart from the Center, Arthur remains the "dead king," no longer controlling the medium of exchange but being controlled by it. His deadness as king for the kingdom is emphasized by the rhyming of *head* and *dead,* and the limits of the new values, by *back* and *pack.* Arthur is losing the good of intellect.

The word *teemed* suggests animality rather than loving generation (44). Men, nevertheless, isolated and competitive, look on the coins with the same worshipful intensity as that with which Bors regards Elayne's thumbs. Contemplating both corn and thumbs, Bors recalls Jesus' command to Peter, "Feed my Lambs" (46). Bors, however, imagines the coin as devouring dragons that "leer and peer" (49). Under their weight house roofs, covering and protection for families, "creak and break," and a shadow falls over the towns: "I saw that this was the true end of our making; / mother of children, redeem the new law (50, 52–53). Another kind of engendering, the loving begetting of children into families, is required if the new law is to be redeemed. The word *redeem* is important. The fault does not lie in the coins. Matter is not evil. Money, rightly used, could express exchange, but for that to happen in Logres a radical reorientation is required as lines 54–56 make clear. In the past Kay, the king's steward, argues, kingdoms have been ordered either by military power or by religion. Now both have become obsolete, although, no doubt, both are still tolerated. In their place, he contends, money should become the new medium of exchange and control. Gold has power, he says, to dance deftly across frontiers, to speak a universal dialect (the antidote to the calamity of Babel), to replace the logothetes who in the beginning passed continually between the throne and the Themes (the provinces). Under the new system, Bors counters, instead of being fed, the lambs will be given the choice of purchase and the rich that of setting the prohibitive prices. At the turn (end) of the day and at the day of the turn (the termination of all days) the many will pay and the few will earn. "Money," Kay has argued, "is the medium of exchange" (64).

Taliessin's looks darken and his hand shakes as he actually touches the dragons. If economists who mint coins were poets, he muses, they would know that symbols are only symbols, coins only coins, carriers of values and not values themselves. When the symbol becomes autonomous, it is deadly. Parts break loose from the whole and become ends in themselves; souls are raped, organicism lost. When sensation is cut adrift from intellect, social tyranny results. The poet can find no joy in the "convenient" heresy of the autonomous image newly brought to Logres. We are reminded of the archetypes that are loosed in *The Place of the Lion* and the sculptured figures dislodged from the stone in "Lamorack and the Queen Morgause." Autonomous coins, released archetypes, loosed figures, represent the division of the indivisible, a de-incarnation of spirit from matter.

The answer to Kay's new medium of exchange comes from the archbishop in a passage that serves as the intellectual and emotional counter to Kay's rational defense of the coins. Might, folly, and greed might claim precedence over exchange, but, says the archbishop, the God who is occasionally hidden for man's pleasure or convenience will become hidden essentially. The archbishop's words go "up through a slope of calm air" in contrast to the noisy rout of the coins across the countryside:

> this abides—
> that the everlasting house the soul discovers
> is always another's; we must lose our own ends;
> we must always live in the habitation of our lovers,
> my friend's shelter for me, mine for him. . . .
> *dying each other's life, living each other's death.*
> Money is a medium of exchange. (76, 79–83, 88–89)

A medium but not *the* medium.

The last word is Bors's. He comes back to kiss Elayne's magnanimous thumbs and to assure himself that her face is still corn, substance of which bread is made, and not gold coins. She still affirms compact (covenant) over contract, a distinction that is being lost in the kingdom. Indeed, says Bors, security lies in order (God geometrizes) but one that emanates from and is sustained by the Center rather than human authority from without. The burning houses outside the kingdom, brutal display of force, result inevitably in enslavement within and without the city.

The poem ends, however, not with a judgment but with a provocative question: can law live? Can the dead king live? Can the view from the top of the porphyry stair of orderly co-inherence be sustained? In short, can the law of exchange that rules the relation of families and friends be made effective in the larger social unit? Here the reference in line 43 is picked up and elaborated in light of line 99: "Christ the City spread in the extensor muscles of your thumbs." The dead king refers both to the head on the coins and to the Body on the Cross, to the earthly and the heavenly kingdoms. The two are inextricably related. It was to preserve the law and to restore the orderly co-inherence that Jesus gave his life in exchange for man's. That act looked beyond the law to an end of which law is an earthly paradigm. Jesus accepted death and reaffirmed exchange and substitution as the principle upon which all societies are to be built. "By that central substitution," Williams wrote, "which was the thing added by the Cross to the Incarnation, He became centre of, and everywhere He energized and reaffirmed, all our substitutions and exchanges" (Essays 137). The poem ends with an acknowledgment of man's limits and of his need for divine aid. Pray, Bors urges, "mother of children," source of all compassion and community, that the coins become merely a medium of exchange to the end that the king and the King may live and that the kingdom may come in Logres as it already is in Sarras.

Percivale emerges as a central figure in Williams's myth for the first time in the three poems that follow: "The Star of Percivale," "The Ascent of the Spear," and "The Sister of Percivale." Williams wrote: "Percivale is at once Taliessin in his highest degree, and a virginal lover (because he and Blanche-fleur have no time for anything else); but also the spiritual intellect concerned with the significance of things and with the Quest" (Essays 177). We learn in "The Crowning of Arthur" that his emblem is a star on a deep azure background. That star is Venus, which the Greeks called Phosphorus when it appeared in the eastern sky in the morning and Hesperus when it was visible in the western sky in the evening. Following Dante, Williams identified Venus with the Third Heaven, a symbol of redeeming love; Percivale, specifically, is Phosphorus.

In the first poem, as Percivale plays his harp at the western magical door facing Broceliande, all distances and all sound seem to coalesce, and through a round window he sees a star ride by. The coalescence, the star and the round window, introduce the imagery around which the poem is structured. Below in the court, among the people, Taliessin sings words to Percivale's music ("he played / a borrowed harp"), turning heavenly sound into human speech. Throughout *Taliessin through Logres* we are reminded of this interplay between the poet and the heavenly vision, between Taliessin, the imagination of this world, and Percivale, the imagination of the other. Here the strains of that otherworldly music, translated into human speech by Taliessin, stirs a "languid" (spiritually unawakened) maid and she falls adoringly at the poet's feet. Mistaking the image for the imaged, she asks, echoing the biblical words "Lord, art thou he that cometh?" (10). Alarmed, as Saint Paul was at Lystra when he was mistaken for a god, Taliessin hastens to assure her that he is only human, a poet whose speech, to which she has responded, is less than the music: "*More than the voice is the vision, the kingdom than the king*" (14). And as Taliessin reached to lift her to her feet, an act of exchange was consummated: "the cords of their arms were bands of glory; the harp / sang her to her feet; sharply, sweetly, she rose" (15–16). The harp was the power; the human voice, the instrument.

Shortly she is standing by the king's gate when the archbishop, on his way to mass, sees and is startled by the flush of adoration on her face. When he asks how that "light of Christ's glory" came to be there, she attributed it to the "light of another." Affirming the laws of the kingdom, the archbishop responds, "Also thy joy I wear" (23). Wiser in the ways of the mysterious spirit than the new convert, he anticipates what might follow and asks, "shall we fail / from Percivale's orbit, we there once hurled?" (24). Can such an experience be sustained? Defending himself from C. S. Lewis's criticism of the word *hurled*, Williams wrote, "[B]ad perhaps. But the Archbishop does mean we are flung into this apprehension of exchange violently at some odd moment" (Notes). The word remained.

The question itself stirs unrest, and the poem takes a dark turn. The sun had risen, dimming the bright glow of the star, and now the clouds come, blotting out the sun. In the darkening court, the king's household talks discordantly and loudly of their fight while they await the lighting of the candles for the mass. The archbishop, nevertheless, sees as in a vision a new heaven and Earth coming through the mediation of the bread and wine, the Body and Blood of Christ whose life was given in exchange for man's.

That vision is neither understood nor shared by the entire waiting household. Lord Balin the Savage, "through-thrust with a causeless vigil of anger," moves restlessly biding his time when he will strike the Dolorous Blow (34). Arthur looks at the elevated host and loves himself and not the Christ as crowned king. Lancelot gazes on the mystery and sees only the ghost of Guinevere for whom he has an adulterous love. In short, each sees in the Sacrament his own most revered illusion of self-glory.

In the midst of that gloom, however, there is still hope. The candles on the altar will be lighted. Taliessin hears Percivale's harping and sings to his music, his words still heard by the few. This poem, beginning with the awakening of an individual, broadens toward its finish to encompass the entire social order, a reminder that salvation is never merely personal.

This critical state of apprehension prepares for the next poem. Our lives are inextricably interwoven with those of others. The girl in "The Ascent of the Spear" is the same who responded so enthusiastically to Taliessin in "The Star of Percivale." There her relation with the poet remained personal, but now we see her in a larger context where the earlier lesson no longer seems applicable. The first step toward the kingdom, secular or religious, Williams says, is to admit that others, however distasteful, do exist and have as much right to their views and habits as we have to ours.

Much of the poem's meaning comes through the interplay between the words *assent, ascent,* and *spear.* The first signifies acceptance and the second upward movement. The third, basically an instrument of division and possible death, is more complex. Williams uses it here to mean, in one sense, the division brought about by the Dolorous Blow and, in another, the death of self by which that division is healed. To what does the girl assent? How can it be said that the spear ascends? What is the significance of that to her? Williams might have attempted to answer these questions so as to satisfy our philosophical or theological curiosity, but, since he was writing a poem and not a tract, he took as his subject an experience with the purpose of understanding and communicating a sense of that experience, intellectually, emotionally, and sensuously.

Taliessin discovers the girl in the stocks, sitting angry and defiant. The guard, image of law and order, laughs and chaffs, but snaps to "rigid attention" when Taliessin appears and lightly—in contrast to the guard's rigidity—takes the spear from his "manned hand." The hand is manned in that its power, derived from the king and not from God, must give way to the higher law of grace that Taliessin represents. When the guard is dismissed, the crowd, up to this point united in their torment of the prisoner, fell into disarray, as leaderless mobs do. Deprived of the guard and unprepared for or unwilling to accept Taliessin's authority, their

> lifted arms fell askew; jaws gaped;
> claws of fingers uncurled. They gazed,
> amazed at the world of each inflexible head. (12–14)

Each becomes, in fact, the isolated world that in his ignorance he assumed himself to be. The "sight of each inflexible head" alone and without even cruelty to unite them rendered impotent their arms which in better days had helped build Logres. They were afraid, and that fear, had they understood, might have been the means of renewing their original strength.

Taliessin speaks first to the girl: "Do I come as a fool? forgive folly" (16). Williams often uses the words *folly* and *fool* echoing Saint Paul's statement that the gospel to the Greeks was foolishness just as it was blasphemy to the Jews but salvation to those who believed. To both the crowd and the girl Taliessin's action must have seemed irrational. He bids her once more to adore, the rhyme emphasizing the centrality of adoration (a form of assent) and its nature as a process and not an event. Her own adoration, as the archbishop feared, has been transient. Once more the question is asked: why should such happen? Is it a trick, a flaw in creation? Is it her own intemperance? In her own mind there is no doubt, and she responds with an intensity suggested both through her words themselves and the internal rhyme that gives them emphasis:

> Fortunate, for a *brawl* in the *hall,* to escape,
> they *dare* tell me, the post, the *stripping* and *whipping;*
> should I care, if the hazel rods cut flesh from bone? (22–24; italics mine)

Her tormentors had formed a perverse community, united in their abuse and secured by force, of which she, ironically, was part (unknowingly, unwillingly). The tension between the two confirms each other's necessary existence.

When Taliessin addressed the girl as "Ah Lady," he was seeing her as she was in God and not as the angry woman taking a stick to "a sneering bastard slut, a Mongol ape / that mouthed" her in a wrangle (21–22). He reminds her that, whatever her cause, her intemperance demands punishment according to the high steward's "needful law" (27). He also exposes her own sin of pride; her refusal to respond to her tormentors both negates and affirms community. Jesus on the Cross made the proper acknowledgment when he prayed "Father forgive them for they know not what they do." There is an irony here. Elsewhere Williams wrote:

> He had put Himself then to His own law, in every sense. Man (perhaps ignorantly, but none the less truly for that) executed justice upon Him. This was the world He maintained in creation? *This* was the world He maintained in creation. This was the best law, the clearest justice, man could find, and He did well to accept it. If they had known it was He, they could have done no less and no better. They crucified Him; let it be said, they did well. (Essays 133)

By that act, salvation was brought to man. The girl, however, by refusing to admit her interdependence, asserts her perverse independence, a luxury denied even the godhead. At this point Taliessin pauses to confess a personal fault, his occasional anger with "praters and graters of verse." Thus he acknowledges a common bond with her and with all men, and his judgment, so far as it is judgment, falls equally on all: "Will you be wroth with your own poor kin?" (37). That would include not only Taliessin but the others. Her self-imposed isolation, more radical than that of the law or the mob, was almost complete. She had passed through Gomorrah, the perversion of community, and was nearing the void, the no-community, the sinking floor of P'o-lu. On the brink, she recovers her senses, no doubt recalling the adoration she had shared with Taliessin a little earlier. Recovery of that moment of glory depended on her acceptance of the larger community also. Always the realist, the poet states the conditions for all reconciliation:

> Though the Caucasian theme throb with its dull ache
> make, lady, the Roman motion; undo
> the fierce grasp from the bench; lay on the spear-shaft;
> climb gently; clasp
> the massive of light, in whose point serene and severe
> Venus, Percivale's planet, phosphor and hesper, is here. (38–43)

The separation of the verb *clasp* from its object by an unexpected break in the line gives additional stress both to the action required and to the separateness and other worldliness of the object of her grasp. The description of the Venus as both serene and severe points up the ambiguous nature of the stocks, the Cross, and all forms of discipline as schoolmasters that prepare one for and become one's expression of love.

She must assent, Taliessin says, not only to him but to the whole of Caucasia, including its aches and throbs, for she is an inseparable part of that body. She must accept its guilt because it is also hers, and she must pursue the Way of order and of ordering. The spear becomes then an image both of division and reunion, at once the pain that destroys and the pain that saves. It represents the centuries of suffering that resulted from the Dolorous Blow, the pain that man and God together bear, in substitution and exchange, that the wound may be healed.

The Roman way might refer to the Old Roman manner of acknowledging submission of the captive. Going beyond her initial adoration and submitting, the girl laid her hand under Taliessin's on the spear, and his hand covered it, an act of mutual humility and exchange: "Her heart flowed to the crowd" (47).

Still the story does not end. Taliessin is once again the realist, or perhaps better, the true romantic. The high steward sent Taliessin authority to release the girl if she be his friend. The steward's way is that of the secular, deference to a fellow authority figure. Taliessin refuses, saying that only she can choose complete freedom. There is yet in her something of the old man, a false sense of pride. Faced with full freedom, she hesitates. "They will say—" she begins. But freedom, Taliessin points out, is more than calculating possibilities and acting pragmatically. "Do they—do we—know?" he asks (64). The archdeacon in *War in Heaven,* when asked if he were certain that a chalice were the Holy Grail, answered, "No, but I have decided in my own mind that I will believe that. No one can possibly do more than decide what to believe" (113). "Love," Taliessin advises, "and do what you choose" (64). The girl accepts the steward's grace.

The *celestialling* is apparently Williams's coinage (55). Here it means making celestial the word or seeing beyond the word the Word. In lines 55–65 there are broken lines and incoherent syntax. The impression is of a mind grasping after meaning that eludes language, and, in this case, for words that point beyond themselves to the Word. The importance, however, is that both poet and girl understand each other in spite of the inadequate speech. The fragmentary "Who" in line 57 refers back to Taliessin and is short for "Who says."

To emphasize that love is the fulfillment of the law, Taliessin insists that the guard with the appointed secular authority perform his designated role and release the girl. At this point the spear takes on still other meaning. It represents the power of the earthly city. It is the emblem of discipline that the city must exercise over the secular order. Grasping the spear and awaiting her release, she submits to both the secular and the heavenly order. Guilt is communal, and pardon must be also. She rises, stumbles, falls, and Taliessin catches her. This he can do now that she has made her choice. The grace that she earlier rejected querulously she now graciously receives.

"The Sister of Percivale" is a masterpiece of compactness and precision. It is composed of three-line stanzas that are knit structurally by internal rhyme, alliteration, and rhythmic movement into a three-in-one unity suggesting, like the "Prelude," the Trinity or God as a circle. To be more precise, however, the prevailing figure is a half-circle from which the full circle is inferred. At the opening Taliessin lies on a wall facing the western horizon, which, on the mythical map, runs from spine to head. A flash of lightning, imagistically an impingement of the imaginative vision upon the material world, flicks with unexpected illumination, separating hall and horizon, sensation and spirit, Earth and sky, in a "morn's mist of making" (4). The mist suggests the one that went up from the Earth and watered it before God made man, the prelude to creativity. Taliessin lies in idleness but not sloth, for sloth is a perversion of the will that renders one incapable of receiving and responding to grace. If Taliessin suffered even momentarily from such listlessness, it was dispelled by the flash of lightning. He remains outwardly passive but inwardly alert, open, and receptive. His voice "rove and drove" words to the "troth," a marriage of vision with its embodiment in verse (6).

In the yard below he sees a slave woman drawing water from a well. Her bent body appears to him as another horizon that defines at once the extent and the limits of his own vision. From the half-circle that he sees, he realizes he can infer a whole. To the west, he knows but cannot see, lie "Jura, Alps, Elburz, Gaul, and Caucasia," completing the circle of which only half falls within his actual vision (13). The slave's bent body exposes scars, marks of discipline, perhaps brutality. To his "heightened eyes," however, he sees circles wherever he looks (11). The scars flicker white, not red, and become starlike, images of the cut hazel, the healing disciplines, upon which Logres is built. Williams is not speaking about slavery as a social institution nor about abuses of secular power but is fashioning an image that describes the fallen human condition as it has existed since the Fall. Taliessin's vision expands, becomes universal, and he sees in the old wounds a map of salvation beaten into the back of the slave, a half-circle to be completed in the face of Blanchefleur.

Taliessin sees still another implied circle: "She swung from the hips," and they become the axis around which the radii, the two points of her body, revolve until her eyes break "with the distant Byzantium" (16, 18). In that figure he glimpses the "curved bottom of the world [Caucasia]," and his heart swells with wonder as his eyes, guided by Hesper, wander over the smooth curves of her body, which he identifies with the empire (19). Williams writes:

> and he knows the Caucasian dangers. But he also sees arm and spine and so on as the radii of the half-circle; what is the *full* circle? how do we find it? It must be everywhere, yet. . . . And this kind of thing is felt at such moments as seeing someone drawing water or handling a book or whatever; only water has a suggestion of images and reflections and nourishment and fertility. Her shoulders carry labour. . . . (Notes)

No poet is more securely anchored in the material creation. The scarred body represents all Caucasia, flesh, fallen but subject to redemption.

Her outstretched arms balancing the straight lines of her spine, she brings the bucket of water from the depth. In its rounded surface she sees the reflection of the sun, the fertilizing and nourishing source of all light and life, God himself. The "gain" for which she reaches is both the water and that which it images (24). Taliessin, watching, asks if it is possible by taking Logres as Center to know the proportions that the radii—man's intellectual, moral, and imaginative outreach—bear to the unseen circumference of the completed circle. The implied answer is, no—the Center is everywhere and the circumference is nowhere, or else everywhere, which is no particular "where." Nevertheless, man does assume a center—Logres, if that is where he is—and he reaches out as far as possible and then infers the rest.

Then comes an image in which we find what Baudelaire called a "confusion of the senses," meaning more an infusion or a coalescing than a muddling, precision rather than actual confusion. The trumpet sound from the gate is "round with breath as that [the arm] with flesh," and the sound and sight are patterned as a single diagram that signifies completeness (29). A new fate has ridden from the hidden horizon to round out the circle. If there is indeed meaning in creation, everything that happens, even the seemingly haphazard, must, from the view of eternity, be defensible. Man's peace lies not only in what he sees but in what he can infer.

A new inflowing grace and a seeming rightness, even of the scars, struck the slave girl on her shoulders, which bore the heaviest burden, and relieved her of the weight of the water. Flinging out her free arm, she experienced balance, and, looking into the water, she saw first her own image—and then "passed" (35). The most obvious meaning is that she had filled her bucket and walked away. It may also have a symbolic meaning. The word *passed* is often a euphemism for *died*. She had. She had passed from her own reflection to that of Another, and in that sense she had died to self.

While she gazed beyond her own to the Other Face, Taliessin saw what appeared a double grace in the yard—the scarred back of the slave and the transfigured face of Blanchefleur. A miracle occurred: "hemispheres altered place" (38). The "Back in the Mount" refers to the time when God, responding to Moses' entreaties, permitted him a passing glance of his back, which was all of the glory that man could bear and live (42). It was enough, however, to infer within human limits some notion of the divine fullness. Blanchefleur has become the back, the God-bearer, to Taliessin. He experienced a Beatrician moment, not consummated in the normal sense but to remain with him, an inspiration and joy. He and Blanchefleur become one in spirit and, mystically, one in flesh. Taliessin sees the two as twin sisters, the half-circle of the one closing with that of the other. Both bear scars because, in different ways, both have experienced slavery. And freedom from slavery requires discipline. The girl's enslavement is the more apparent but no more real. Blanchefleur had doubtlessly known the dark night of the soul and bears unseen scars. We remember that she died as the result of giving her blood to save another. Even Sybil, the saintly figure in *The Greater Trumps,* did not come to her beatitude easily but reclaimed her heritage only after "days of pain and nights of prayer" (142). Williams might have dwelt on Blanchefleur's struggles, but that would not have served his purpose here.

Momentarily lost in adoration, Taliessin, chided by Percivale, springs into action and greets the princess, saying, "Bless me, transit of Venus!" (53). The word *transit* in astronomy means the apparent passage of a heavenly body across a given meridian, in this case across Taliessin's vision. "The star and the scar," Williams says, "are the same identity in two categories" (Notes). Indeed, the scar as Taliessin has seen it under the lightning is not the raw wound, the hurt and shame of discipline, but rather what remains after that has been transformed and glorified. We do not forget our sins, not even after they are pardoned. Williams writes, "The new union can hardly be scarless; the original Unity, so again unified, must bear the marks of its wounds—as indeed it does: say, to name but one, of the spear-thrust in the side" (Essays 104).

Thus we remember our sins as occasions for celebrating forgiveness. "Hence," Williams writes, "T's outburst. B's greeting (like Beatrice's) is the always-approaching, never reaching relation of the divine part to the divine whole" (Notes). The scars and the lightning, the discipline and the grace, are the wheel on which the rope is wound until the plane revolves, the circle closes, and "peal breaks from the bone and the way of union speaks" (57). Morgause's eyes, we recall, had bruised Lamorack to the bone, to the depth, and so from the same source will the peal of release be sounded.

The penultimate stanza is unified and, in turn, unifies the poem, to a great extent by internal rhymes (*axis, taxes,* and *waxes*): the Center, the disciplinary tension, and the illuminating grace that transforms the whole when the full revelation is experienced and the circle closes.

The precise proportion of the diameter to the circle remains a mystery, however, like Blanchefleur's smile, an asymptote—which is a straight line always approaching but never meeting a curve short of infinity but which at that point becomes tangent to it. In Blanchefleur's greeting, Taliessin hears the "one note of the infinite decimal," that is, something that is always recurring but never finished. Alice Mary Hadfield says, "CW once referred to the decimal as an image of the unit of measurement through Creation, containing all distance and all capacity, large or small" (Supl. 10). The greeting is a beginning in time that will reach completion only in eternity but that, along the way, will provide moments of foretaste by which that state of beatitude can be experienced.

3

A Shoot of
Your Own Third Heaven

> mean
> of the merciful Child, common of all rites,
> winged wonder of shell and stone, here
> a shoot of your own third heaven takes root in Logres.
> — "The Coming of Galahad," 127–30

T he next three poems beginning with the birth of Galahad and ending
with his arrival in Camelot, and the appearance of the grail, are the
high moments toward which events up to this point have moved. Between
the two poems, "The Son of Lancelot" and "The Coming of Galahad," is
placed one of Williams's finest poems, "Palomides Before his Christening."

Galahad, man's capacity for divine things, never forgets that he is the
son of Lancelot, a chivalrous knight and faithful lover. Williams recalls
Galahad's words to Bors as Bors departs from Sarras as one of the finest passages in Malory: "Fair lord, salute me to my lord Sir Lancelot my father, and
as soon as ye see him bid him remember this unstable world." Williams comments: "The times have been changed since the love of Guinevere and the
enchanted darkness of the chamber of Elayne, but Galahad derives from
all. 'The unstable world'—yes; but it was thence that he himself came" (Essays
194).

In "The Son of Lancelot" we are asked to see events normally experienced sequentially and to grasp concepts most often arrived at rationally
as though they existed simultaneously. The problem is compounded by the
length and complexity of the poem. Williams depends heavily on recurring
images as communicating and unifying devices. The temporal and thematic
form of the poem is summarized in the Lent (Advent), Christmas, and
Easter seasons of the church calendar, which are considered here both as

a sequence and a simultaneous happening. The poem begins with the Quinquagesima season, the last Sunday before Lent. Lent, along with Advent (regarded by the medieval church as a "little Lent") are reminders of man's fallen condition and his need for redemption, the one anticipating the birth of Jesus, and the other, his death and resurrection. In chronological time, these seasons stretch from the prehistoric moment of man's Fall to the birth, death, and resurrection of Jesus. The Judeo-Christian religion is anchored in history, some of it, indeed, indistinguishable from myth but based, nevertheless, on a core of fact. Yet on another level all these events—the anticipation, birth, death, resurrection—are simultaneous occurrences, an eternal present, accomodated to "the mind of the tribes" and played out on the stage of time and space. Williams's sense of the simultaneity of eternal time makes him sometimes seem careless in handling sequential time, as, for example, his identification of the Dolorous Blow with the Fall in the Garden. In line 190 he makes Manes (founder of the gnostic heresy of Manichaeanism, who lived ca. 216–76) contemporary with Arthur. Williams defended such incongruities by saying that they are at once past happenings and also recurring realities.

The first section of the poem introduces a number of complexities (1–7). The lupercalia (from the Latin *lupus* for wolf) was an annual Roman fertility festival held on the Palatine on 15 February at which the *Luperci* (priests) ran around the walls of the city wielding thongs cut from animal skins, which, it was supposed, would cure sterility in any woman who received a blow from one of them. The festival took place on the spot where the Lateran Basilica was to stand and at a time roughly approximating the beginning of Christian Lent. Wolves, images of barbarism, appear frequently in Williams's poetry.

Old Rome with its magic is everywhere regarded as a precursor of the new Rome with its magic transformed into mystery. There are two myths of the founding of Rome. One, given by Virgil, is here mentioned only in passing. The other, more ancient, is that of Romulus and Remus, twins who were abandoned as infants, suckled by a wolf, and grew up to found the city. Their birth of the virgin Rhea Silvia, who was raped by the god Mars, established a parallel with the professed birth of the founder of new Rome. Significantly, in the year 494, the Lupercalia was changed by the Christian church into the Feast of the Purification.

In contrast to the Luperci's benign regard, the pope sees the wolves as ravaging the empire and his eyes glaze with "terror of the Mass," seeing the wolves as the savagery operative in men since the Dolorous Blow. Even Virgil could not exorcise them. In "the heart breaking acts" of the Mass, the pope sees a reenactment of Jesus' death and recalls the unnatural darkness that shrouded Calvary and anticipates the one that will enwrap "that chamber where, as in the Dark Night of the soul, 'all the windows and holes were stopped that no manner of day might be seen'; and where the princess of the Grail abandoned her virginity and Lancelot was defrauded of his fidelity, so that the two great Ways might exchange themselves for the begetting of Galahad" (*DD* 116–17). This opening passage, with its interplay of light and dark, sets the tone for the poem. Lines 8–70 recount Merlin's divination, which is not, Williams says, black magic: "it is not contrary to grace, though Merlin himself is somehow apart from the whole question of sin and grace. He is rather as if time itself became conscious of the future and prepared for it" (*Essays* 191). The "chamber of union" is the place where Galahad was begotten by a magical ingress through "the window of horny sight" (early windows were made of thin sheets of horn) (11). His magical wand is cut hazel, image of doctrine and discipline, "balsamed with spells, blessed with incision—ritually set apart and stamped with the emblem of Christ (13). We infer this from line 244 in which the hazel is said to be the "cross-stamped hazel." It is the instrument of vocation. Williams writes, "[Merlin] remained a white magician, a theurgic power, and the rod of a magician is not a toy. It is energy and direction" (*Essays* 182).

In lines 14–15 Williams borrows occult symbolism. The "Body of light" apparently refers to what is called the "astral body," man's conscious self as opposed to his physical self, which, through magical/mystical powers, can be detached and projected into realms ordinarily beyond normal perception. (Saint Paul spoke of being caught up into the third heaven and hearing words so secret that human lips could not repeat them.) Those capable of such powers belong to the "higher grades," another occult term for those who achieve extraordinary insight and mastery. Merlin's mystic vision penetrates three circles, or "spheres," reminiscent of both the Cabala and of Dante's *Divine Comedy*. Beyond the three levels on the Sephirotic Tree lies the incomprehensible God. In *The Divine Comedy* the third circle of paradise is Venus, the last sphere tinged with the Earth's shadow and beyond which lies another kind of reality. Merlin is pushing to the outer limits of time, beyond which no man in a normal state can go. There lies mystery.

In the first circle Merlin lays bare the present state of Logres in images of antithetical fire and ice. The red glow (compared with the red grail of line 30) of brute famine, the "packed [intense with animal energy] eyes of the forest-emerging [Broceliande] wolves," and the "heaped fires of man's kindling" form the first cluster. In the second cluster, the Earth lies flat, frozen, trapped, "under desecrated parallels [sensuality and substance in division], clawed perceptions [filaments ripped from the web of being], denounced to a net [the web become a snare] of plunging eyes." In Camelot "the squat snow houses" and the "huddled guards" signal the fallen and impotent state of Logres. The first circle depicts the dangers from within Logres.

The second circle details the threats from without. Merlin looks into the "accumulated distance" and sees "tidal figures / shaped at the variable climax of temperature"; that is, unstable figures shifting positions just as the tide ebbs and flows in response to forces from without (28–29). The king, lost to reality, dreams of a "red Grail" in an ivory Logres, no longer an emblem of the spilled blood, but an object of aesthetic wonder. He sees himself as rival to the emperor, object of men's "thuribled and throated worship" (32). It is a daring image, and Merlin breaks off in apparent disgust— "magic / throws no truck with dreams" (32–33).

Merlin sees Taliessin reading a letter from Bors telling how the Moslems, implacable enemies of the Incarnation ("harried God and soul out of flesh"), are building a fleet that will withstand the "stress of sea and air" in preparation for an attack on Christendom. The defense, a quality of adoration, is exemplified in Blanchefleur, the nun at Almsbury. Lines 42–44 are a tightly interwoven passage of subtle variations on a mesh of images. "Veiled passions" refer to the monastic veil and also to the subordination of earthly to heavenly passions, the renunciation of marital love for the sisterly bond of the community of nuns. That the nuns are "earth's lambs" suggests not only innocence but also substitution and sacrifice. Then comes a startling juxtaposition. They are also wolves, at once lambs and wolves—the closing of the circle. They are open to the inflow of grace, and at the same time, tenacious as wolves in their desire to overcome division. That defense alone, the poem says, will withstand the onslaught of the Moslems. Wordsworth glimpsed the unity by means of what he called the "feeling intellect," that unity of faculties in which the intellect and emotions are proportioned and immediate and lasting and gracious." The "vital principle" in occult tradition means the life force, source of health and vitality.

As Merlin ascends, words and sentences give way to a humming, a unity and a music beyond normal speech, but, when he turns his ear back toward Earth, sounds become separate, a cacophany of discord: the women's cries, the pope's voice, the howl of the wolf (40). And then, anticipating things to come, the sounds of Lupercal and Lateran cease, and Merlin is led by the wolf's howl to locate on the frozen snow the imbruted form that had been Lancelot.

At this point the poem drops back and picks up the action at the time of Galahad's conception. Lancelot is the predetermined father of the High Prince, because, Williams says, he is "(*a*) eighth in succession from Christ (8 is the number of the Christhood), . . . (*b*) the strongest and greatest knight alive . . . (c) . . . concerned with love as a thing of dolour and labour and vision" (Essays 176).

Moreover, "he will not have to do with any woman but the Queen . . . [and remains] the 'best knight,' labouring in that threefold consciousness of God, the King, and Guinevere" (Essays 189). Williams finds the substitution of Helayne for Guinevere thrilling because of the kind that it is. There is an ambiguity in Lancelot's love for Guinevere, his faithfulness being a kind of spiritual chastity, and yet, for all that, a betrayal of his king and the kingdom. It is also a betrayal of himself. He will not reach Sarras, but he will become, in that mysterious chamber of the soul's dark night, the father of Galahad. "There is no compromise with the sin," Williams writes, "but there is every charity towards the virtues" (Essays 190). At this point, Williams departs from Malory. Instead of returning to the hall to quarrel with Guinevere, Lancelot realizes the deception and suffers such a sense of betrayal that his mind is overthrown; "he runs into a delirium of lycanthropy," a form of insanity in which the victim imagines himself to be a wolf (83). The image is especially appropriate. Lancelot became the antithesis of the ideal knight, a mere animal. He "grew backward all summer," words that recall the description of P'o-lu in "The Vision of the Empire." Obsessed by guilt, Lancelot haunted the environs of Carbonek for the full winter while his "contrarious mind" was twinned and twisted with the "beast's bent to feed" (91–92). Even in his depravity, however, he is unable to extinguish entirely his better impulses:

> rumble
> of memories of love in the gaunt belly told
> his instinct only that something edible might come. (96–98)

The good of intellect lost, he slavers, howls, and lusts for food, his son's flesh—Galahad, man's capacity for Christ.

In line 105, the word *they* must refer to the wolves and the Moslems who isolate and enclose (circle) the themes. The "Crescent," standard of the Moslems, cut the narrow seas, and Manes, the Christian heretic, preaches dualism from Cordovan pulpits. Nevertheless, Byzantium is secure in the partial vision of Lupercal and its fulfillment in Lateran.

Meanwhile, Merlin and Brisen time and space the birth of Galahad. They see mirrored in Helayne's flesh the contracting and dilating empire and, in her birthing pains, the outrage of the wolf in the flesh. When the child is born, however, Merlin sees "over the Empire the lucid flash of all flesh," a brightness that makes the snow sullen, and in the child he recognizes the means for restoring unity in Logres (124). From that birth Merlin returns to the "royal doors of dream," the court in which there is neither accuracy nor honesty.

Arthur cherishes the grail "for gustation and God for his [Arthur's] glory"; proclaiming himself the aesthetic climax of Logres, he softly sleeps. Here *aesthetic* means form without substance. The queen was merely an ornament to adorn the king's office. She is, however, "tormented unaesthetic womanhood"–womanhood deprived of her natural function, restlessly giving expression to an inner turmoil. She sees herself "swathed by tentacles, her breasts sea-weighted" (133). Held by that undergrowth of P'o-lu, her breasts will never suckle Lancelot's son. In her eyes her lover appears "a grotesque back, the opposite of a face / looking backward like a face" (135–36). Lancelot's back is the obverse of the back that revealed to Moses as much of God as man can bear. Guinevere "bursts the swollen sea"–a contrast to the "flat, sole change / in her everlastingness" (134, 139–40). The everlasting diminution of Lancelot is reminiscent of the sinking floor of P'o-lu and of the void into which Virgil was everlastingly falling. As time passed, "The hoary waters / laughed and drowned her tongue" (141–42). She loses the power of speech and all sense of co-inherence even with her lover, who now is a mere speck on the distant horizon, always diminishing but never diminished.

Williams often uses fragmentary sentences and ellipses to suggest meanings that elude formal statement. In lines 145–52, however, there is obvious confusion. The thought of the sentence is difficult to follow, but this, I think, is its meaning:

> For a blade's flash [the courteous recognition of his coming] he smiled and
>   blessed their [soldiers] guard,
> and went through the gate, beyond the stars' spikes [pointed poles com-
>   prising the fortification around the compound seen imaginatively as
>   spikes for the stars]–
> as beyond palisades [within which lie civility and security] to everywhere
>   the plunging fires [reference to line 19, the chaotic countryside]
> as from the *mens sensitiva* [feeling intellect], the immortal tenderness,
> magically exhibited in the ceremonial arts [guards' ritual greeting]
> to [its contrast] the raging eyes, the rearing bodies, the red
> carnivorous violation of intellectual love,
> and the frozen earth whereon they ran and starved.

The "dumb queen," her tongue having been drowned, saw the dwindling back of Lancelot; in contrast, the soldiers saw something quite different. They saw "him." The referent might seem to be Lancelot, but in line 159 "the tall form on the frozen snow" is certainly Merlin. There is a sense, however, in which the pronoun refers to both. Both become wolves, one gray and one white, one a back and the other a face, one Lent and the other Easter, a composite figure through whom will come the "second working," the restoration of the first creation that was spoiled by the Dolorous Blow. As Lancelot diminishes, Merlin dilates to monstrosity, drops on all fours and becomes a "loping terror," a mystery to their eyes that is quickly lost on the "dark horizontal edge / of a forest" that encloses their bleak world (168–69).

In line 170 and following we have a sobering definition of love. When Williams talks about love and romance, he takes for his prototype the man on the cross, not the image on the silver screen. The "manner of the second working," the recreation by the second Adam of the original order fragmented by the first Adam, is a "fierce figure / of universal consumption" at once Lupercal, the taunt, and Lateran, the truth (158, 71–72). In the "wolf-hour," the time of man's division, even his greed and grief become graces, his gain, "the measure pressed and overrunning"; if, that is, they remind him of his need and propel him to seek salvation (176). At this moment the whole empire listens in quietness to the wolf's howl, signal of the cosmic battle being waged on the outskirts of Broceliande between good and evil, white and gray wolves. The divine archetype has become a wolf in order to restore in the wolfish his original image. The armies move to "renew the allegiance of Caucasia" (197). The forces engage and the gray wolf is "twisted and tossed into vacancy"–vacancy because, as evil, he had no substantial being, was never more than the dark side of good (208). Lancelot's head strikes the ground, and Lancelot remains "senseless," awaiting the restoration of intellect and manhood.

Throughout the turmoil Blanchefleur preserves a "dreamless adoration" at Almesbury, a sense of reality not found in the halls of Camelot (217). Deep in exchange with the world, although apart from it, she prays for the kingdom. Into her hand Merlin delivers "the child of grace in flesh" to be nourished and prepared to assume the Perilous Siege (233). Unlike Lupercal and Lateran, Galahad is not the taunt and truth but the "taunt of truth," man's capacity for Him who saved others but could not save himself (173). Having finished his task, Merlin disappears, "fled, moving white upon the motionless white," invisible, leaving only darkened paw marks as evidence that he had been there (242).

The blood glowed in the child's cheeks, as in Merlin's, which have been chafed by the speed of his running, or as in the fire kindled in Lancelot's chamber in Camelot. Blood, fire, and wind anticipate the coming of new life, images at once of death and rebirth–the child's birth and Lancelot's death and rebirth. Meanwhile, the court prepares to celebrate Easter.

Palomides is baptized on the day that Galahad appears before the court, thus establishing a relation between the two events. "He is in some sense an image and shadow of Galahad," Williams says of the Saracen lord. In an earlier poem, "A Song of Palomides" (*Heroes and Kings*), Williams had Palomides appear in the hall and actually sit in the Perilous Chair, an act that in the myth is strictly reserved for Galahad. The High Prince is recognized in Palomides in this act related to the healing of the wounded king, and through which all the court is "lost and found in Christ the truth." In a headnote Williams speaks of the coming of Galahad as an apparition, suggesting that Palomides is the physical manifestation of the spirit that is Galahad. This represents an early stage in the development of the myth, leaving open the possibility that Galahad is the spirit of Christ and that Palomides is his embodiment. Williams came to reject that version. Galahad was a man representing the human capacity for Christ. In 1941, after the publication of *Taliessin* in 1938, he said that the talk about Galahad "being bloodless and so on" was nonsense. In the mature myth the two events, Palomides' baptism and Galahad's appearance, are separate, and yet their full significance is seen most clearly in light of each other. There is between the two much the same relation as that between Blanchefleur and the slave girl. Palomides is initially the dualist and Galahad, the Incarnationalist. Galahad grows up in an atmosphere of adoration, and, if he had doubts about the Unity, they were subordinated to his natural disposition to believe. Palomides, on the other hand, finds belief difficult. To commit himself to his momentary vision of Iseult runs counter to both his training and his inclination not to believe. He is not swept into the believer's camp by great emotion but rather brought, painfully, slowly, by a deepening conviction that short of the Incarnation nothing else would do. His decision to return to Camelot and be baptized is largely a matter of will. C. S. Lewis describes him as "the dry convert – until the last moment the almost sulky convert" (*Arthurian Torso* 164).

Williams was aware of Palomides' feeling. "It was the consciousness," he writes, "of the extreme surrender and the sadness which must accompany it that caused one Christian poet to compose a hymn with the refrain: Jesus Christ is our Redeemer / And we wish to God he weren't" (*HCD* 135). The two men are best described as a composite character.

The first two stanzas, therefore, written in the present tense, are preparation for Palomides' retrospective probing of the events that led to his return to Camelot. The first line suggests how radical a change that decision was: "When I came out of the cave the sky had turned." In "The Sister of Percivale," Taliessin says that by mystical imagination the partial horizon became a complete circle, the part inferring the whole. Palomides is not a mystic.

It seems to him at least momentarily that the sky has actually turned, independently of anything he has thought or done, and he finds himself in an alien world. He too has changed, however, and, although he has not recovered the vision of unity that he had seen fleetingly in Iseult, he realizes that he must retrace his steps, going back to that moment when it all started, if he is to find peace. Everything between that time and the present seems dead, irrelevant, "fossils of space in the petrifaction of time" (3). Coming to understand the futility of his own efforts, even the capturing of the Blatant Beast, which he did as far as man can, he knows that he must now follow the track of the "slant-eyes' edge" (4). Thelma Shuttleworth suggests plausibly that this might refer to the fact that astrology is associated with the East, and that Caucasia was considered the city of astrologers (Supl. 12). It might also have an additional meaning. Later in the poem Dinadan speaks to Palomides of the path that slides "to the edge not the front of the eyes," meaning perhaps not the obvious but the unexpected, perhaps even the "foolish" as the union of flesh and spirit had seemed to the Moslem Palomides (95, 79–80). His new destiny is in "the city of the astrologers," a place founded on mystery and not Greek rationalism, which was his heritage. In the cave to which Palomides had withdrawn, neither astrology (magic or mystery) or astronomy (rationalism or science) could survive. The rocks are too hard for living roots to penetrate, and no "earth-shock" alters the smooth surface to create handholds by which a man may lift himself. The word *earth-shock* might be an oblique reference to the quake that shook the Earth, opened graves, and rent the veil of the temple following the crucifixion.

Palomides' thoughts return to Iseult and to his resolve to trap the questing beast and achieve honor, not through affirmation of the unity, but by exorcising the flesh that had become for him consuming lust. Having done that, he believed, he could accept christening and come to the table (hall or altar) on his own terms, thus providing, through his triumph, an example for Christendom of a salvation that the bleeding wounds of the Grail King seemed impotent to effect.

This was his plan. "But things went wrong" (17). Tristram won Iseult. The word *accurate* refers to her failure to respond to him with a love corresponding to his love for her, a love he felt transcended that which she gave the "plausible Tristram" (20). Palomides never forgets that he is an alien in Logres and that his differences, racial, religious, and cultural, made him an inferior in the eyes of the natives. He is motivated, consequently, by a smoldering resentment and a perverse sense of pride. This is never more apparent than when he cheated in order to overthrow Lancelot in a tourney. His shame and his pride are intensified when, fleeing in a rage from Logres, he is captured by pirates and later rescued by Lancelot. It is perhaps human that he should smile when he hears that Lancelot, "my savior," has gone mad.

In line 25 he returns once again to Iseult's arm, but, as he now recalls it, the arm lies desolate, mere flesh, around which, in his imagination ("brain") bees buzz, and gnats and mosquitoes whir. The "cream," the glorified flesh, dissolves and becomes, with the whirring insects, part of a "spinning cloud" (27). If he were able, he speculates, to conquer the beast, something neither Tristram nor Lancelot had done, the City would be so amazed that their mouths, agape with wonder, would swallow that spinning cloud, and it would vanish. With that resolve, he began his pilgrimage. He followed himself from the city—not the vision of Iseult's arm—his journey from the beginning a repudiation of co-inherence. Significantly, however, he goes "up a steep trail," suggesting not a descent into hell but a scaling of the Mount of Purgatory (35). Shuttleworth writes: "Palomides climbs through Iseult's skeleton. (CW says somewhere that physical delight should grow inward; that to measure the beloved's frame is to measure the Empire, and P. had made that actual journey from Ispahan to Logres)" (Supl. 12). His understanding is partial and his means misdirected, but his unconscious aim from the beginning was union with the City, albeit on his own terms.

Dinadan, passing, calls, "Friend, the missing is often the catching" (36). Williams remarks, "Dinadan realizes that loss may be a greater possession than having; and P. who would be quite incapable of believing believingly believes unbelievingly, by means of that more-than-irony" (Notes). Under the power of that more-than-irony and with yet unbelieving mind, Palomides goes on toward his unanticipated end, bruising ankles, knees, wrists, and thighs, seeing imaginatively the mountain as a human body over which he climbs from feet to head. He also pictures himself clambering over rooftops, like the little dragons in "Bors to Elayne: on the King's Coins." On the blank side of the roofs he sees the king's knights as flat, rubbed patches, gray blobs. Men are dehumanized. Of the two images, Williams says, "Romantic love and social order have both become entirely blanks" (Notes). He arrives finally at the cave, traditionally a symbol of internalization. Yet, ironically, even there co-inherence is present. He builds a fire from twigs left by a previous traveler, and the two, whoever the other, are united in an act of exchange that neither one willed—indeed, that neither would have recognized as interdependence. The fire is both an image of burning lust and cleansing flame. Moreover, the beast that he set out to pursue becomes his welcome companion and an instrument of his conversion. We are reminded of the words of the skeleton in *Thomas Cranmer*. The skeleton has haunted Cranmer throughout his career as, it would seem, an adversary, but as the action reaches its climax, he reveals his actual identity, saying to Cranmer,

I am the delator [announcer, revealer] of all things to their truth, . . .
I respect you, Thomas; I heard; I am here.
Do not fear; I am the nothing you meant.
I am sent to gather you into that nothing. . . .
Stop me loving, would you? stop me proving
the perfect end in the diagram of the bones?
You believe in God; believe also in me;
I am the Judas who betrays men to God. (46–47)

The ambivalent flesh will yet betray Palomides, against his will, to a recognition of the Incarnation and lead to his christening.

There follows in lines 49–72 an account of the soul's dark night. While the fire burns, he sits, and, like the beast, scratches. The fire—"flesh-fire coloured"—dissolves into a thick, greasy smoke until finally the beast disappears, and Palomides is left alone, mere aching bones on the cave's floor. Reduced to the most elemental state, he discovers that in the absence of flesh there remains still in his bones a need for fellowship. "Skeleton dreamed of skeleton it loved to neighbor"—a skeleton that was there because his instinctive need created the illusion of its reality (61). There follows a parody of the natural attraction of thigh for thigh and humerus for humerus as the remains of what was a man displays in infinitesimal jerks and sideway thrusts its irrepressible attraction for "the shining cates it imagined" (64). It is a union not to be consummated in that way. The bones grow brittle, sinews snap, and a movement of the air through the cave causes the bones themselves to crumble. There follows a masterpiece of understatement: "It was a dull day."

It was a dull day, indeed, but it was a dull *day*. A new wind, symbol of Pentecost and of new birth, had begun to blow. Spirit, which was left after flesh was consumed and bones broken, clung batlike to the stones, and less than batlike sucked the hollow cavities no longer filled with marrow. The broken bones are a contrast to those of the Crucified: "He was stretched, He was bled, He was nailed, He was thrust into, but not a bone of Him was broken" (Essays 136). In Him the pattern held. At least the bats, spirit disincarnate, image of nothingness, frightened him and caused him to leave his "pretties," his fancies. The "realist" is beginning to discover what reality really is. He was blown by the wind as ash to the cave's mouth. Before him, he saw the track, leading now toward, not away from Camelot, less attracted, it is true, by what he sees there than repelled by what he has experienced in the cave. He can think of no reason why he should not be christened, even though in doing so he might appear a fool. The Chi Rho, Greek emblem for Christ, scratched by early Christians on the catacomb walls, is on a rational level like all other scratching, but for those for whom the sky has turned it appears the only scratching. This is the implied thought of the elliptical line: "but in the turn of the sky the only scratching. . ." (82). We are left in a world of smooth rock and the Blatant Beast to finish the sentence: "that matters."

Once more Palomides' thoughts turn to Dinadan and to a time when to gain honor he had compromised honor. Dinadan on that occasion had called to the lords, "This is his day," but to Palomides he said ambivalently, "Catch as catch can." So Palomides had. "But," Dinadan continued, "absence is a catch of the presence" (92). So Palomides was to learn. If ever, Dinadan promised, in the blank between "this and that"—the two kinds of catching— "the sky turns," and you recognize in the absence the real catch, come and be christened, "I will stand your godfather . . ." (96). It was still a "Dull, undimensioned" day. The word *undimensioned* is the same as that used in "The Coming of Galahad" in a similar context but with greater specificity. In western magic the pentagram is an important symbol, four of its sides representing the elements earth, air, water, and fire, and the fifth, the spirit. When the five points are connected by lines, the result is a dimensional surface, symbol of integration and unity. If, however, there are only five points and no connecting lines, as stated there and implied here, relationships are lost and the pentagram is undimensioned. Palomides has not yet made the connections. The ideal co-inherence that he had glimpsed in Iseult's arm is yet to be achieved. Nevertheless, he rides. We must assume that at this point he has acted so far as to climb down the mountain and back to Dinadan. In Dinadan he finds a sympathetic figure. He too is an outsider; he knows no lady, and his conduct is not rigidly controlled by the chivalric code of the court. Dinadan might play the fool, but he stands apart from the courtiers, Palomides says, because "he has not the honour and the irony of the court of culture" (100). Palomides' irony here is Dinadan's defeated irony.

Williams's notes on "The Coming of Galahad" conclude with this summation: "But this kind of experience when it *happens* is beyond all formulations. . . ." He speaks of the vision with which the poem ends. Galahad's coming represents the climax of the myth as Williams reconstructed it. Either Logres will or will not become the resting place for the grail, Camelot will or will not be reunited with Carbonek. It would have tried the skills of even the greatest poet to have described adequately the appearance of the grail. Williams does not try but instead recounts its impact on those who saw its veiled appearance in the banquet hall. He writes, "All had the food they chose," a psychological rather than a factual statement. The grail itself remains a mystery.

When the meal is finished and the grail vision has passed, the king,

Lancelot, and the queen lead Galahad to Arthur's bed. Taliessin, on the other hand, finds his way to the "skied hall" of the guards, grooms, and scullions, among the jakes and the latrines. Through the windows of the hall he sees the torches as the procession winds its way from floor to floor up to the king's chamber where Galahad will replace the Old Adam in Arthur's bed. "G. in A's bed," Williams says, "is (i) a Rite (ii) substitution of this defeating kind" (Notes). "The third heaven heard / their declarations of love, and measured them the medium of exchange" (21–22). Arthur got Mordred; Guinevere, an intense but self-destructing passion; and Lancelot, the love that he wanted but not as he wanted it. Neither Arthur nor Lancelot nor Guinevere was to achieve the grail.

Inspired by the scene, Taliessin sings an old nursery rhyme: "Down the porphyry stair the queen's child ran; / there he played with his father's crown. . . ." (25–26). The king is Arthur—but the queen? Morgause, not Guinevere, bore Arthur's son, Mordred, who was already plotting to seize his father's crown. The poet's grim foreboding is interrupted by Gareth, legitimate son of Morgause, brother of Gawaine and Agravaine. He is at court incognito, his identity known only to Taliessin and Gawaine. He has been sent by his mother to work for a year as a scullion in the king's kitchen for the purpose of learning discipline. Line 34, "a face too soon to be dead," is capable of double meaning. Taliessin sees in Gareth a resemblance to his mother, and, possibly, in a flash of foresight, anticipates Morgause's murder, and possibly Gareth's own slaying later by the unwitting Lancelot, an incident that would hasten the final conflict between Arthur and Lancelot.

Asked about the new knight, Taliessin is evasive, saying only that there is something strange about him. Gareth, picking up the clue, makes the only direct reference to the grail in the poem. He has seen from the kitchen

> a mystery sitting in the air—
> a cup with a covered fitting under a saffron veil,
> as of the Grail itself. (44–46)

The cup is hidden, being itself so bright that it must be viewed only from behind a veil, saffron-stained by the glory. What had Galahad, Gareth asks, that he was permitted to lift the "Great Ban," something that the king could not do? The Great Ban, it has been assumed, refers to Arthur's excommunication for incest, but it must also refer to Galahad's assumption of the Perilous Seat, and, in anticipation, the end of his quest when he will see the grail itself. Taliessin answers indirectly. His fathers, the Druids, he says, "touched poems in chords" (sounded a combination of notes together) that told "of everywhere a double dance of a stone and a shell, / and the glittering sterile smile of the sea that pursues" (51–52). Williams is borrowing imagery from book five of Wordsworth's *Prelude*. In a note he explains,

> Stone and shell = mathematics and poetry (as in *The Prelude*) = the hard exploration of romantic states and the beauty of romantic states. The beauty comes before and after; which is why the shell has be to fitted to the stone, to breed there, and afterwards burst from the stone (eight lines from the end); this is the finding of Identity. Without it man is a mere pseudo-romantic. Galahad is the supreme (humanly) of both states. (Notes)

The poet, in short, works both with facts and imagination. He grasps the facts by an act of imagination and, by an act of imagination, transforms them. In *Reason and Beauty in the Poetic Mind* Williams states that "in more exalted moods Reason is the faculty by which Power discerns the life of things. But it discerns those principles not as a mere plan but as poetry" (23). The "life of things" lies in the paradoxical unity: mathematics and poetry, fact and imagination, flesh and spirit, the cut and the uncut hazel, Broceliande and Byzantium, Nimue and the Third Heaven, Logres and Carbonek, Arthur and Pellas, stone and shell, alleyway and the king's bedchamber. Gareth is obviously the appointed instrument to that unity in the absence of which Logres is only "the glittering sterile smile of the sea that pursues" (53). Gareth, too, has heard the poem "by a northern poet, read" (Wordsworth, by implication, in spite of the violation of chronology), and even more important, he has seen for himself sterile Logres, torn by division, bereft of vision, and without "measurement"–the perception, that is, of pattern upon which the kingdom might build. "I found myself weeping there," he says, "like a fool" (61). Taliessin hastens to assure the young man that in Galahad the stone has been fitted to the shell there to breed. The impregnation has occurred, although a period of gestation must precede birth.

The way toward that end, however, will be difficult. Taliessin describes his own experience through astrological imagery. He has seen everywhere five houses (not the five to which he refers later). They represent aspects of experience in which the division of shell and stone are most apparent and where reconciliation is required. They include the Druid oak (poetry), Caucasia (sex), parchments of Gaul (intellect, theology), altar stone (religion), and Byzantium (Porphyry stairs, vision, kingdom). Once again he refers to the newel posts, which he described in "Taliessin in the School of the Poets" and here identified with shell and stone, saying that only through reconciliation will the Acts of the Throne become known to the "mind of the tribes."

Gareth asks elliptically, clearly smarting from his present position, how he can achieve unity in the jakes. Taliessin tells him that the city includes the whole, both jakes and hall. Be content, he advises, to be there for the present. Achieving identity, socially or personally, requires openness, willingness to try and prove; a wise rejection of the undesirable and a choice of the good. These images have their source in the human body, and Taliessin and Gareth are standing in the place of rejection, designated on the mythical map as Ispahan. The words themselves are the physical counterpart to the spiritual terms in line 84: "adore and repent, reject and elect." The two sets of terms are in reality interdependent, and reconciliation is the outcome of the tension between them. Choice is possible, however, only when there are alternatives to choose from. The creative dynamism lies precisely in the tension: "without this alley-way how can man prefer?" (85).

The slave girl, with "feminine curiosity," breaks in to ask what food, given choice, he had fixed on. Did he, she asks by implication, so much as consider in food the equivalent of the jakes? He understands and replies, "More / choice is within the working than goes before" (88–89). One can anticipate and prepare just so far. The opportunity for wise choice must come "in the working," in the situation as it presents itself, right choosing being always existential, a matter of responding to each situation as it comes. She presses: does that mean that all situations are alike, that taste never varies? He hastens to assure her that, indeed, there is variation but that each change comes "from its centre" (93). It lies, that is, within the individual and his relation to the Center, the source of all wise choosing. To put the matter in light of the prefatory quotation from Dante, the choice of being scullion or knight, serving maid or poet, is less the issue than the manner in which one does his task. One's felicity is determined by "sense and more" (83). Arthur's failure, for example, was in using the kingdom for his own ends, and his condemnation would have been equally great had he been a scullion and so acted. The knight, scullion, poet, serving maid all exist for the sake of the kingdom, and no one by virtue of his vocation alone is farther from the Center of all felicity, which lies in experiencing fully the relationship, than any other. Williams paraphrases: "'When I could have anything I wanted, I wanted nothing but what was there.' All moments are equally good . . . and nourishment is in all" (Notes).

The girl, however, is still not satisfied. What food had there been for Palomides, she asks, in whose eyes the pentagram glistened only dimly when he had been christened? Is there any solace in Taliessin's words for those who, like Palomides, have really suffered? Taliessin responds by saying that suffering is universal, that he too has suffered: "I have known" (109). He proceeds to describe the process of integration in astrological images, referring to five kinds of experience, which he calls houses and has known as five "undimensioned points" (105). The pentagram eluded him so that often even the good in each slipped through the open spaces, "the gates of the winged prince of the jakes." The word *fluttered* suggests insubstantiality, lost glory, like that of the dreams of the king and queen, which Merlin describes in "The Son of Lancelot" (106). Taliessin knows that such dreams often turn into nightmares. When the shell and the stone cease to breed, a child lies dead, the potential for new life is lost. At that point there is nothing left for the cut hazel to measure. This speaks directly to the girl. Perhaps, then, she suggests, the stripes on her shoulders, marks of discipline, were the "blessed luck" through which she was led to discover the shell and the stone. It might be, the poet assures her

> if the heart fare
> on what lies ever now on the board, stored
> meats of love, laughter, intelligence, and prayer. (115–17)

Galahad's eyes, Taliessin remarks, are "the measure of intensity / and his arms of action; the hazel [discipline], Blanchefleur's adoration [the fruit of discipline], he [the wholeness, completion of the pentagram]" (121–22). Just as the emperor's clerks "study of the redaction / of categories into identities" (reduction of abstract to concrete), so must we, he says. Her hand, at Messias's disposal ("if Messias please"), becomes also an instrument ("office") of light, representing all hands so disposed from lowest to highest, from Gareth to Gawaine to Galahad. Such hands are love's means to love and the "common of all rites." They are the winged wonder of "shell and stone" through which "a shoot of your own third heaven takes root in Logres" (130).

This image of hands is further elaborated. Gareth reports that, when Galahad washed his hands before the meal, "the water became phosphorescent." Sanctity, Taliessin replies, is "common [present in all things] and crescent" (133). The word *crescent* refers obviously to the moon, which is often a symbol of fertility, the Great Mother, the God-bearer. Taliessin has seen Blanchefleur walk dropping light, as, indeed "all our beloved do" (136). Such sanctity—that seen by Dante in Beatrice, Bors in Elayne, Palomides fleetingly in Iseult, Taliessin in Blanchefleur—is "the shell of adoration and the grand art"; it is regenerative (137).

In contrast, however, Taliessin had looked at the queen's hands and seen in them no office of light. The bones of her fingers showed through the flesh, reminiscent of the unfleshed bones of Palomides when he struggled with the Blatant Beast in the cave of self. They were claws, like those of the beast, gripping the stone and fitting it not to the shell but to its echo, a perversion of love's means to love (142–43). Perhaps it is this terrible image of destructiveness that causes the girl to cry, "Lord, make us die as you would have us die" (145). Make us, she implored, die the death of your choosing into life and not that of our likely choosing of death into hell.

The last lines are a summary (146–64). The sense of the process and the achievement that Williams so obviously wishes to communicate, how-ever, prove still elusive. The passage begins with a series of elliptical phrases: "Proofs were; roofs were: I / what more? creeds were; songs were" (147–48). Questions arise. Proof of what? What is proof? Of what are roofs images? Why the asyntactical "I"? By proofs Williams could hardly mean logical or demonstrative proof. In *The Descent of the Dove* he refers approvingly to a statement by Lorenzo Valla who, when questioned by the Inquisition, replied that he believed all that the Holy Church believed but hastened to qualify that by saying, "She did not *know;* She believed." Williams adds, "and with her, he" (190). He laments what he calls "the tyranny of aggressive reason," which characterized medieval theology and suggests that there is a way by which "Reason can avoid that brutality": "It consists of saying, at the very beginning, as that other great rationalist Euclid said: 'Let us sup-pose. . . .' We cannot begin to prove anything without supposing some-thing" (122). Williams began by supposing that it is possible to fit stone and shell so as to bring the undimensioned houses into an image of cosmic co-inherence. That such an order exists, of course, remains a supposition not subject to factual demonstration. In the novel *Many Dimensions* Lord Arglay, chief justice, confronted with a mysterious and miracle working stone, image of the first matter, suggests, "that amid all this mess of myths and tangle of traditions and . . . and . . . febrifuge of fables, there is some-thing extreme and terrible" (128). Williams had subjected his own hypo-thesis to the test of experience; he had accepted its mythological embodi-ment as having the truth of myth if not of historical or scientific fact. He concluded that, in ultimate matters, intuition and vision penetrated beyond the reach of the rational mind and of demonstrative skills. "Renounce the myth [any one version of it] and the vision [the Myth] remains," (*HCD* 14) he asserts. This is the "proof" to which Taliessin points.

"Roofs were" is more elusive. In two other poems roofs serve as images. Bors imagines the "little dragons" scampering over house roofs that creak and break under their weight. Palomides pictures himself clambering over roofs on houses without doors. On their blank sides he sees the king's knights as flat undimensional figures. There is neither relationship nor points of en-try. Personal, romantic, and social values have been lost. In both cases, the roofs are coverings for houses, places where families live, images of co-inherence. They are being destroyed. Here he refers to roofs "slanted to each cleft" on the five zodiacal houses (149). In line 12 he had used the word *cleft* to describe the division between bedchamber and alley; in lines 100–109, he referred to the undimensioned points that when joined compose a pentagram. He returns to the image: five undimensioned points with two lines from each that slant outward toward a common center so as to form five detached roofs. If the clefts between them were closed and all lines joined, they would form both a pentagram and a star. Taliessin must discover a means for bringing that unity and wholeness about. The word *roof*, it is worth noting, occurs in the literature of alchemy and mysticism. Regardie, for example, quotes Thomas Vaughn, the seventeenth-century hermeticist, as saying, "Thou must prepare thyself till thou art conformable to Him Whom thou wouldst entertain, and that in every respect. Fit thy roof to thy God in what thou canst, and in what thou canst not He will help thee" (I, 73). Taliessin is concerned with relating the five areas of experience represented by the five zodiacal houses so that their roofs "fit" to form the pattern of co-inherence. There follows the asyntactical I, emphasized by its isolated position at the end of the line. It seems to hang in space. In absence of rational and scientific proof, Williams implies, man is in some sense alone, thrown back upon himself to hypothesize and, ultimately, to make a choice of whether to believe or not to believe, to act or not to act. The decision is personal and existential. "What more?" he asks. There are some things. There are creeds, intellectual formulations, songs; there are poetic visions, mythic structures. They help, but are they enough? The dynamic that brings them all together is suggested by the image that follows.

The five zodiacal houses are Mercury, Venus, Earth, Jupiter, and Saturn. The throne's firmament is the Earth, surrounded by the other zones. The first of the Sephiroth, Earth (Malkuth), is known as the kingdom. Mercury and Venus lie within the Earth's shadow in this Semi-Ptolemaic scheme. In the poem Taliessin describes Mercury as "thirsting to theft," but Williams characterizes him more explicitly in his notes as touched by "desire and greed." Dante places the planet second lowest among the circles of paradise and assigns Justinian to it as an example of rulers whose pride and delight in their own fame mar their service to the kingdom. Williams does not associate this planet with any one character but demands of everyone complete devotion to his function. He identifies Venus particularly with Percivale, and here the image stands for "preference" ("election"), albeit for selective choice: "of the greatest," love (151).

Beyond Mercury and Venus, Jupiter and Saturn circle. Earth, in between, is "seen and strewn by the four." *Strewn* is used in its root sense meaning to be covered over by something strewn. The astrological assumption that the planets exert influence over man is taken as an image of cosmic meaningfulness and of divine providence. There is, Taliessin says, a pattern of relations among the houses, a sense of unity that may be described as "an authentic poetic vision." With these two planets, which lie beyond Earth's shadow, we enter a realm beyond man's normal apprehension.

Jupiter, with its two moons of "irony and defeated irony" is represented by Lancelot and Blanchefleur (153). Lancelot, irony, could not relate what he sought, fidelity in love, with what he got. Blanchefleur, on the other hand, perceived, beyond Lancelot's understanding, the divine plan for the union of Camelot with Carbonek, or the vision with the reality. Her hand and head (effort and will) were the shell bursting from the stone. A reference to Dante is helpful here. He makes Jupiter the image of justice but distinguishes between human and divine justice, the latter being, he says, beyond human intellect. That justice, Blanchefleur's, is defeated irony.

Logres has come into Jupiter with the coming of Galahad, Taliessin says, and now, with the other planets, circles Saturn, which is "girdled by turned space." The image of "turned space" is a repetition of that in "The Sister of Percivale" and "Palomides Before his Christening." The horizons come together to form a circle. Saturn was associated with contemplation and the mystic vision. In *The Divine Comedy* a golden ladder ascends from Saturn into the heavens beyond where it is lost in the mystery. Galahad represents man's capacity for wholeness. Jupiter, the present state of Logres, is the stone awaiting union with the shell, Saturn. In a moment of mystic vision, it all becomes clear to Taliessin, whose eyes are "non-human; he sees 'The Throne' and his eyes resemble the Throne" (Notes). Emeralds of fire, seemingly points emanating from the throne and sinking through all Logres, catch everything up in a single web of glory. That vision, however, is the poet's alone and remains blank to scullion and serving maid. The image of the eyes is similar to that of the cone found in "The Vision of the Empire" (86). Both are derived at least partially from what in occultism is called "a cone of energy," claimed by adepts to rise from the magic circle in a spiral of silver-blue light.

4

The Moon Waxes and Wanes

the moon waxes and wanes in the perilous chair,
where time's foster-child sits, Lancelot's son.
> —"The Departure of Merlin," 55–56

The first three poems of the five that are the subject of this chapter, "The Departure of Merlin," "The Death of Palomides," and "Percivale at Carbonek," are united in tone. Time has passed. The grail quest, for most of the knights, has failed. The kingdom has disintegrated. The king, Mordred, Gawaine, Agravaine, Gareth, Dinadan, Lot, and Morgause are all dead. Lancelot remains, but, although having come close, failed to achieve the grail. Guinevere is in a convent, a penitent. Even the entering of Carbonek seemed an anticlimax. Logres is on the verge of fading into mere Britain. These three poems mark a transition from the bright expectations with which "The Coming of Galahad" ended and that which follows in the two poems with which this chapter ends, "The Last Voyage" and "Taliessin at Lancelot's Mass." Two notes seem necessary before discussing these five poems: one, a comment on the moon as image; and second, a further statement about Merlin as a symbol of time in relation to eternity.

Williams found the moon an attractive image because, I think, like the hazel, it was "capable of more than one significance." As with so many of his images, the moon represents materials from varied sources out of which he constructed a device of many thematic and emotional uses. Basically the moon is the feminine counterpart of the masculine sun, giving off no light herself but reflecting that of the other. She was called the "funnel" (in Cabalistic lore—located on the Sephirotic Tree immediately above Malkuth, feminine Earth or kingdom) through which divine energy flows downward to man. The moon is also a symbol of fertility and of the vital forces of nature. For centuries farmers consulted the position of the moon before planting crops to determine when conditions were right for best germination and growth.

In astrology the moon was considered the most important celestial body after the sun since it moves through all the signs of the zodiac and was assumed to influence everyone's horoscope. On the Sephirotic Tree it symbolizes the reconciling forces that harmonize polarities. In all traditions it represents mystery and the supernatural. Williams used it particularly as an image of the regenerative power of divine grace, the reconciling element between opposing forces in man and between heaven and Earth. He saw it also as an image of visionary and creative imagination.

In yet another way the moon must have appealed to him especially. It can be at once an image of change and of changelessness. The fact that it enters a new sign of the zodiac approximately every two and a half days and is seen on Earth as a continually waxing and waning object has made it in popular culture synonymous with irresponsible change. On the other hand, since its changing phases are part of a stable recurring cycle, it can be seen just as readily to represent a changeless order of which the phases are patterned images. From this point of view, the moon is seen as the means of increase and decrease, growth and decay, life and death in a never changing, life-sustaining process.

Nowhere are the moon's multiple meanings so dramatically portrayed, however, as in the tarot cards. There it falls between the Star, symbol of aspiration and hope, and the Sun, the source of light and life. The card itself portrays a wolf and a dog (the animal nature) howling at the moon, while beneath a crayfish crawls out of a pool of water, symbol in modern psychology of the impingement of the unconscious on the conscious.

With the general failure of the grail quest, the problem of the relation between time and eternity becomes a pervasive concern. It is brought into focus in the first of these five poems, "The Departure of Merlin." The word is *departure*, not *death*. By the time Williams came to write these poems, as we have seen, he had come to think of time and space (Merlin and Brisen) as the human manifestations of the simultaneity of events and the accumulation of distances on the eternal level. Time neither dies nor sinks into shameful perversion, as Merlin does in Malory and Tennyson, but is brought eventually into synchronization with eternity, and space is not obliterated but made one with spacelessness so that all things are at once "near and far infinite and equal" (39). The omission of the expected comma further suggests the identity also of time and space.

"The Departure of Merlin" begins with the pope standing at "Lateran's stone," a reference that, coming as it does, is difficult to dissociate from the stone of the previous poem. The pope presents himself, in the "heart-breaking manual acts" of the sacrament as a vicarious offering before God in substitution for all men ("Vision" 97). The themes are "pointed" by the appearance of Galahad from Trebizond (a city on the Black Sea that marks the boundary between Christian and Moslem empires) and Archangel (city far north on the White Sea), from, that is, the sunlit to the frozen. Throughout, the empire "befriends the World's ends," and, in the action of the Mass, the heretical doctors, Moslem and Christian, are refuted. In "time-spanned" (temporal) Logres, the end approaches, and the destruction of the round table is imminent. The "method of phenomena"–the medium through which sense perceptions are manifest–is about to be indrawn, not withdrawn, to Broceliande. Although Logres will dwindle into mere Britain, the emperor will continue to be seen on occasions as "flashes of perfection."

Merlin's immediate work, preparing for Galahad's birth, is completed when he delivers the High Prince to the "moon of white nuns." The word *moon* refers to the nuns as reflection of the divine light, the God-bearers. In line 9 it refers also to the mysterious power that pointed the themes with a new brightness, a reflected power that could transform a secular government into a "web of wood," the "coeval rooted world's idea." It could be the means by which the Holy Grail was brought to Logres.

In line 13 the waxing moon refers to the hope promised in a moon of increase, the appearance of the Holy Grail, signaling that Merlin's work is done and that the "blessed young sorcerer" may return to the "heart's simultaneity" (16). The verb *span* is ambivalent. One of its meanings is to measure and to reveal the pattern of the eternal in the phenomena. It means also to bring distant points together, or, "to accumulate distances." Merlin is being indrawn and made one again with Broceliande. There he, foster father of Galahad, is met by Joseph of Nazareth, the foster father of the womb, and Joseph of Arimathea, foster father of the tomb. According to legend, Joseph of Arimathea received the blood of Jesus in the cup from which he drank at the Last Supper and which Joseph later brought to Britain. The two Josephs are foster father in that both presided at a birth not of their own engendering. They are "twin suns," earthly types of the Sun, the father from whom all life comes.

Broceliande, the "coeval-rooted world's idea," is the archetype of that which time and space were to have synchronized in Logres, a place not only of simultaneity and accumulation, but of both lively action (the Josephs came dancing) and of repose (18). There is no strife except growth from the roots and no reaction to that growth but repose, joyful acceptance. It is a state reminiscent of that described in "The Coming of Galahad": "Felicity alters from its centre" (93). The "rich-ringed moments" of line 23 is an image based on the growth rings of a tree trunk that, indeed, follow one after another in what might be called sequence and yet are all part of an organic whole, an integrated pattern of growth from the center. Their voices are "young-leaved," expressive, that is, of joy and renewal, the perpetually young, like Merlin.

The moons that wax and wane have come away from sequence, the changing phases lost in the stable, recurring cycle, a perfect circle. Even the sun and moon are brought into oneness in Broceliande where all is cause and effect at once. The laws of Merlin's boyhood, time and space, cause and effect, accommodations to human limitations, are unknown in the place of making.

Taliessin enters the poem in his own person in line 29, seeing in a vision from the deck of a galley the figure of Merlin among the trees. At the same time the form of the headless emperor fades, not dies, because he never had substantial being. The flat djongs, without sails, in contrast to the galley, and thus unable to catch in and be driven by the wind, drift aimlessly toward P'o-lu. To describe their moving as floating is accurate. The journey to P'o-lu is an easy one. We are reminded of Evelyn's protest (*All Hallows' Eve*) when she is dead and drifting deeper and deeper into hell, "Why are we here like this? I haven't done anything" (22). Precisely. It is that easy. The sight of alive and joyful Broceliande had diverse effects on the sailors who viewed it from the galley. One, ghastly and gaping, despaired of joy and leapt into the phosphorescence (the deceptive glow of P'o-lu), his mind shattered, his capacity for love extinguished. Others, however, hearing the sea call bidding tack, sprang to the oars and with the help of the purple sails made for Byzantium, an effort at once human and divine. The sails of the galley, purple because that is the symbolic color for spirituality and effort, are caught by the winds and driven toward port, not in place of but as a necessary supplement to the sailors' efforts. There is no place in Byzantium and beyond in Sarras for the drifting and fearful. For those who position their sails ("tack") to catch the wind and apply themselves to the oars, Byzantium is at once "near and far infinite and equal" (39). Williams writes: "And the distance from the antipodes is no greater, in grace, than from, say, Camelot" (Notes).

Williams introduces another complex image in lines 41–42: "More than the fable of Dryads is troth to the Table / in the growth of hazel and elm, oak and bamboo." The Dryads, according to legend, are born and die with the trees they inhabit, their identity being that of the trees. So must one's troth to the table be. The word *troth* suggests a sacramental relation and an indissoluble union. The table might be the Round Table, but, in this case, it is more likely the "stone" upon which a type of the Holy Grail is reserved (1). Is there a particular meaning in the words, their pairing and their ordering? The hazel is associated with discipline and grace and the bamboo with P'o-lu. In between the two are the building materials of elm and oak. Is Williams saying that the spiritual powers are operative everywhere, among both hazel and bamboo? ("If I ascend up into heaven thou art there: if I make my bed in hell, behold, thou art there" [Psalm 139:8].) This interpretation is suggested by Williams: "Those in the antipodes (not formal hell) even feel Broceliande; they become aware of all moments besides the P'o-lu one, and 'hope springs eternal' . . . *unless,* like the one sailor, you really do hate the good" (Notes). Man can will damnation, however. By "formal hell" Williams means that state of self-willed lostness beyond which there is no turning back. *Descent Into Hell* closes with these lines, referring to Wentworth: "Presently then the shape went out and he was drawn, steadily, everlastingly, inward and down through the bottomless circles of the void." The suicide in the same story, however, on the verge of the void, encounters and responds to love and is drawn back. The voice of all moments is one voice, and it is heard by those with ears to hear. Its message is one of rejoicing: "Behold I make all things new."

Lines 45–48 bring Broceliande into focus largely, as Ridler points out, through a linking of abstract and physical terms (lxvi). The result, for the reader, is a sensed total experience of a world much like our own and at the same time strangely heightened and intensified by an illumination not of itself. Time, of course, is Merlin. His "president" and "precedent" (that which is prior in order and that which establishes the pattern of what follows) floats through all things when his grace is "ungrieved" (not spurned), to bring "membraned and tissued experiences [multiple and diverse]" into unity (47). Ridler reports that someone once told Williams that a lime tree lets the light through its leaves, and that a beech tree holds it back—"an observation," she says, "which does not seem to me to be accurate" (lxvii). The image here of golden light piercing the one and being banked behind the opaque green of the other, however, is an accurate representation of the varied experiences that by time, are smitten into simultaneity. Nimue joins the unjoined, accumulates distances, and brings "natural becoming" to her "shape of immortal being" (51). In a flash of revelation, she, archetypal womanhood, is recognized "in the world's base" (52). The image is borrowed perhaps from the lore of the Sephirotic Tree. The woman represents material Earth located at the base from which all creation begins its ascent toward reunion with the divine; she is the feminine element in God.

Merlin has spoken his last spell—Galahad has assumed the Perilous Seat; worked his last image—the veiled grail has hovered momentarily over the king's hall. Beyond that Merlin cannot go. Once again he seeks repose in his native land where both sun and moon have come away from sequence. In Camelot, however, there is still work to do. The moon waxes and wanes over the Perilous Chair in which "time's foster-child sits, Lancelot's son" (56). For the time being action in Logres seems suspended.

"The Death of Palomides" has as its background three related but widely differing traditions: Jewish (particularly medieval mysticism), Christian, and Moslem. Williams's approach is comprehensive, and his conclusion, although Christian, is inclusive. The poem is especially indebted to Cabalistic writings, which are discussed in the Introduction. A pervasive image is the Sephirotic Tree. The poem begins: "Air strives with wings, wings with air," a reminder of the right and left side of the Tree, separated but still necessary counterparts one of the other. The air and the wings are images of Palomides' internal tension and his struggle toward consciousness and integration. The "space of glory" reflects the imagery of the Tree and anticipates the conclusion of the poem (2). For the present, however, he remains on the underside of that glory, in the kingdom (Malkuth), having ascribed to (acknowledged) the power but still awaiting the consummation. By "heart's revolution" he means both the twisting and the turning along the interminable paths and his long contention with the power (3). Now the sky has turned round and Palomides has been christened. The "backward wings" mean that he will look back over his life, returning again to the two old Jews at Monsalvat to join them, as earlier he could not, in reconciliation with the Unity (4). Perhaps on a profounder level, he is aware of approaching death. "In my end is my beginning," Lady Julian said.

The work *quickens* is rich in associations (4). We recall it from the "Prelude": "Galahad quickened in the mercy"; and from Jesus' statement: "For as the Father raiseth up the dead, and quickeneth them, even so the Son quickeneth whom he wills." Quickening is not birth itself, however, but a prelude to birth. It is that stage of pregnancy in which movement of the fetus is first felt. It is also associated with the eagles of lines 1 and 40–44 and with a virtue Williams called "Speed," a subject to which I shall return.

In stanza 2 Palomides begins a review of his past, not a chronological recital of events, but a movement back and forth, an interweaving of present with past, which melds bitter and sweet of both into a unified experience. Only three times does he mention the Prophet, here and in lines 45 and 54. He recalls the Prophet's shout, "Alla il Alla"; he states "I left the Prophet" with a starkness suggesting both grief and guilt; and, finally, he reconciles himself with the Prophet as nearly as a converted Christian can: "sharply the Prophet . . . [calls] to me this at my dying, and I to [him]" (5, 45, 54–55). Palomides left the Prophet and rode north. That occasion was for him a time of instability and also of creative change, which at the time he could not understand. Palomides was from the beginning a reluctant aspirant.

He stops for a night under Monsalvat in the lodging of two old Jews, twins of Levi, of the tribe of the Jewish priesthood. His sheltering with the Jews is credible since Judaism was allied with Islam in the attempted conquest of Spain. Monsalvat was the site of an eighth-century monastery in which there was an allegedly miracle-working Virgin Mary. Moreover, it was later connected with the grail legend.

One of the twins was "sea grey . . . sea-wrinkled," and the other "burned sun black" (10). They pronounced "Netzach," which suggests their identity. One represents the third Sephiroth, water, and the other, the fourth, fire–the opposing forces that must be reconciled before the seeker passes from a lower to a higher spiritual state. Their chant is an invocation "poured into channeled names" (12). According to Cabalistic teaching, there are ten names for God in the Old Testament, each associated with one of the Sephiroths, that serve as channels through which the divine flows down to man. One strain of mysticism consisted of the use of divine or holy names, the permutation and combination of Hebrew letters for the purpose, among others, of hastening the advent of the Messiah. "The first mathematics of Ispahan," Persian dualism, trembles before the "intoned formulae" (13). In contrast to the rationalism of Ispahan, the old Jews "cast totals," reached conclusion, based on a myriad of mystical sources.

The first reference to eagles comes in line 16. The passage is literally a description of what is happening. Figuratively, however, it has a mystical meaning also. Devout Jews, considering the name of God too holy to be written down or spoken, replaced it by four letters called the Tetragrammaton, JHVH. In one tradition, developed at length in *The Place of the Lion,* each letter is associated with an animal or bird that represents a particular virtue. The first three are the lion (strength), the snake (subtlety), and the butterfly (beauty). The fourth is the eagle, which signifies what Williams calls "Speed." In general, the eagle stands for transcendence and, in Williams, specifically, for integration, commitment, and action. He was fascinated by the incident of the unasked question in Cretien's *Conte du Graal* in which Percivale fails to heal the wounded Grail King and restore the kingdom because he does not ask the meaning of a strange pageant enacted before him in the Grail Hall. Why does he not ask? Williams suggests that it might be because, having been involved in partly causing his mother's death, he was incapable of asking questions concerning holy things: "There is the first faint hint . . . of a natural but unhallowed impulse which fails before holiness" (FA 66). Failing to ask, he did not receive.

The eagle, on the other hand, is symbolic of taking the initiative by asking so that the power of grace can become operative. A passage from *The Place of the Lion* explains:

Quentin was leaning on the other side of the window, or whatever opening it was, in whatever world, through which the light poured, and more
than light. For the light changed as he remembered again that it was not
Quentin but the thing that was between him and Quentin, the thing that
went with speed, and yet, speeding, was already at its goal, the thing that
was for ever new and for ever old . . . that issued from its own ardent nest
in its own perpetually renovated beauty, a rosy glow, a living body, the
wonder of earthly love. The movement of the Eagle was the measure of
truth, but the birth of some other being was the life of truth, some other
royal creature that rose from fire and plunged into fire, momently consumed, momently reborn. Such was the inmost life of the universe, infinitely destroyed, infinitely recreated, breaking from its continual death
into continual life, instinct with strength and subtlety and beauty and speed.
(185)

The eagle is a type of the phoenix. Palomides has at last learned to act
through the strength of another. At that earlier time, however, the eagle's
scream was no more than ugly sounds. Palomides sat aloof in his young
seed-mail, "young arrogant militancy," Williams explains (Notes). Aloofness
was to remain an impediment. He was instinctively drawn to what was taking place but scornful of himself for his attraction. He heard "Netzach" and
cried, "What is Netzach?" Netzach is the victory, but over what he could
not or would not understand. He did remember later, however, the statement that eventually destroyed his dualism: "*The Lord created all things by
means of His Blessing*" (27). *All* things.

Though separated in time from that early experience, Palomides can
still feel the struggle that he then suffered. In his imagination he sees the
two old men lifted from one spiritual level to a higher one, the path having
opened mysteriously before them. For him, he reflects, the interminable
paths had been ends in themselves upon which, in contrast to the speed
of the eagle, he loitered with "unangelic speed," alone. Only Dinadan, he
remembers, saw clearly, noted his error, smiled, and waited for the sky to
turn. He recalls his rejection by Iseult and his victory by cheating over
Lancelot; he dwells upon his longings, fears, fights, and anger—none of
which led anywhere. Now, he says, although the old emotions, particularly
the fear, return, he is no longer their captive because he has learned that
the paths are only paths—as paths, that is, they are not "terminal." Still the
way is difficult, no soft voices—only the harsh screams of the eagles—drive
him, backward it seems, toward the "primal station," reunion with him who
created all things. Nearing Netzach, he is aware of a "scintillation of points"
emanating from a fire that is a type of the Fire (42). It is falling all about
him. The image of the rays of light and fire from above intermingles with

the "points of the eagle's plumes, plumes that are paths" that sweep upward beyond the symbolic fire and the symbolic plumes to the "unbelieved symbol" (43, 44) – unbelieved in the sense that it transcends the rational mind. The image is lost in the imageless. The interminable paths terminate.

For Palomides, salvation still comes hard and without sustaining emotion. He recalls the Prophet, Iseult, the Blatant Beast, and Lancelot's pardon, remarking that, if in that pardon he has been christened, it was "half because I was a greater fool so" (48). At last he recaptures that elusive moment, unrecognized at the time, when at Monsalvat he heard the old men sing, and now he senses in their words the meaning of all that followed. Now he can join them all in proclaiming the rightness of creation. If that is the meaning of the kingdom, the power, and the glory, he resolves, his heart offers the kingdom, endures the power, and joins with the eagles in a cry that is at once defeat and victory: "That Thou only canst be Thou only art" (60). By rejecting all else, Palomides has come at last to discover that there is nothing but He.

So far we have seen Galahad, through the bedazzled eyes of others to whom he appears, if not as pure spirit, at least something more than, perhaps different from, mere man. Williams associates him with Percivale and Bors, referring to the three as "the hierarchy." On one level, we could rank them in ascending order: Bors, Percivale, and Galahad. But as with all hierarchies, that order is not static but constantly changing since at one time or another each holds primacy because of his function. There is a sense in which the three become a composite character. Williams says, "the hierarchy was one, for all three reached Sarras, and if Galahad alone achieved, yet it might be held that the Galahad-in-Bors achieved as much as did the individual High Prince" (Essays 180). Williams surely felt, however, that to round out the character of Galahad it was necessary to give even greater emphasis to his humanity than up to this point he had been allowed. Thus we have the poem "Percivale at Carbonek."

At this high moment of the Prince's triumph we see him as the son of Lancelot in what seems to the speaker, Percivale, something like a crucifixion experience. Galahad carries his humanity right into Carbonek.

The poem begins with stark simplicity and completeness: "In the rent saffron sun hovered the Grail." It is the given of which the rest of the poem is the result. Only once before, in "The Coming of Galahad," has there been an attempt to describe the grail and that, as we have noted, was incomplete. In Malory and Tennyson the grail is described as light or luminosity, but Williams speaks of it as an object, a cup, hidden under a saffron veil. It would seem that the light emanates from the sun through the cup and that the veil, stained by the intense rays, protects human eyes from an inhuman brightness. The veil hangs over the Body and Blood as it had over the Ark of the Covenant, the old rite. The image of radiating beams occurs often in Williams. The word *hovered* in one of its meanings suggests lingering in a state of suspension and expectation. Galahad, at the gates of Carbonek, is only steps from the hall where the grail is to appear. To everyone's consternation, even the "astonished angels of the spirit," Galahad pauses, and for a moment action is suspended and salvation seems to hang in the balance (7). Yet another matter demands attention before the gates are entered. Joy (Galahad) remembers joylessness (Lancelot) and kneels under the arch, where Lancelot had run, to share with his earthly father his guilty frenzy and to ask, as it were, pardon for the divine from the human as the human entreats pardon from the divine. *"Pardon, lord; pardon and bless me, father"* (8). Williams wrote to Ridler:

> Only once does the Joyous Prince weep, and that is when he comes to Carbonek, the place where he was born, and Lancelot went mad. And even Galahad doubts if even eternity is quite worth it. But at least he implores his father to forgive him – not Lancelot alone, but Arthur and all Logres; . . . Do you not conceive that to be a very moving episode? Joy having to be forgiven for the necessity of its own birth? (Supl. 16)

The myrmidons, astonished angels, attendants on Pelles's household, pause. Their beauty is "unremitted," unforgiven because in their case forgiveness was not necessary. Lancelot has not recognized and accepted his son. Williams avoids sentimentality and remains realistic, refusing even at this emotionally intense moment to sacrifice intellectuality. The blind and seemingly unjustified suffering of Lancelot, who represents mankind, demands some justification. Galahad feels himself caught and held by the "fibrous infelicity of time," incapable of escaping the grip of the temporal and of experiencing eternity (11). Momentarily, his implacable resolve to enter Carbonek is pierced. The health of the wounded king must wait, while he, the now subdued glory, implores the kingdom (the Earth and his earthly father) to pardon the power that both permitted and sustains the "double misery of Logres," the Dolorous Blow and the destruction of the table (16). Of the Fall Williams says "it is not credible that a finite choice ought to result in an infinite distress; or rather let it be said that, though credible, it is not tolerable (to us) that the Creator should deliberately maintain and sustain His created universe in a state of infinite distress as a result of the choice. No doubt it is possible to Him" (Essays 131).

Under the arch, Galahad wept for his father. Indeed, from the human view, Lancelot had been betrayed by Merlin and Brisen: "he saw not; he was false to Guinevere" (20). Moreover, we are told, he was not ever wantonly lewd. He was betrayed; yet that betrayal, on one level, was to truth. He had secured fidelity by sacrificing fidelity itself. As with Palomides and Cranmer (*Thomas Cranmer of Canterbury*), he had encountered "the Judas who betrays men to God." Percivale, the imagination of the other world, understood at least partly what was happening. He hears the padding of the paws and the howl of the wolves, "woven between us"–that is, making him, along with Galahad, a sharer in Lancelot's misery and that of all fallen flesh (23). This is the cold that causes Galahad to shiver at the point of the "bleak conjunction" (24). It is a conjunction of Lancelot and Brisen, Camelot and Carbonek, Arthur and Pelles, God and man. It is, in short, all the acts of substitution and exchange by which the great reconciliation takes place. For his "botched" creation, God, Williams says, shared man's guilt: "He became as helpless as we under the will which is He. This is the first approach to a sense of justice in the whole situation. Whatever He chose, He chose fully, for Himself as for us" (Essays 132). Lines 25–28 are brought into focus by the verb *rattled,* a word used commonly in combination with "death-rattle." The entire picture, indeed, is that of a man dying, the head that of a skull and the dry voice little more than a noise: "Pardon, Lord Lancelot; pardon and blessing, father" (28). All effective pardon must be an exchange between man and God, between man and man, for until man both gives and accepts pardon the "Host in Lateran" will lie hidden in a sepulchre awaiting resurrection.

Galahad turns mechanically, "slews," to Bors and asks if he, in the name of all fallen humanity in Camelot, will "bear" pardon to–not from–Carbonek. He asks Bors to share with him, to bear the cross of reconciliation. Bors's answer is the natural human one: "What should we forgive?" Galahad's answer summarizes the charge Bors might have made:

> "Forgive Us," the High Prince said, "for Our existence;
> forgive the means of grace and the hope of glory.
> In the name of Our father forgive Our mother for Our birth." (37–40)

And Bors's response is complete. He avoids what might seem blasphemy by refusing the word *forgive,* for, he says, God alone can do that. Man is, after all, His creation. Yet, Lancelot is a lover and kind, capable of responding to love out of love. For himself, Bors says, "I assent to all," the means and the glory (42). This response makes proffered grace operative. Having his last act this side of Carbonek completed and Bors made ready, Galahad commands, "Go," and Bors steps forward, Galahad, significantly, following in his steps. Carbonek was entered.

Williams drew much of his information for "The Last Voyage" from A. E. Waite's *The Hidden Church of the Holy Grail,* which he read as early as 1915 and regarded highly. Waite wrote:

> the royal prophet of Israel had learned by a message from heaven that the last knight of his lineage would exceed all other chivalry as the sun out-shines the moon. By the sage counsel of his wife, he built this ship to last for 4000 years, with the double object of making known to Galahad not only the royalty of his descent, but the fact that the wise king was aware of his birth in due time. . . . The Ship was launched; the king saw in a vision how a great company of angels descended and entered therein, as it sailed far out of sight. (301, 303)

The ship, laden with a number of sacred relics, came in time to represent the Christian church. Waite continues: "The sea over which it sailed signified the world; the bed was the Holy Altar, on which the Divine Son is con-secrated and offered daily; in another sense, it was also the Cross of Christ" (303).

The first line of the poem embraces both the Jewish anticipation of a coming Messiah and the Christian belief that the coming had been realized. The "hollow" represents the organs of generation, the location on the mythical map of Jerusalem, the place associated with the beginning of the Jewish, Christian, and Moslem religions. Jerusalem, the source of life, is the reverse of Ispahan, the alley of rejection. Both are located, however, in the area of the thighs where Pelles received the Dolorous Blow, possibly, Williams admits, a wound in virility but with the qualification that it was spiritual as well as physical.

The ship appears in the poem from two points of view, the artistic (2–19) and the factual (beginning with line 20). The first is a painting of Solomon against a distant backdrop of a small city and temple; "all on a deck floated in a sea of dolphins" (5). The dolphin, also associated with Dinadan, in early Christian art stood for love and swiftness, motivation and action (89). With his right hand lifted in blessing, Solomon "whelmed" (turned over, covered up) the *djin,* an order in Moslem mythology higher than man but lower than the angels who were said to rule the Earth before the crea-tion of Adam. Believed to have special architectural skills, according to the Koran, they helped build Solomon's temple. Perhaps they assisted in building the ship before they were whelmed. He stretches his left arm to Balkis who tastes "effectual magic, / intellectual art arm-fasted to the sensuous," that is, brought into material being by the arm that lifted the magical wand (9–10). Solomon is master of necromancy – the summoning of spirits thought to foretell future events for those who have "no necessity of existence in themselves," those who do not possess, as Galahad does, the indwelling spirit of God (13).

The second painting depicts a laureate ceremony in which Virgil stretches to Taliessin a shoot of hazel, the discipline of poetry, which he had received from Homer. Around Taliessin on one level stand images of continuity and on another of simultaneity. Spiritual and imaginative powers are part of an order untouched by change.

The actual ship, on the other hand, drove and clove the wind that blew from unseen shores, an object driven through time, beyond empire, past Carbonek, through Broceliande (part water and part land, "trenched"). It is propelled by a power not human ("with no mind's sail reefed or set, no slaves at the motivated oars") (24). Line 26 begins a sentence that ends with the line that, with slight variations, is to recur as refrain throughout the poem: "the ship of Solomon (blessed be he) drove on" (34). Regardless of the change in the temporal order of Logres, the ship moves inevitably toward its destined end and will eventually draw all Logres into itself. The long series of modifiers that precede this main clause suggests the speed, "Swept from the altars"; the efficiency, "the shortest way between points"; the power, "the wrath that wrecks the pirates"; and the confidence, the inevitability, "the thrust of the trust" with which the ship drives "to the point of accumulated distance." A sense of that destination is conveyed through the image "the knotted web of empire" and through the paradoxical description of its being "multiple without dimension, indivisible without uniformity." Sarras itself is a paradox.

The word *alchemical* introduces the central thought of stanza 3 (34). The "alchemical Infant" refers specifically to the High Prince but also to that quality in Percivale and Bors that they share with Galahad. The alchemists were ancient scientists who sought the Philosopher's Stone, the so-called *prima materia* from which all matter derives, and which, if found, could be used to transmute base matter into gold. Their hope was worldly and spiritual, both to create material wealth and to enhance, perhaps to generate, life itself. Belief in the stone derived from the conviction that all creation came from one central source and possessed power to effect man's material and physical transformation. Basil Valentine, a medieval monk, described alchemy as "the investigation of those natural secrets by which God shadowed out eternal things." Williams uses the idea of the Philosopher's Stone as a central image. He represents Jesus as the real stone and Galahad as man's capacity for divine things. He is the transforming and unifying power of the Spirit.

The word *infant* is used in the Spanish sense meaning the son or daughter of a king and recalls also the obsolete English use meaning a young man training to be a knight. It refers by implication also to the Infant Jesus, since Galahad is the capacity in man for Christ. The word *burned* suggests the "Burning Babe of Love," popular in Christian tradition as one of the names for Jesus, nowhere expressed more graphically than in the poem by Robert Southwell:

> My faultlesse breast the furnace is,
>   And Mercie blows the coales.
> The mettall in this furnace wrought,
>   Are man's defiled soules;
>
> For which, as now on fire I am
>   To work them to their good.
> So I will melt into a bath,
>   To wash them in my blood.

Here the alchemical Infant stands in the prow burning red by "celerity"—as a result of the ship's speed and his response to the Spirit—but turning white, being transformed. Percivale stands behind him, his hand on the High Prince's shoulder, "the folded column" (36). *Folded* is related to "closed wings of flight" in the next line, meaning that he has achieved victory over self and stands in receptive contemplation and "philosophical amazement," no longer acting but acted upon. The silver may signify the moon, reflected light, or it may have reference to Percivale's association with Phosphor. Bors is mailed in black, mailed because he is a warrior, and, in time, he will return to Britain where his real work remains. *Black,* I assume, is a description of the appearance of his armor. He kneels, the flesh of fatherhood, a universal figure, as important as his companions in the divine scheme, and prays for the common needs of his household, daily bread and forgiveness of sins. Through the three, by three ways of exchange, the city of Camelot by way of Carbonek and Broceliande drives toward Sarras.

Stanza 4 begins with an image of a flight of doves. Williams explains: "all that was Logres and the Empire has become a flight of doves driving the ship on its way" (Notes). The long sentence, because of its complexity and its importance invites analysis:

> An infinite flight of doves from the storming sky
> of Logres—strangely sea-travelers when the land melts—
> forming to overfeather and overwhelm the helm,
> numerous as men in the empire, the empire riding
> the skies of the ocean, guiding by modulated stresses
> on each spoke of the helm the vessel from the realm of Arthur,
> lifted oak and elm to a new-ghosted power. (46–52)

The simple subject flight comes in line 46. The complete subject is "An infinite flight of doves." The predicate verb, *lifted,* is delayed until line 52. In between is a series of modifying phrases and clauses which present a rapidly revolving kaleidoscope of images that, in the swiftness of their movement, suggests the speed of the flight and, in the process of their transformation from one form to another, something of their mystic significance. The predicate object is "to a new-ghosted power." It is important to note that, according to Williams, this is the way things appear to the lords. They are passing beyond sight of land, but we know that land is not literally melting. Sarras, their destination, embraces both body and soul, two modes of designating an inseparable whole. Bors will return to the kingdom, changed though it will be. Even for Galahad and Percivale it is less dissolved than transformed. It has become a flight of doves. Galahad carried his humanity into Carbonek, and he will carry a transformed Logres into Sarras. To describe that state Williams must rely on imagery. The dove traditionally symbolizes the Holy Spirit and is associated with those spiritual powers discussed in relation to Palomides' death. The flock "overfeather and overwhelm the helm," pointing and guiding the ship beyond man's capacity as it drives forward through the mysterious waters. The doves are agencies of that which transforms common oak and elm of the man-made ship into a "new-ghosted power" (52).

The sentence beginning with line 53 also presents difficulties. The main clause reads, "The hosted wings trapped the infant's song." What follows is a series of modifiers: "blown back, tossed down, thrown / along the keel . . . hastening the keel / . . . the helm fastening / the . . . ship / . . . as the fine fair arm of . . . Cymedocea / . . . thrust the . . . Duke." The key word is *hosted* in line 53. It is an extension—and also a contraction—of overfeathering and overwhelming in line 48. As a noun, *host* has been used variously to mean a gathering, a multitude of angels that attend on God, the victim of a sacrifice (as the Host of the communion). As a verb, it was once used to mean "to gather into a host." As an adjective, and in this context, it is complexly suggestive. The birds gather into a flock—their wings spread protectively over the ship. They are a source of power and direction. As a sacrifice and sacrament, the doves represent that part of Logres that the three are bringing into Sarras. Galahad's song is transformed and returned as speed and balance and subtlety and beauty. The hosted wings stand in contrast to Percivale's "closed wings," a spiritual power before which Percivale stands in "philosophical amazement" (37). There follow two similes, one secular and the other religious. The first refers to the movement of Aeneas's ship up the river Tiber where he was to found Rome; the second, to the mystic Ship of Solomon, one the secular and the other the sacred city. Both are types being now returned and made one with their archetype.

The "wonder that broke" is, literally, the hallowed sword of David that Solomon placed in the ship with instructions that it not be used unworthily (63). The Dolorous Blow involved an unworthy use of a sacred hallow. All creation now, however, is being "returned" and set right. Williams comments: "'The hollow of J.'–the generative organs of this life are no more than the shoulder-hollows of G. What *his* generative organs are, no one has begun to imagine" (Notes). We recall Williams's suggestion that the thigh wound represents a diminution of man's physical and spiritual virility. The ultimate generative power, whatever that may be, is not man's to exercise. The "new birth" is the work of the spirit. That power flows through Galahad, who bears in his own body both the ban (the Fall) and the blessing (the Redemption).

The ascending-descending (annually rotating) sun "lay in quadrilateral covers of a saffron pall" over the bier of Blanchefleur (71). It lay, it would seem, about the four sides without shadow. She who died that another might live becomes the type of substitution, like Galahad, of man's capacity for Christ. She who lies under a saffron pall, like the grail, becomes a type of the archetypal shedding of blood on Calvary. Significantly, Williams assumes that hers was a wound, like Pelles's, in the thigh. In the kingdom, while it is still "to-night," before Logres has faded into mere Britain ("the last candles"), the woman for whom Blanchefleur gave her life dances for her friends, Blanchefleur's blood burning in her cheeks. We remember Williams's statement about Blanchefleur and the slave girl: "Blanchefleur cannot be perfect without the slave." Nor can she be complete without this dancing woman. Together they illustrate the two ways along the one Way: the affirmative and the negative. The word *measure* might mean, as it often does, that their action reveals diagrammatically the divine pattern for the redemptive exchange between heaven and Earth (79). It might also relate to the dance of the following line. For Williams the dance was the perfect image of simultaneity of time and accumulation of distance, man's union with God. It was autonomous, not a means to an end but the end itself. One does not dance to go somewhere. The dance merely is. So with the spirit. The dead woman awaits the turn of the dance until they both are at one with the heavenly. The word *throe* is often used in relation to both death and childbirth.

Sacrum in line 81 means literally "holy bone," because, formerly, it was often used as an offering in sacrifice. In human anatomy it is part of the pelvis, a basin-like cavity formed by four bone structures. It lies in the area of the reproductive organs and, because of its cuplike shape, suggests that the pelvis is the container of human life as the grail is of the spiritual. The interpretation is merely an extension of the image of Blanchefleur as substitution in lines 70–75.

Over against the example of co-inherence is juxtaposed the "deep schismatic war" in Logres (85). Gawaine is one of the causes of Logres's downfall. In him we see, Williams says, "honour run mad." He and his brother Agravaine murdered Morgause in order "to clean their honour's claws in the earth of her body" (93). In defense of the "Throne's honour," the two exposed the relation between Lancelot and Guinevere, demanding that she, according to law, be burned. They pursued Lancelot when he attempted to rescue her, and, in the fracas that followed, Lancelot unwittingly slew his friend, their brother, Gareth. In revenge the two brothers persuaded Arthur to make war on his old friend. While the king was away from Logres, Mordred seized the throne. The table was "hewn in twain." The saddest victim of this honour madness was Dinadan, "the king's dolphin," who was caught and broiled "on a bed of coals" because Gawaine and Agravaine could not abide his "pertinence of curiosity" (94–95). Dinadan was the one member of the court who could distinguish between pretense and reality. He recognized Gawaine's professed honor as a guise.

The first and second parts of the stanza are united by the repetition of the word *thick:* "the merciful heaven drove the thick smoke to choke him. / But the Infant's song was thick with a litany of names" (96–97). The word gives sensuous and emotional embodiment to an intellectual concept. First we are presented with the thick smoke, smelling of burning wood and human flesh, ascending in a mercifully choking cloud, mitigating the horror somewhat by speeding Dinadan's death. In the second it is the song, thick with names, including surely that of Dinadan for whom Galahad offers himself in substitution, that ascends, turning death into life. The smoke eventually bursts into flames that unite the heart of Dinadan with the head of Percivale, flushing the silver with new color.

The penultimate stanza is one of the most audacious in Williams's poetry, comparable in its provocative daring with the essay "What the Cross Means to Me." Galahad's song becomes a variation upon the opening lines of Psalm 43: "Judge me, O God" (*Judica me, Deus*). But Galahad sings *Judica te, Deus,* and in response the wind picks up the song and drives the words back against themselves. It is a daring challenge and an unexpected response. "This then is the creation," Williams writes, "that 'needs' (let the word be permitted) justifying" (Essays 132). The only possible justification, Williams argues, is that God did indeed accept the challenge and become himself the victim of his own law, offering his life in exchange for mankind's.

As the ship draws closer to Sarras, however, the time for all justifying passes. "Prayer [Percivale] and irony [Dinadan] had said their say and ceased" (112). Now all speech gives way to speed, the "necessity of being" (118). The human instruments by which the ship was directed become superfluous.

The ship has moved from Logres, past Carbonek, through Broceliande, and now nears Sarras where time is brought into synchrony with eternity. The hierarchy has reached the point where Galahad is so united with Christ that he has almost a necessity of being in himself.

While the ship drives on, back in the old kingdom time and distance remain just time and distance. With the death of Arthur and the return of Logres to Carbonek, the kingdom fades into mere Britain.

The delay of the Parousia, the Second Coming of Christ, Williams says, prefigured a kind of reconciliation between the church and the "ordinary process of things." In the second chapter of *The Descent of the Dove,* "The Reconciliation with Time," Williams speaks of the necessity that the church felt to prepare for drawing unto itself the whole of normal human experiences. The accommodation to process rather than event required a change in the church's method of operation: "She suffered, she manipulated, she hierarchized, she intellectualized" (27). When it became clear that the Second Coming would be indefinitely delayed, the church accepted the conditions imposed by time and continued to celebrate the Presence under the form of Bread and Wine, types of the Body and Blood, and to pursue in the everyday world the way of substitution and exchange that the Sacrament affirmed and empowered. "Taliessin at Lancelot's Mass" is an explication of that change of method.

The poem is written in couplets and divided into four-line stanzas. The only other poem so structured is "Lamorack and the Queen Morgause of Orkney." It is a witness to Williams's technical skill that he could use this form to express so sensitively the very differing themes of the two poems. In "Lamorack," the structure takes on some of the unyielding hardness of the rock; in "Taliessin at Lancelot's Mass," it is manipulated so that its greater flexibility expresses a sense of one's being himself "manacled by the web, in the web made free" (51). In "Lamorack," the release of the sculptured forms seems an aberration; in "Lancelot's Mass," the manacling and the freeing appear part of the co-inherence.

Lancelot, originally a knight and not a priest, begins the Mass at an altar of "ancient stone laid upon stones" (3). Williams sees commonality among the great myths as types in varying degrees of the one archetype. Lancelot's altar has immediately back of it "Carbonek's arch" (home of the Grail King), "Camelot's walls" (Merlin's effective magic), and the "frame of Bors's bones" (the diagrammatic pattern of human hands at work). But beyond these lie still further reaches. Lateran itself is built where the Lupercalia were celebrated, where "Rods of divination between Lupercal and Lateran" link new with old, Christian with pagan Rome. Beyond the empire is Broceliande, Carbonek, and eventually Sarras. All creation in the beginning was one, and its destiny is to become again one web around the Heavenly Center. Just as Galahad had taken his manhood into Carbonek, and the three had carried what remained of Logres into Sarras, Lancelot brings to the altar all that he has been. He wears his armor, but without helm or sword; his hands are bare "as Lateran's to the work of the Lord" (8).

In stanza 3, the dead lords leave their graves to gather about the altar so that the celebration of the new co-inherence may begin. God, whose power is not limited by human categories, gathers all time around the one Center, the resurrection of the Incarnate Word. God's grace, not limited by the accident of time, reaches both backward and forward, stretching from eternity to eternity. Those visionary men stand as on the mystic Ship of Solomon, between Nimue of Broceliande, natural grace, and Helayne of Carbonek, spiritual grace, still in a state of making. In Almsbury, at the same time, Queen Guinevere occupies Blanchefleur's old cell in an act of exchange that recalls the archbishop's words that of necessity we live in the habitation of others. Blanchefleur had become foster mother of the child that might have been, but was not, Guinevere's. The queen looks back, and her memories, Williams says, are "sharp and dear" (14). Ambivalence remains, the sharpness of regret and the seeming rightness of a love so tragically flawed. Now, from an enlarged perspective, she feels the mystical milk rise in her breasts and, in an act of reverse substitution, she becomes as it were the mystic mother of the High Prince. Out of that substitution came Galahad, through whom the wounded and dead king (Pelles-Arthur) assumes the double crown of Logres and Carbonek and is seen as one at the altar. Pelles, going to the altar, is recognized as the true ruler, and Arthur, who had thought the kingdom was for the king, steps down. This new unity transcends time and is experienced only momentarily around the altar just as man occasionally glimpses the emperor riding in the sky.

"Lancelot and Arthur wove the web" (21). Together they had begun the building of the kingdom, and, now, in a more exalted sense, they are weaving a new web of co-inherence. The sky opens on moon and sun, the receptacle and the source, and in that brightness "the unseen knight of terror stood as a friend" (23). Although Williams pondered long over the meaning of the Invisible Knight, Garlon remains a shadowy figure in his work. In the *Commonplace Book* he identifies the knight with the "Unasked Question." He was fascinated, as we have already noted, by the episode in the *Conte du Graal* in which Percivale fails to heal the Fisher King by not asking the meaning of the strange pageant enacted before him: "What serves the Graal?" "The question asked," Williams states, "is equivalent to the question of the Virgin ('How should these things be?'): it releases the energies frozen by the Fall: . . . the lack of the question would mean the lack of

an answer, and hence an ignorance of the true nature of the Invisible Knight"
(Essays 170). In this case it meant that the wounded king was not healed
nor the kingdom restored to fruitfulness.

The Invisible Knight, then, is that good that man by nature seeks, but
which after the Dolorous Blow he sees not at all or partially or distorted.
Yet as late as March 1941, Williams wrote to Ridler, "I think, on and off,
of our Taliessin and the Dolorous Stroke—the method of the Invisible Knight
evades me still" (Ridler lxv). There are two other statements, however, that
indicate how he is to be interpreted here. In a listing of subjects for the
projected volume, *Jupiter over Carbonek*, he notes: "Garlon invisible outside
Broceliande; wherein he is seen 'with a black face'; in Sarras—the Holy Spirit?
Azrael?" (Essays 175). In "Notes on the Arthurian Myth," he writes: "in the
shape of a little viper, Garlon, the Invisible Knight—who is Satan to us but
the Holy Ghost to the supernatural powers—provokes the last battle" (Essays
178). It becomes a matter of perspective, less what is seen than how it is
seen. In this poem the knight has much the same role as that of the Skeleton in *Cranmer*, the Accuser in *Judgement at Chelmsford*, and the Flame in
The House of Octopus. To man's eyes, distorted by the Fall, the knight seems
the opposite of what he actually is, and also the opposite of what unregenerate
man thinks he wants. Only when the sky turns round and new light breaks
does he appear in his natural guise, not a terror but a friend.

With the recognition of the Invisible Knight, events move toward consummation. Lancelot comes to the prayer of consecration while Taliessin
and his household stand at the earthen footpace "to be blessed and to bless,"
each performing his function in the constantly shifting hierarchy (27). At
the singing of the holy names evocative of the Spirit, flames fall from a new
sky to a new Earth, in reenactment of Pentecost. The imperial lands are
renewed in bands of "bitter glory" (32). Logres has been withdrawn, but
the means of grace are yet present in Britain. At the Epiclesis, the invocation of the Spirit, Lancelot-Arthur-Pelles "invoke the making of man" (34).
The last phrase held special significance for Williams. We recall its use toward
the end of *The Place of the Lion* when Anthony names the beasts and restores
the natural order of creation.

In the *Commonplace Book* Williams speaks of Galahad's moment of
achievement and of Bors's vision of a choir of voices, saying, "let us make
man" (Essays 170). In times simultaneously apprehended, we are made present at the creation when God made man; at the Incarnation when God
was made man; and at the emergence of the new heaven and Earth when
the Holy God once again is made flesh and blood in the Bread and Wine.
Each level of meaning, "all the ways the Theotokos conceived by the Holy
Ghost," floats as petals from the blossoms of the Host, the bread of the

Sacrament (36). "We exposed." The Host is elevated in the ritual of the Mass so that the Unity—web, path, points—are shown forth as in a prism. The language recalls that of "The Coming of Galahad" where the points of the pentagram are connected by paths and the resulting whole frames a web of interrelated, interdependent parts. Even the antipodean zone is retrieved under that power, and the acts of the emperor are recognized throughout creation. Evil is exposed as having "no substantial being." Over the elements on the altar, Galahad spirals upward, "gyre on burning gyre" as a "flame of anatomized fire," that is, in a form that reveals the true structure of creation, pushing back the night so that in the light of day the intertwining glories are revealed (41). In *The Figure of Arthur* Williams quoted from Rupert of Deutz:

> Because the Virgin conceived him of the Holy Ghost, who is eternal fire, and he himself through the same Holy Ghost, as the Apostle says, offered himself a living sacrifice to the living God, by the same fire is the roasting ("roast with fire"—that is, burnt by the travail of the Passion) on the altar, for by the operation of the Holy Ghost the bread becomes the body and the wine the blood of Christ. (17–18)

The table, symbol of the co-inherence, ascends. The infant becomes "the passage of the porphyry stair" by which "lordliest and least" are lifted into unity (48). The movement of the cycle reaches its climax in this transcendent celebration.

In *The Figure of Arthur* Williams defines the achievement of the grail as consciousness of Christ rather than of self, "the perfect fulfillment of the thing happening"—the reconciling life, death, and resurrection of Jesus as being "remembered," made present in the Bread and Wine of the Sacrament. Galahad is drawn by an irresistible magnet, into reunion with God. In an essay not published at the time of this writing, Joe McClatchey has remarked cogently:

> At first, to achieve the Grail meant Asking the Question. With the invention of Galahad it came to mean seeing a vision of the transubstantiated Christ. . . . In . . . "Taliessin at Lancelot's Mass," Taliessin experiences in that Holy Eucharist a consciousness of the Incarnation and the Sacrament so acute that he feels himself to be completely at one with the Mysteries. It is the supreme moment of his life and doubtless with "The Prayers of the Pope" the summit of Williams's lifelong calling. ("Lecture" 16–17)

Taliessin is gathered and "manacled by the web, in the web made free" (51). He has served his function as the "imagination of this world." That which is happening at the altar transcends his powers: "there was no capable song for the joy in me" (52). Like Virgil on the threshold of paradise, Taliessin has reached the limits of poetic imagination. In his poetry he had made "joy to a Joy unknown," but now he submits to the Joy Itself, to that which is beyond poetry (54). Lancelot pronounces "*Ite missa est*"—the mass is over. The Mass has just begun. The images are all being caught up and made one with the imageless, a fact accomplished already in eternity. The poem celebrates a process stretching in time over perhaps centuries, as it were, as it indeed is—a momentless eternity. It remains now only for man "to discover in the process of time the conclusion that we have implored in time" (*HCD* 4).

What, in light of such eschatology, is the destiny of the poet? The only tragedy in Christendom, Williams has said, is that of art. There comes a time when even the greatest poetry becomes "meaningless sweet sound," and the poet must be reconciled to seeing his "infinite images, dropping pell-mell" into the void. In the presence of a greater Power the poet becomes "superfluous." His compensation for the loss of so glorious a "means" is the envisioned end that, in this poem, has just been proclaimed.

The volume concludes:

Fast to the Byzantine harbour gather the salvaged sails;
that which was once Taliessin rides to the barrows of Wales
up the vales of the Wye; if skill be of work or of will
in the dispersed homes of the household, let the Company
    pray for it still. (57–60)

The last two lines are unclear. They seem to mean that, like Merlin, Taliessin, of the temporal order, the imagination of this world, is returning to his origin. The Coming is not yet. He leaves his unfinished task in Logres (now become Britain), whether of work or will, to his dispersed but continuing household of poet/prophets, charging them to continue to pray for the envisioned consummation when time is brought into synchronization with eternity as it was momentarily experienced in Lancelot's Mass.

5

"Behold a Radiant Brow"

Well, they took up the leathern bag, and he
who opened it saw the forehead of the boy, and
said to Elphin, "Behold a radiant brow!"
"Taliessin be he called," said Elphin.

— *Mabinogion*

Williams says in his preface that the poems included in *The Region of the Summer Stars* are related to those in *Taliessin through Logres* but "are incidental to the main theme," the reign of King Arthur in Logres and the achievement of the grail. The title of the second volume is borrowed from a section of the Welsh *Mabinogion* called "Taliessin," translated by Lady Charlotte Guest. There we find these lines: "Primarily chief bard am I to Elphin / And my original country is the region of the summer stars." The visionary and transforming imagination of the poet has its origins in the place of the summer stars, and, in such poems as "Taliessin in the School of the Poets," "Taliessin on the Death of Virgil," and "Taliessin at Lancelot's Mass," Williams explored the limits of poetry. Taliessin, he says, was the measure of what the poet could and could not do. In a letter to Joan Wallis on 20 August 1943, he wrote, "I can see dimly in the distance the point at which Taliessin is no longer enough, and We proceed to Percivale" (Supl. 24). This statement suggests a shift in his attention from the work of man's imagination to the operation of the spirit.

The title of the new poems focuses attention on the region of the summer stars, located beyond Venus, the third heaven, rather than on Logres, even less upon external action and more on contemplation of the sources of action. The statement suggests that in the new poems Percivale will be the central consciousness through which the action is seen, although that expectation is not met. Here Percivale is an even more minor character than in the earlier volume. It must be remembered, however, that *The Region*

125

of the Summer Stars was part of a projected cycle to be called *Jupiter Over Carbonek*. In the list of subjects to be treated in that volume, left by Williams and included by Ridler in *Image*, however, there is no mention of Percivale (174–75). No doubt Williams referred to the character himself less than to that which he represents.

The poems were to be contemplative in tone, correlative to rather than an expansion of the action of *Taliessin through Logres*. This is the sense in which Williams could refer to the new poems as "incidental to the main theme." The meaning of Jupiter can be inferred from the poems. In "The Coming of Galahad," Logres is said to "come into Jupiter," and the planet symbolizes defeated irony. In "Taliessin in the Rose Garden" we read:

> Pelles bleeds
> below Jupiter's red-pierced planet; the taunt
> yields to the truth, irony to defeated irony. (173–75)

And in "The Prayers of the Pope":

> Jupiter rode over Carbonek; beyond Jupiter,
> beyond the summer stars, deep heaven
> centrally opened within the land of the Trinity;
> planetary light was absorbed there, and emerged
> again in its blissful journeys. (239–43)

Some of the differences between the two volumes become apparent when we compare the preludes of the two. The first embraces action beginning with the coming of Taliessin, through the building of Logres, to the fading of the kingdom, and ends with the poet's return to Wales. The second centers less on action than on meditation, the emphasis shifting from what man may do to what God has done.

The first stanza of the "Prelude" to this volume juxtaposes temporal against timeless. Although Christianity is of timeless origin, it is, nevertheless, firmly anchored in history. Its background is Judaism; its administrative and organizational skills are Roman; and its intellectual indebtedness to the Greek, whether by borrowing or in refutation, is obvious. It denounces those, of whatever origin, who "most prattled cunning preventive doctrine" as beside the point—man's redemption, not his behavioral control (6). The crucial moment in the development of Christendom came, according to the "Prelude," when Paul embraced Athens' unknown god, whom the Greeks ignorantly worshiped, as a type of the Incarnate Christ whom he preached. Thus the Incarnation, as it is manifest in creation and redemption, became the central focus of this volume.

The next stanza, beginning "The crooked smiles of the Greeks," is reminiscent of Paul's statement that the Incarnation was folly to the intellectual Greeks (11). The word *crooked* suggests something awry, inaccurate. Against the "defensive inflections of verb and voice"—manipulation and distortion of language—their "presaged frustrations," and "sterile projections," Paul preached the twofold "Nature of the Golden Ambiguity," the man-God (13). The puzzled Greeks saw in Paul, "thorned-in-the-flesh"—inflicted, that is, by a physical handicap—an ironic refutation of his teaching that material creation is good and that God is just (12). The defeat of Greek irony lay, of course, in the Incarnation, an act that does not explain human suffering but makes it both endurable and glorious in the context of divine sharing and in light of redemption. Paul "invented the vocabulary of faith" in his teaching about the "physiological glory," an oxymoron (18). "The young Church breakfasted on glory; handfasted." *Breakfasted* refers literally to the communion, which was followed by the breaking of the preparatory fast, and *handfasted*, to the physiological glory through which the union between man and God and man and man was secured.

The "ancient intellect"—Hebrew, Greek, Roman—demurred. Some of the converted pagans returned to their old faiths, and the church itself was torn by strife. Nestorius, the "careful," attempted to bring peace by seemingly embracing both sides of the controversy, preaching that there was indeed in Christ two beings, but that they were united only in moral union and that Jesus was not in substance one divine person, the Word made flesh. While he preached and the metaphysicians listened, blood was shed in the city. Was Mary "theotokos," Mother of God, or "Anthropotokos," mother of man? The controversy raged, and Nestorians surrendered "the ground of faith and earth" for what they mistook for peace (35).

The orthodox, in contrast, seized their heritage and, through a union of Roman polity and incarnational faith, founded the empire, seeing everywhere grace translated into glory. Beyond the ancient lines of the imperial shapes of Greece, Judea, and Rome, Christendom saw "almost (in a cloud)" the face of the Sublime Emperor as John on Patmos had seen Him (44). The Acts of the Throne became manifest on Earth as hazel, corn, and wine—discipline (human intellect and will) and bread and wine (mystery)—and were made substantial.

So great was the excitement that perfection seemed imminent and the Second Coming at hand. Only a few—monk, nun, slave, princess, poet, pope—knew more wisely that it would come "centuries belated" (52). They expected not an immediate apocalypse but the coming in time "from the world of the Three-in-One," the container, the chalice, the Blood of the *Deivirilis* (60). The word *Deivirilis*, Greek in origin, means at once divine and human. It would be communicated in "the morn of the Trinity rising through the sea to the sun" with Lancelot's altar as its focal point (63).

Stanza 5 communicates a vision of the Unity that emanates from the throne in a diagram of light and is enfleshed in the "golden cream and the rose / tinctures," and, also, in qualities that are only names until they are embodied in "the golden day and the rose-gardens of Caucasia" (69–70, 72). The rose garden, symbol of the natural beauty, Caucasia, is a recurring image given centrality especially in "Taliessin in the Rose Garden" and "The Queen's Servant." Over against that vision of unity, Williams juxtaposes its antithesis, the headless emperor, "in a foul indecent crimson" as he walks the "vile marshes of P'o-l'u" (79, 81). (This is the spelling throughout the volume.)

In the last stanza, Williams once again states the ground upon which faith is defensible. Whether the story is fable or truth is not to be confused with "fact." The Grecian irony, a rational quality that pronounced the Incarnation folly, gave way to the defeated irony that recognized truth in the taunt: "He saved others; himself he cannot save." There was a story that Joseph of Arimathea, "ere the Deposition," caught a cup of Jesus' blood, which eventually he brought to the western coast of England. That the actual cup is yet present somewhere in England is almost certainly a fable. That the power of the sacrifice is yet operative is a fact that Williams makes the theme of the novel *War in Heaven*. His great interest in seeing parts of the human body as types of the divine archetype led him to suggest here, and elsewhere, that women in their periodical menstruation "shared with the Sacrifice the victimization of blood" (109). This statement may be physiological fable, but Williams still held to the mythic truth that it embodies.

On one level the Incarnation and on another the place of women as Theotokos in the world's base are recurring themes in *The Region of the Summer Stars*. As Theotokos and base, they stand as opposing forces to the floorless void and to man's falling into spacelessness.

The first ninety-two lines of "The Calling of Taliessin" are based on materials found in the *Mabinogion*. Williams retains the sense of magic and mystery of the original. In line 20, for example, he describes the movement of "river-mated rhythms," meaning apparently the rising and falling pulsations, the recurrent soundings, of the flow of water downstream. Something of the same effect is achieved in, say, the first ten lines of the poem. They rush forward, often to be broken in midline, a series of undulating movements emphasized by the frequent internal rhyme and alliteration, each so much a part of the sense that one is almost unaware of their presence. They sweep sensuously into that mystery that surrounds Taliessin's birth.

Williams borrows heavily, as a series of lines from the *Mabinogion* illustrates (corresponding lines from "Calling" are indicated in parentheses):

And my original country is the region of the summer stars: (54, 61)
I have been loquacious prior to being gifted with speech; (63)
I have been on the galaxy at the throne of the Distributor; (56)
I am a wonder whose origin is not known. (50)
I have been with my Lord in the manger of the ass; (62)
I have been in the firmament with Mary Magdalene; (58)
I have been bard of the harp to Lleon of Lochlin. (51)
I have suffered hunger for the Son of the Virgin, (55)
And it is not known whether my body is flesh or fish. (64)

Williams modifies the spirit and character of the Welsh original, however. The poet in the *Mabinogion* is unabashedly a magician, uninhibited by common restraints. If his poetry fails, then he falls back on magic. Taliessin, however, relies on what he himself is, a poet, "the imagination of this world," and not on magical control over people and things.

In Williams's poem we see Taliessin in his youth while he is still caught in "the fated cycle" of eternal repetition before he has been freed by the "doctrine of largesse in the land of the Trinity" (31). The Druids, Williams explains, represent a kind of natural poetry and Taliessin is the finest example of its furthest reach. His song, then, becomes in Williams's reconstruction a new poetic creation.

The next passage, lines 71–91, closes with the statement "he was caught by a rumour." What rumour? The word is, no doubt, a borrowing from the Old Testament of a statement used by both Jeremiah and Obadiah: "I have heard a rumour from the Lord." For them it signifies a divine message breaking into human consciousness. Taliessin's rumor was partly cultural, but primarily it came to him somehow from "over the dark rim of the southern sea" (80). The rumor is, in contemporary terminology, those primordial images stored in the "collective unconscious." They came from the "southern sea," consistent with the universal symbolism of water as both the origin of life and the unconscious. Moreover, Byzantium lies over a southern sea. Christianity is rooted in something shared elementally by all humanity, but its fullness was only guessed at by the pagan Druids. The full revelation awaited Byzantium. The rumors, however vague, were Taliessin's incentive to break out of the fated cycle into the freedom of eternity. There follows something more than statement—the communicated sense of Christian redemption summarized in a mere five lines:

> he heard
> tales of the tree of Adam, and the rare superfluity
> of moral creation, till the will of the superfluity

> turned the tree to a rood for itself and Another
> and envenomed its blood with mood; then the will of its Origin
> shared the blood and fared forth well from the tree. (73–78)

The rare superfluity is man; rare because he was created in God's image, and superfluous because his existence is not essential to God's completeness. The "will of the superfluity," by choosing, turned the Tree of Life into a Cross of Crucifixion for himself—and Another.

There were tales in ancient myths of magic trees and dying gods; there was magic and there was ancient verse, but all these seemed "poor . . . beside the thickening dreams" of the empire and of the coming grail (85). The passage is given unity partly by skillful use of rhyme and near rhyme. The words *heard* and *word* throw emphasis on the rumor and by association point toward the Word, the rumor made fact. Much the same purpose is served by *till* and *will,* underscoring the point that the Fall was indeed man's own willed action. The result of the Fall is expressed in *rood . . . blood . . . mood,* pointing up the poisoning of man's blood and that of his progeny through an act that resulted in universal "mood" or grief. The word *blood* also anticipates the blood shed on Calvary. *Shared* and *fared* combine into one action. The cluster of stressed words in "fared forth well," and the consequent breaking of the rhythm of the line, which in the immediately preceding one is regular, forces us to linger over the meaning of *well.* God reunites himself with His creation, and man is made well by His act of substitution. Taliessin was drawn toward the "healing metaphysic," and he sought the sea and the city.

Between the Wye and the city, however, lies Broceliande. Taliessin finds himself on the edge of the forest beyond which lies the place of Making. In the opposite direction he can discern the outlines of Logres, a place "without form," an echo of the biblical description of the Earth before God moved upon the face of the water and spoke order into existence. Most telling of all the kingdom's many woes is the fact that "transport had ceased, and all exchange stilled" (108). This meant not only that commerce was stifled but, more seriously, that man had lost contact with the throne. Co-inherence had failed.

Within Broceliande reside the powers by which Logres might be made a co-inherent theme of the empire and prepared as the abiding place of the Grail. Taliessin sees Broceliande through the eyes of a poet:

> there the divine science and the grand art,
> if at all below the third heaven, know
> their correspondence, and live in a new style. (114–16)

In a limited sense the "divine science" is theology; more broadly, however, it is the "fact" that theology attempts to formulate, the divine pattern of the structured universe, and the key, were it understood, to the meaning of creation and of man's place in God's scheme. The "grand art" is poetry. In Broceliande the correspondence between the image and the imaged is most clearly understood. The description is, as nearly as possible, of the object itself and, more importantly, a record of Taliessin's experience of its presence and power.

From here to the end of the poem we see the action from Taliessin's perspective. That experience is deeply disturbing. Broceliande is a dangerous place for an ordinary man. Among those who venture into its depth, some few, we are told, return "by grace dumb / and living, like a blest child, in a mild and holy / sympathy of joy" but most "loquacious with a graph / or a gospel, gustily audacious over three heavens" (120–23). And, reminiscent of the theme of "Taliessin's Song of the Unicorn," he foresees loneliness and alienation as his lot as a poet and wonders if any man can give himself wholly to the discipline of verse and at the same time love and be loved by a woman. Thus, in a state approaching despair, he imagines himself

> flung alive where only
> the cold-lipped mermen thrive among staring creatures
> of undersea, or lost where the beast-natures
> in a wood of suicides lap at the loss of intellect. (141)

There are two borrowings from Dante's *Inferno*. In Taliessin's mind, yet untutored Broceliande takes on the aspect of Dante's forest of bleeding trees, the symbolic end of those guilty of taking their own lives. As punishment they lose all semblance of the human form. Taliessin faces the choice of entering the wood and becoming either "blest," or "fanatic," or so "brain ravished" that life becomes spiritually sterile.

The phrase "loss of intellect" recalls Virgil's remark to Dante before the gates of hell that they have arrived at the place where he would see those who had lost "the good of intellect" and were thus rendered incapable of making the saving choices. The word *intellect*, Williams says, "is not a matter of worldly education, but of sensitive apprehension and spiritual knowledge" (*Beatrice* 123). The passage closes with a striking image. The "dark rose sunset" that Taliessin had earlier glimpsed between the trees becomes an "angrily rose-darkened [flood] down the inlets of the wood" (147). Here the color rose represents the outthrust of hell, in contrast to another of its meanings when it is used to describe the porphyry stairs, the ascent to the heavenly throne. According to Williams's understanding of

evil, hell is heaven known perversely. In lines 326–29, the image appears
again as a

> tiny, dark-rose, self-glowing, as a firefly's egg or . . .
> the entire point of the thrice co-inherent Trinity
> where every crown and every choir is vanished,
> and all sight and hearing is nothing else. (333–34, 337–39)

In that exalted state, the image is lost in the unimaged, and Broceliande
is recognized as the medium through which divine light is transmitted.

Byzantium, we begin to feel, is less a place than a state of being, trigonometry rather than geography, diagram rather than map. From here to
the end of the poem we are given an account of Taliessin's spiritual awakening, his initial vision of Logres, the coming of the grail, and his mission
as the king's poet. Merlin directs and empowers his vocation.

Williams again draws upon astrology and Cabalism, seeing in both a
poetic vision of cosmic ordering: in the Ritual of the Pentagram, a means
for evoking spiritual powers and of restoring relations, and in the Sephirotic
Tree, a diagram representing man's spiritual ascent.

The changing time of day–the deepening of the rose sunset and the
falling twilight–is an image of Taliessin's troubled inner state and prepares
for the next major turn in the poem:

> The sun had sunk,
> the rose vanished from the under-sea–and he
> banished there between Logres and Broceliande
> to feel before him the road threaten ravage
> and the power of universal spirit rise
> against him to be wild and savage on his lonely spirit;
> all things combined, and defined themselves in that moment
> hostile to him and the burning homes of Logres. (152–59)

The internal rhyme links lines in a single rhythmic movement and suggests the simultaneity of the falling darkness and Taliessin's deepening sense
of alienation, an impression intensified by the words *ravage* and *savage*.
At that moment all things appear hostile and "the burning of the homes
of Logres," the external fact, becomes an image of Taliessin's inner turmoil.
Without and within there is only fragmentation and loss of meaning. He
sees in the distance the approach of what appears a single figure, which,
when it draws near, grows double and materializes before him as Nimue's
parthenogenetical twins, Merlin and Brisen, time and space. The first Adam,
too, was according to legend, parthenogenetical, single, both male and fe-

male. In the poem "Lilith," from *Heroes and Kings,* Williams writes of how in that state of singleness, the Adam, who by nature yearned for companionship, conjured up as a figment of their imagination a phantom creature, a projection of themselves, whom they loved incestuously. Whereupon, God, appalled by the perversion, divided the one Adam into two beings, a male and a female, so that their love might be directed outward rather than inward, and that love might become exchange rather than self-idolization. That relation would be the earthly type of the co-inherent Trinity. The two, Adam and Eve, Merlin and Brisen, are images of that union that, according to rumor, existed between Mary Magdalene and Jesus, she to him in his grief and he to her in her sin. Both foreshadow the bond of exchange that would come to exist between the poet and his household:

> Taliessin
> felt before him an accumulation of power
> tower in the two shapes, so deep in calm
> that it seemed the word of the heart and the word of the voice
> must find, in each and in both, correspondence there
> more than even the grand art could know or show for all similitudes. (181–87)

Taliessin's intuitive sense of correspondence, the identity of the image with the unimaged, goes beyond that which poetry itself can reach. The phrase "so deep in calm" is a sharp contrast to Taliessin's earlier turmoil. He hears Merlin's speech "flow . . . as the south wind, stirring the tiny waves, shows / and shakes the stillness of the wide accumulated air" (187–90). This is one of the many recurring images in the poems of motion in stillness, a preparation here for the linking of the energy and activity of Broceliande with the third heaven, the place of the "living unriven truths" (252). Merlin describes what is to come, the founding of Logres, and begins the ritual by which the young poet is initiated into his office as king's poet: "I make haste to Logres, to call and install King Arthur; / at whose board you and I, lord, again may meet" (200-201). Lord indeed! The rhyming of *lord* and *board,* immediately following the calling and installing of the king, places enormous stress on Taliessin's new title. Surprised, he asks Merlin who he is, mortal or immortal, friend or foe. Merlin replies, "A friend, mortal or immortal, / if you choose" (206–07). The offer of friendship is contingent on Taliessin's acceptance, the importance of choosing emphasized by the break in the line. There is only good and man's freedom to choose whether to know it as good or evil. When, continuing, Merlin speaks of the coming of the Hallows from Sarras, Taliessin asks once more "Where is Sarras?" Merlin mildly rebukes:

> Hush; formulae and rhymes are yours
> but seek no more; fortunate the poet who endures
> to measure in his mind the distance even to Carbonek;
> few dare more—enough. (216-19)

Whereupon, Taliessin falls asleep and hears, first, mere noises that become shortly a voice repeating names that mean little: "Thames, Camelot, Carbonek, Pelles and Arthur, / Logres, Wye, Helayne, Broceliande, / Byzantium, the Empire . . . the Empire" (238–40). In occult tradition, to discover the name means to penetrate its power. Suddenly, the noises become substantive and begin to shape themselves into the image of the empire. Then comes a crucial step. Taliessin asks a question, "What serves the Empire?" We are reminded of Percivale's failure to ask the expected question, which delayed the coming of the grail. Taliessin asks, the frozen energies are released, and the answer comes. "The rite opens" (248).

In a vision Taliessin sees, in other than space, the third heaven, Broceliande, and Logres in organic relationship, each in descending order, each, in its own degree, an image reflecting the one above it. The Earth's shadow pushes back the boundaries of space and finds its point in Venus; at the base of the cone, between Broceliande and Logres, Merlin and Brisen stand, children of the Mother of Making, to mediate heaven's grace to Earth.

On the ground Merlin draws a pentagram and begins his invocation. At four points, those representing the elements, all that is to go into the forming of Logres, he drops the sacred herbs, said by occultists to possess magical healing power. Under Merlin's hands they become "flame of potential intellect becoming actual, / allaying the mortal air with purification" (266–67). At the fifth and upper point, Brisen, feminine source of potential birth, stands naked, open, receptive: "the impassioned diagram of space; her shadow fell / east into Logres, cast by the fourfold fire" (271–72). Thus she defines for Merlin the place "to prepare, and himself to fare to the preparation" (276). Through an act of imagination, the truth within the image is actualized. Merlin lifts the "five times cross-incised rod," cross-incised because his work has been transformed from magic into mystery; five times perhaps with reference to the five sacred wounds of Jesus. The elementals (spiritual creatures personifying the four elements) moved by his invocation, become the "magical continuum" through which the feeling intellect of the third heaven "fasten[s] on earth's image" (256). Taliessin, the poet, can see only by means of those images:

> The weight of poetry could not then sink
> into the full depth of the weight of glory.

> For all the codes his young tongue bore
> Taliessin could not think in Merlin's style,
> nor his verse grow mature with pure fact. (284–88)

"Pure fact"–the Holy Trinity and the Incarnation, for example–is a mystery for which human speech at its most incisive can never be more than a code. The operation of Merlin, we are told, "passed through his sleep / by accidents, not by events" (295–96). Williams uses the word *accident* in the medieval sense of an entity that by its essential nature adheres in another entity as its subject. An accident is thus dependent on something other than itself for meaning, while, in contrast, a substance has being in itself. The two words here are *accident* and *event*. The event exists in eternity and is substantive; accident is the corresponding (and derived) image by which the event is perceived in time–for example, the pentagram, the sacred herbs, the divining rod, the figures of Merlin and Brisen, and the vision of Broceliande, the third heaven, and Logres. Taliessin, the poet, is to be the imagination of this world, the artificer of these images of eternity in time. Thus he will serve his function in the kingdom.

He sees Brisen's body as the map of a road that will lead him throughout the empire from Byzantium to Caucasia and, eventually, almost to the "city and the light / [that] lay beyond the sun and beyond his dream" (309–10). But that final station is beyond his reach:

> on the brink of the last depth
> the glory clouded to its own covering and became
> again the recapitulatory body of Brisen,
> the engine of the First Mover, fit to his wit
> that works in earth the birth of superfluous good:
> fair let the creature follow that Nature. (312–17)

The phrase "recapitulatory body" is arresting. In embryology the word is used to designate the stages of growth in the embryo that are said to resemble the evolutionary development of the species to which the embryo belongs. Here the full glory is "clouded to its own covering," but something of its substance, fit to man's wit, may be seen in Brisen's body. Directed by that image, Taliessin began subconsciously to share in the doctrine of the largesse (311–18). He looks once more toward the "wide waste of Logres" and now sees, in the play of fire and shadow, "the stones of the waste glimmer like summer stars" (323). The pattern will be the third heaven, but Taliessin's labors will be in the wasteland of unmade Logres. His commissioning follows:

> Go son of the bards; king's poet,
> go; propolitan are the porphyry chambers; see
> and know the Empire [the contemplative life, vision] . . .
> rescue the king at Mount Badon [the active life]; stand by the king [as his
>   poet-soldier, the imaginative life], . . .
>
> . . . until the land
> of the Trinity by a sea-coming fetch to his stair [Camelot returned to
>   Carbonek]. (342–47)

There are two unusual words in this passage. *Propolitan* is obviously a coinage. Anne Scott comments on its origin and meaning:

> C. W.'s own coinage from "propolis," the dark red substance, also called "bee-glue" which bees use for making their hives cold and wasp-proof. Whenever he spoke of the City he would quote the line about bees from *Henry V* "The singing masons building roofs of gold" as illuminating all that it meant to him. "Prophyrogenitus"–born in the porphyry chamber–was a title of the Byzantine Imperial family, and to find that propolis connected the two ideas must have pleased him very much. (Supl. 22)

The word *fetch* is used in its nautical sense meaning to approach or to arrive at a particular point or port. This charge by Merlin is the second critical moment in Taliessin's calling. The first came when he asked the question; the second, when, after viewing the third heaven, he looks toward Logres and sees it in light of the eternal and accepts his role as poet in its building.

The passage that follows, especially the thirty-six line sentence beginning with line 365, is difficult. Williams attempts to communicate through Taliessin's own consciousness a sense of the simultaneity of a series of events. The coherence of the sentence is more psychological than logical or grammatical. The poet is at once asleep within the pentagram, by the king's side in Logres watching the approach (the fetch) of the grail-bearing ship from Sarras, both watching from a distance and himself on the ship, and, finally, once again safe within the pentagram. He foresees events yet to come and is assured that the outcome, because those events are within the frame of the pentagram, is part of some divine purpose. At the same time, his imagination is feverishly at work. He sees himself as part of some high destiny, "and even in a sleep within a sleep Taliessin trembled" (337–38).

He fears that he may be destroyed by the newfound powers, or, at least, he may return from Broceliande a "blest child," or perhaps he even foresees his fated love for Blanchefleur who was to be "farther from and closer to the king's poet / than any" (369–71, 377–78). Perhaps "among all the phantas-

magoria" Merlin reveals something of the awesome "final term and firm purpose of heaven" (380–81). At this point his thoughts become especially intertwined and convoluted. He sees but fails to distinguish clearly (he had
not yet been to Byzantium) between the role of Helayne and Blanchefleur,
one the symbol of divine and the other of human substitution. He speaks
of the "daughter of a king," Helayne or Blanchefleur or both–which, perhaps, it does not so much matter. Williams himself said that their identity
was not only possible but probable. The daughters rightly stand on the visionary ship speeding toward Sarras:

> holding an unseen thing
> between her hands, but over her hands a veil,
> the saffron veil of the sun itself. (383–86)

The scene shifts and Taliessin finds himself again safe within the pentagram, secured not only from malignant forces released by the Dolorous Blow
but also from the humanly unbearable light of heaven. The vision of the
transformed empire though mediated through its accidents is clear:

> through the reach of Logres
> the stones of the waste glimmered like summer stars,
> as if the king's poet's household of stars
> shone, in a visible glory. (397–400)

Yet there are contingencies. If, Merlin promises, the great design fails, "ambiguous rites" have been prepared to assure that the doctrine of largesse will
be kept alive within the household of the king's poet.

The discovery of the meaning of substitution and exchange is the third
stage in Taliessin's enlightenment. He said, within limits of natural grace,
before leaving to pursue the rumor, "I am a wonder whose origin is not
known." Merlin now enlarges and focuses that wonder and mystery by placing
it in context of the co-inherence:

> they who shall be called and thralled
> by Taliessin's purchase and their own will
> from many a suburb, many a waste; say
> that they are a wonder whose origin is not known,
> they are strown [overcovered, protected by] with a high habit [both a
>   covering and a way of behavior], with the doctrine of largesse,
> who in his house shall be more than the king's poet
> because of the vows they take. (425–31)

6

Multiple Levels of Unity

> let the hazel
> of verse measure the multiple levels of unity.
> —"Taliessin in the Rose Garden," 130–31

T aliessin in the Rose Garden" is a meditation on images of womanhood on the human level and of the Incarnation on the divine level. The rose garden is symbol of Caucasia and of the human body, the configuration Taliessin sees in the garden. The color crimson (or some shade thereof) is a recurring motif—the color of the roses, of the veins in Guinevere's arms, and of her ruby ring, "royally runed." It signifies the blood that flows through her body; that drops from Pelles's wound; that rages envenomed in all Adam's children; that is shed by all women periodically and at the time of birthgiving; and, archetypally, the "timed and falling blood" of Christ (149).

Here, as in "The Coming of Galahad," the astrological myth, the Sephirotic Tree, and the Sacred Pentagram are all reflections of the manifold levels of unity. The twelve zodiacal houses image cosmic unity, the sun passing through the houses (lunar months) once each year ("as," Shuttleworth suggests, "the blood circulates through the veins, arteries, organs of the human body" [Supl. 23]). It is believed that the celestial bodies influence men's lives and characters and even the physical structure of the Earth. They diagram the interrelation and interdependence by which all creation is joined in one co-inherent web. Stanza 6 suggests man's climb toward God by way of paths along the Sephirotic Tree. Finally, the five planets to which Williams gives special attention represent the points that, when connected, form the sacred pentagram. The two linking forces are poetry, the imagination of this world, and divine grace, the power of the other.

Taliessin walks among the roses "(all kinds all minds taking) / making verse, putting distance into verse" (3). As a poet he enters sympathetically into all minds, remaining at the same time detached, tracing the diagram,

139

enfleshing the pattern, translating the Greek minuscula. The specific blossom *Rosa Centifoliae* with its one hundred petals, each individual and yet all part of the whole, images the co-inherence of creation in its pristine state. Taliessin sees first, at the garden entrance, a "rush of crimson," a single manifestation of the undifferentiated life as though it were part of the garden itself (10). Closer inspection reveals the three women, each a petal in the one rose, all of the same womanhood, but each having her own function: the queen to exhibit glory; Dindrane (Blanchefleur in religion) to exemplify contemplation; the maid to affirm natural beauty by tending the rose garden. Dindrane is the unifying figure, for, in her, "an eidolon of the slaves," is the co-inherence most explicitly expressed: "The air was clear, as near as earth can / to the third heaven, climax tranquil in Venus" (19–20). Venus, love and tranquility, is a state of being. In contrast, Broceliande, the place of making, seethes with the energy of becoming. Taliessin's senses are stirred, and he trembles in concert with "the infinite and infinitesimal trembling of the roses," caught in a creative energy from both Broceliande and the third heaven (25). The scene is reminiscent of that described in Jonathan's painting of the city (London and yet not London) in *All Hallows' Eve:*

> The spectator became convinced that the source of that light was not only in that hidden sun; as, localized, it certainly was. . . . The eye, nearing that particular day, realized that it was leaving the whole fullness of the light behind. It was everywhere in the painting—concealed in houses and in their projected shadows, lying in ambush in the cathedral, opening in the rubble, vivid in the vividness of the sky. It would everywhere have burst through, had it not chosen rather to be shaped into forms, and to restrain and change its greatness in the colours of those lesser limits. It was universal, and lived. (30)

Taliessin sees Guinevere as the "sensuous mode," the feminine counterpart of the masculine sun (27). In the language of the Cabala she is the world's base, the Binah and potentially the cut hazel, the bearer of fruit. She wears a green gown, symbol of natural forces and living things, and on her finger a ring, "the single central ruby" in which is concentrated, for the poet, all that the rose garden and the feminine body symbolize—"the contained / life of Logres-in-the-Empire" (36, 37–38). For only a moment she stands the intended "hollow," and then the pure blaze of glory breaks in an "unrestrained rush." Taliessin foresees the bloodletting war loosed upon the kingdom because of her failure, and he sees the ring both in and circling that war, both its cause and the summary image of that prior and determining cause of all wars, the Dolorous Blow. Taliessin recognizes the path of the rose garden as verse (an image) into the "secrets of Carbonek and the queen's majesty" (49). The reference is most obvious to the Grail King's wound but also to the glory that is by nature woman's because she shares in her body the sacrificial shedding of blood made perfect on Calvary—a matter made clear in lines 160–62. He hears himself saying, "The Wounded Rose [Pelles and Guinevere] runs with blood at Carbonek" (51).

Stanza 3 anticipates the poem's conclusion. While Taliessin speaks to the queen about her role in Logres, she talks, laughs, and looks furtively for Lancelot. He is reminded of Iseult and of Mark, Tristram, and Palomides, who loved her, and of himself who loved Dindrane and sighs for "the zodiac in the flesh," the possession of the vision of co-inherence that romantic love should bring. Paraphrasing Saint Paul, he remarks that such union of flesh and spirit to men like Mark and Tristram is a scandal and, to women like Iseult and Guinevere, folly. Yet for all that, he concludes, it is still Palomides and himself, unrequited lovers, who see "everywhere the hint, / in a queen's shape or a slave's" of the diagram of glory (61–62). Rejected, they are left only with bitter comfort of the law of exchange. The beauty they coveted for themselves falls to another.

In stanza 4, Taliessin draws upon the zodiac as another symbol of co-inherence. That which appeared a scandal to pious Jews and folly to sly Greeks becomes credible to him in light of his Druid birth and his Byzantium schooling. The pattering of the sacred names is drawn from various sources (75). The Book of Revelation tells of four beasts with different faces and many eyes who "rest not day and night, saying 'Holy, holy, holy,' Lord God Almighty." In both Old and New Testament the name of God is held in special reverence. In Cabalistic tradition the various names by which He is called (his one name never spoken) is held to communicate special virtues to those who repeat them devotionally.

In Byzantium Taliessin saw how the city, the bride, was faced toward the emperor, the one waiting to receive and the other to give the impregnating seed of life. They are symbolic of the interrelation of all orders of creation, queen to king, slave to lord, Caucasia to Carbonek. The vision of Unity is further represented by the twelve houses, the lunar months, which describe the path of the sun around the planets annually. In its circular and cyclical course, the sun, image of eternity, both measures the temporal limits within which the planets operate and impregnates them with life. The emperor is the "sun sign," the name given to the sign under which one is born, for all creation. God is indelibly stamped on everything that exists. The universal sun sign is accompanied by lesser ones, individual and particular, and the whole, like the *Rosa Centifoliae,* is an organism of perfect order and balance.

Four of the twelve houses are named in this stanza: Aquarius, Gemini, Scorpion, and Libra. Each is associated with a part of the body: Aquarius, with the eyes; Gemini, with the arms and hands; Scorpion, with the genitalia; and Libra, with the buttocks. Traditionally, Aquarius is also related to the air, and it is believed that those born under the sign possess clarity of vision and penetrating insight. Taliessin, the poet, has the ability to detach himself from action and view the human scene from outside (1–2). Here, in "the clearness above the firmament," he studies the pattern of the universe "in the stellar clearness." He sees

> the rosed femininity
> particled out of the universe, the articled form
> of the Eve in the Adam; the Adam known in the Eve. (89, 90–92)

Particled, a verb, derives from the noun meaning a portion that is withdrawn from a whole – in this case, the "rosed femininity" of Eve that was originally part of the universe and, specifically, of Adam. *Articled* carries the meaning of being bound as by a treaty or by slavery. Eve remained an articled form, interdependently related to Adam and, both Adam and Eve, to God. Co-inherence is the natural law of creation. The particle remains articled to the whole. Taliessan permits his "visionary eyes . . . to pass through the themes and the houses." Can even the poet, he asks, communicate what he sees, the queen in the glory that surrounds her in that vision? "Eyes then are compacted power," Williams writes; "they are an index of vision; they see and refer us to greater seeing" (Ridler 85). It is of that thing greater that Taliessin struggles to speak.

The question unanswered, perhaps unanswerable, he turns to Gemini, the Twin, associated with the arms and shoulders. He sees power running down the arms and being caught up in and made effective through the hands. He thinks of the queen's two hands, potential instruments of the feminine graces; he recalls the myth of the founding of Rome by Romulus and Remus who were suckled by a wolf and humanized by their own efforts "to labour, making muscles and thumbs," those human thumbs that dis-tinguish man from beast and permit him to become the intended god-image, a creative force (100). The desired end is that the twin arms and hands "each might neighbor the other to instruments and events" (101). "The Scorpion-contingency, [when] controlled and ensouled in Jerusalem" becomes the means of all life (102). The words *contingency, controlled,* and *ensouled* are care-fully chosen, and the latter two are given emphasis by rhyming. As the source of generation, Jerusalem is a holy place, but its sanctity is contingent on its proper use. It might be the means of uniting men and women, a type of the relation of the Heavenly Bridegroom with the bride, the church. It might be the power by which woman exercises her role as the world's base, the source of new life. The Scorpion, however, also carries in its tail a dangerous sting. If sex is sometimes considered man's greatest danger, that is because, being his greatest good, it carries the contingency for greatest perversion. By creation, however, the queen's body is solidly based on Libra, the sign associated with the buttocks and represented by the scales, symbol of balance and justice. There is a relation between the genitalia and buttocks, the latter being the subservient back or base of the other, and each functioning in its appointed role as part of one glorious body, to use Saint Paul's image of the church.

In stanza 5 the Sephirotic Tree serves as image. The Way weaves about the human body, the city. In some of the diagrams of the tree, a figure of a human body was superimposed upon it, and parts of the body were associated with the Sephiroth, which receive emanations from the divine Sun. Taliessin, from the "clearness above the firmament," pursues the progress of the emanation downward from the eyes through the arms to the hands where the light is "swallowed" (in line 98 it is "laired") and contained in the hands—that is, controlled and made effective toward the shaping of events. "There is not much difference apparently between the Adam and the beasts," Williams writes, "except that he (or they) control them" (*HCD* 16). In the human body that emanation is a type of the creative power by which all things were made. It is manifest potentially in the queen's outstretched hand, in the slave's trimming shears, and in Dindrane's prayers. Proceeding still further downward, Taliessin's eyes fix upon the house of Libra, the physical creation, represented by the buttocks, "the imperially bottomed glory" (122). Libra, the scales, represents balance and justice "needful to all joys / and all peace" (124–25). The subject here is human justice, "between man and man, and (O opposite!) between man and woman," but particularly the latter (126). Justice in their relations lies precisely in their divinely willed differences and in the reconciliation of opposites in a unity of flesh and spirit. Only "the hazel of verse," the disciplining and shaping imagination, can suggest those "manifold levels of unity."

In stanza 6, Williams turns to arch-natural justice, from the buttocks to the "privy parts and the sexual organs" (*Essays* 83). The contrast is startling. The rays suddenly range wildly, and the "roseal pattern" of unity is distorted. The color becomes "botched and blotched" like blood "inflaming the holy dark" (135–36). We are confronted with a simultaneity of images of disaster. The Adam, dissatisfied with zodiacal unity, preferred to experience the strongest bond of their unity in antagonism and bade the scorpion sting. The curves (their position in relation to the circle that is

God) of their identity (their individuality but also their union with each other) is "crookt" (as a planet wrenched out of orbit). That finite choice, perhaps—indeed, something so trivial as eating an apple—had infinite consequences, a paradox that deeply troubled Williams. The Adam's blood envenomed by the scorpion, however, was passed to children and children's children. Cain, moved by self-centered ego, slew Abel, substituting his own version of earthly for heavenly justice. From his fallen view his own safety demanded elimination of his brother. His eyes had become bloodshot so that he could no longer discern the true pattern of human justice and felicity, the co-inherence. Aquarius, the Twin, Cain and Abel, Remus and Romulus, Balin and Balan, Arthur and Pelles, the two arms, Everyman experienced antagonism in the blood and in the shedding of blood. The irony, defeated on Calvary, is that purification and return lay precisely in the identity they spurned.

Over against the bloodletting, as Taliessin sees, there is another Way. The poet is still climbing the Sephirotic Tree, or, as one image fades, another emerges, and he is ascending the porphyry stair from the "pit and the split zodiac," climbing "against timed and falling blood": that of the second Adam, who came down "by a secular stair," God made flesh, to lift man up to God (153, 149). In the pit from which he emerged he sees the empire "stretched," and he hears the women sob "as in a throb of stretched verse" (156-57). The word *stretched*, in this context, suggests images of the medieval torture rack upon which men's bodies were broken and calls to mind also the cross upon which Jesus was "stretched, . . . bled, . . . nailed, . . . thrust into" (Essays 136). Women everywhere "share with the Sacrifice the victimization of blood" (162). Redemption by the shedding of blood is a fact then known by both flesh and spirit with the difference that the spirit knows that it knows and flesh does not. The spirit carries, therefore, greater responsibility than the flesh. It was spirit that brought about the Fall. Flesh and spirit, however, are really one, each a category of a single identity, names by which men speak of the unspeakable. Woman's flesh

> lives the quest of the Grail
> in the change from Camelot to Carbonek and from Carbonek to Sarras,
> puberty to Carbonek, and the staunching, and Carbonek to death. . . . (165–67)

Guinevere fails to come to terms with reality, to reconcile Caucasia with Carbonek, and to achieve maturity by undertaking the journey. The closing lines of the stanza are an oblique reference to Mary, who, in contrast, not only asked the proper question but made the desired response: "Behold the handmaid of the Lord; be it unto me according to thy word."

Stanza 7, with the image of the Virgin Mary in the background, is a song of praise to all womanhood. The word *travel* refers to the spiritual journey, and, by sound association, with *travail,* suggests the sacrifice of holding in her body "the image of the supernatural," the measurement of the archetypal Body in terms of the natural (166–67, 170–71). Williams sees in Pelles's bleeding wound and in the bright spot on the planet Jupiter, imagined to be a wound, types of the Wounded King on the Cross, and he recognizes the truth of the taunt, the yielding of irony to defeated irony, in "Others he saved; himself he cannot save."

An additional comment about Jupiter is perhaps necessary. The projected *Jupiter Over Carbonek* was to have emphasized meditation more than action and to have been written from the perspective of divine grace rather than poetic imagination. Williams perhaps had in mind Dante's treatment of Jupiter in *Paradiso* where the planet is identified with kingship and with justice and peace, but with a sharp distinction between human and divine justice, between Cain's "cure" and Christ's sacrifice (142). Here Jupiter also is an image of the highest type of bleeding wound short of the archetype Himself. He provides the last of the five points that, when connected, form the Sacred Pentagram.

The light of Percivale's philosophical star shines on Logres and Broceliande, enabling the responsive woman to feel man's capacity for divine things, Galahad, rise in her flesh and to see her flesh bright with the Christ-presence. All this is manifest in the turn of her body and in her heart that finds its own healing in the healing of others. Jesus both energized and reaffirmed all substitution and exchange and in his example established anew the pattern by which creation was to be brought again into co-inherence. There is no other way. Christ alone heals Himself without others. Blessed is she, however, who hears with "touched ears"–ears opened by His touch– the preparations for the rite of Galahad "and the fixing of all fidelity from all infidelity" (189). The reference is to the coming together of the two great ways, affirmation and negation, in which "the princess of the Grail abandoned her virginity and Lancelot was defrauded of his fidelity, . . . The High Prince has remained an intensive symbol of the two ways; he is not on them, but they are both in him" (*DD* 116–17). And women are the God-bearers.

There follow two brief stanzas that stand in tragic juxtaposition. In the first Taliessin sees the queen as the feminine headship of Logres intended to exhibit the glories of womanhood to all her subordinates, bringing "to a flash of seeing the woman in the world's base." That is the vision of the queen from the throne. The reality of the queen in the rose garden, talking sideways to Dindrane and looking furtively for Lancelot, foreshadows the tragedy to follow. She dismisses the poet's words with the majestic scorn of a queen and the ironic unawareness of a frivolous woman: "Has my lord dallied with poetry among the roses?"

7

The Ways upon the Way

> she saw the lords
> riding before her, the Ways upon the Way, . . .
> the two great vocations,
> the Rejection of all images before the unimaged,
> the Affirmation of all images before the all-imaged,
> the Rejection affirming, the Affirmation rejecting.
> —"The Departure of Dindrane," 83–84, 86–89

The action of "The Departure of Dindrane" centers around two women and two events, one accomplished and the other immanent. Dindrane, determined on a vocation in the convent of Almesbury, is on the point of departing Camelot; the slave girl anticipates an appearance in seven days before the king's bailiff to make a choice that will determine her future. The departure of Dindrane is presented as an action effectively accomplished. She has made her decision, and we are given only "the poetic result" of it. The slave girl, on the other hand, has yet to decide, and we see her struggling. The theme is vocation and the manner in which one follows the Way. The poem is specifically a treatment of the various ways upon the Way and of how the ways are at once separate and intertwined. The two ways, Williams writes,

> were to co-exist; one might almost say, to co-inhere, since each was to be the key of the other: in intellect as in emotion, in morals as in doctrine. . . . The Way of Affirmation was to develop great art and romantic love and marriage and philosophy and social justice; the Way of Rejection was to break out continually in the profound mystical documents of the soul, the records of the great psychological masters of Christendom. (*DD* 57–58)

The first two stanzas are expository. The household awaits in the court for the appearance of Dindrane, accompanied by Taliessin and Elayne. The second stanza explains the practice in Logres, based on old Levitical law, that gave a slave, after seven years of service, a choice among three freedoms: return to the home country; a dowry for marriage for a woman and, for a man, a farm or a job; or a willing continuation of servitude in the household the slave had served.

The next two stanzas introduce the central characters: the slave girl from whose perspective most of the action is seen and in whom the significant internal action is being worked out; Dindrane who, here as elsewhere, appears in the company of the slave girl, not necessarily the same one, without whom, Williams says, she "cannot be perfect to understanding." The two women are complementary: prayer and action, negation and affirmation, saint and slave. Near freedom the slave girl "brooded on choice" in a stanza that ends significantly with an unanswered question (25). The word *brooded* with its overtones of uncertainty and anxiety is precisely descriptive of what is happening. It is also suggestive of incubating and nurturing. She is presented with the three alternatives and the responsibility for choosing. She is moved initially by the consideration of self-interest. The first two possibilities are straightforward. The third, however, is uncertain. Were she to choose it, she would give up claim to self-control and be forced to "leave / what end would to come" (31–32). Could she be certain that even in Taliessin's household she would not chafe at the restraints and look back with grief on lost opportunities? Taliessin, she knew, lightened no heart that was not already quickened–open and receptive–to his will. Even if her heart were so heightened at the moment, would it, she wondered, endure the uncertainties that time might bring, or would she regret not having chosen a seemingly less conditional freedom? Did her security lie in individualism or in co-inherence?

The slave girl uses the word *doom* with reference to what might prove a regretted decision (35). At the beginning of the poem we learn that the "day was curst / with a rain that had not abated since first dawn" (1–2). At the beginning of stanza 4 we are told: "The gloom of the day hung over the porch." Her language and the "curst" external gloom are symbolic of the girl's troubled mind prior to her enlightenment, which comes after the arrival of Dindrane. Dindrane appears between the "two she loved" (41). One was the mistress of a household, a wife and mother, a bread maker; the other, although a unicorn, was nevertheless, a doer, an affirmer of images. He both fought battles and wrote verse. Both the bread maker and the poet stood in seeming contrast to Dindrane, and yet the three are bound together on the one Way by their very differences. For Dindrane they represent things to which she might have given her "world's heart" had it not been pledged to God. Theirs is the way of affirmation; hers, the way of negation. Yet between the three there is the bond of "labours and neighbours," the rhyming signifying the intertwining of the two ways (45). In the convent she will exchange with them who are in the world her contemplation for their labors and studies. She has now come to the point, however, where the separation, already affirmed in spirit, will be known in her flesh, and she pauses for a moment to contemplate what the new household will be like. Sensitive still to the demands of the world and of the body, she feels apprehension.

The slave girl watches with, no doubt, bewilderment. She knows and loves Dindrane, knows the severity and finality of the vows she has taken, and she "guesses" the "sword of schism that pierced her lord" (53). The image is meant for Taliessin but also recalls memories of another Lord and another piercing sword of which all subsequent separations for his sake are types. The rhyming of *schism* and *chrism* both emphasizes and links the idea of suffering with healing, death with life, as a single action in the "heightened heart." The slave girl suddenly sees her own state as measured against the "new-treasured servitude" that Dindrane exemplifies. Dindrane is moving willingly to bondage; transfigured, as it were, she passes into a "new-panoplied category" of glory that makes the recent concerns of the slave girl seem trivial (60). What had appeared a cell is now seen as a shell to be broken by emerging new life. What had seemed as joined by fetters, a chain, now appears instead "jointed bones" of a living body, a new creation, "manacles of energy, . . . manipulations of power" (64). All disciplines are recognized as a panoply of God's plenitude. Down Dindrane's arm the power moves to be caught in her hands and flung abroad in hundreds of ways, each a manifestation of the creative spirit.

In an act of substitution and exchange, the girl feels the love and life of Dindrane flood her being and sees the two, Taliessin and Dindrane, not as fallen flesh and blood, but as presences, figures larger than life; as for them so for her: "at once in her heart, / servitude and freedom were one and interchangable" (76–77).

Stanza 5 is about separation and unity with emphasis on separation; stanzas 6 and 7 are also about both but with stress on unity. Stanza 5 begins with a distinction between servitude and freedom, which the slave girl is just beginning to understand. Servitude is obedience to an imaged law. When images are recognized for what they are, as conveyors but not substance, they can be protective and utilitarian. When they become ends in themselves, they are enslaving. Freedom lies either in the unimaged law, followed by the few who pursue the Negative Way, rejecting all earthly images, one after the other, until only the unimaged God himself remains; or, in the "choice of images" exercised by those who see in every image a valid expression of some aspect of the godhead but refuse to regard any one as definitive (79). "This also is thou; neither is this Thou."

The slave girl sees her two lords pursuing the one Way in different modes, he affirming and she rejecting. The ways that appeared separate prove to be intertwined, the Rejection affirming and the Affirmation rejecting. The two figures ride through a cloud "either no less than the other the doctrine of largesse" (91). The cloud as image is the same as that which covered Sinai as God revealed himself through the law to Moses, overshadowed Jesus as he revealed himself through grace to his disciples, and into which Dante entered on the first level of paradise–a cloud, Williams says "as if, living, he entered a still uncleft pearl. He impearls himself. How body enters body, dimension supports dimension (he says), we cannot tell; therefore we should more expressly long to understand the union of our nature with God's, that is, the Incarnation" (*Beatrice* 195). The slave girl is being initiated into the great mystery of the co-inherence, as Williams states it, the "in-othering of men and the in-Godding of men" (*Beatrice* 190). There follows for her one of those moments, the beginning of magic, "when it seems that anything might turn into anything else" (*Witchcraft* 77). That moment has been prepared for by the presences and the cloud. The forms before her take on the mythical shape of centaurs, having heads, arms, and upper bodies of a man and the lower bodies and back legs of a horse, awesomely peopling a world made infinite by a cloud of supernatural creatures that range among the hazel. And "she? slave or free? no centaur" (97). Perhaps, she muses, she might appear so to another, a child, a lover, or God, someone who sees her "new-personed," adoringly, as, she believes, Taliessin had seen her with the impersonal eyes of a poet and recognized her capacity for glory. With the centaurs plunging about her, she glimpses among them "the great personalities . . . close-handed, oath-bonded, word-in-the-flesh-branded" (106–8). The hyphenation suggests the joining of elements not ordinarily considered single. She becomes the nuts from the uncut hazel falling along the hazel's way, natural grace brought to fruition through spiritual discipline–". . . and she it" (113).

She wonders if, after all, she has a choice. Both nostalgia for her native land and the hankering for what is commonly called freedom seem poor choices or no choice along side the alternative. She embraces the co-inherence under which, newly and freely bound, she can enjoy perfect freedom. "Felicity alters from the center," Taliessin had told another. The slave girl hears in the air above the centaurs, as though from the third heaven itself, a voice saying "fixed is the full" (124). Fullness is not quantitative measurement. The language echoes the thought of a passage from Dante's *Paradiso*, which Williams discusses in *The Figure of Beatrice*. In the lowest heaven, the Moon,

Dante asks Piccarda, the sister of Foress Donati, whether in their relatively low state—so to speak—those on the Moon envied the happiness of those on the higher planets. She replies, as Williams translates: "Brother, the quality of love quietens our will; it makes us desire only what we have, . . . we love; we love the divine will, we love as that chooses to love, we are in-willed to will, in-loved to love" (196).

The reference to Wordsworth's *mens sensitiva* and the shell, images central in "The Coming of Galahad," might have a subterranean connection with the image of the uncleft pearl in the passage quoted above from Dante (61, 161). The shell has broken (and for the slave girl is breaking) and the pearl is emerging. The theme of the intertwining ways on the one Way is consummated in the last few lines of the stanza. Over the galloping centaurs and above the noise of their pounding hooves, the girl hears a voice echoing the message that Galahad sent to Lancelot by Bors: "Fair lord, salute me to my lord Sir Lancelot my father, / and bid him remember of this unstable world" (142–43). The admonition is ambiguous. It could be a warning against too close an attachment to images as ends, or, as likely, an encouragement to affirm all things in this unstable world as images of the All-imaged.

Each must choose. Dindrane goes on to Almesbury, and Taliessin returns to Camelot. Although his native region is the summer stars and a part of his "split" voice, his twy-nature, rises to the third heaven, he is also the poet whose present home is Logres to which he must return to prepare for the coming of Galahad. There follows an emotionally taut scene that could have been trivialized by undue stress on personal pathos. The lovers part. Instead of dwelling on the human pain, however, Williams holds strictly to his purpose, giving us what, in context of the poem, is "the poetic result" of the experience (*RB* 5). The personalities are submerged in the impersonalities, and Taliessin wishes for Dindrane a safe passage through the impersonalities (the negations and denials). And she for herself desires a return of the personalities (the reaffirmation) beyond the bond and blessing of their departure: "I will affirm, my beloved, all that I should" (152). He responds: "I will reject all that I should" (153). The way of both Almesbury and Camelot, he assures her, leads to the same "turn" [end]. An enigmatic passage follows: "The grace be with you; / which, as your face made visible, let your soul sustain" (155–56). The reference, I think, is to the return of personality beyond the impersonalities of which Dindrane has just spoken. God, in his largesse, returns abundantly that which man has for his sake willingly surrendered. Taliessin's prayer is that she may be spiritually sustained while she awaits the return. For his part he turns back to his household. "He burned. . . . " C. S. Lewis remarked, "In each of them now the natural passion is not so much 'mortified,' as set on fire, by the spiritual" (*Arthurian Torso* 152). Dindrane yearns for the "cell" at Almesbury as Taliessin burns for his household. In the peace of this "in-willing" and "in-Godding," only the horse tosses its head and snorts.

Seven days later the slave girl commits herself to serve not Taliessin but his household, the community of the co-inherence. She has discovered along with the girl in "The Star of Percivale" that Taliessin too is only a man, an image pointing to a greater. She can now accept joyfully the once feared uncertainties, confident that in love all luck is good. The "jangling bits" of the horses are symbolic of all discipline, imaged laws, to which man is subjected, but from her new perspective they appear more means of direction than of restraint. She says, "They only can do it with my lord who can do it without him" (172). She has discovered the true function of personality and has freed herself from destructive self-centeredness.

The doctrine of substitution and exchange is pervasive in all Williams's work. In a postscript to *The Descent of the Dove* he suggests one way in which the practice might be recovered and made operative among Christians today. He proposes the founding of an "Order of the Co-inherence," a very informal banding together of a few kindred spirits whose sole purpose would be to meditate and practice substitution and exchange in love, a technique, he says, that needs to be rediscovered in the modern church.

In addition to this and his other statements on the subject, Williams obviously felt it necessary to write a poem that would give emotional and sensuous dimension to a set of ideas, an actual sense of something happening—something that prose cannot, or can only in a limited way, communicate. Of "The Founding of the Company," we can say what Williams said about another: "A thousand preachers have said all that Dante says and left their hearers discontented; why does Dante content? because an Image of profundity is there" (*Beatrice* 212).

Much of the interrelatedness of which the poem speaks is communicated structurally through the internal rhyme, functioning abstractly on one level by gathering the whole into oneness through its pervasive sound pattern; and, on another, by heightening and relating concepts through the technique of repetition, elaboration, and contrast. The poem becomes less a statement than a complex image that finds its archetype in the esoteric word *perichoresis* in line 106. Williams uses the word, however, not because it is esoteric, but because it images accurately the experience that he wishes his readers to feel. The poem is less to persuade than to captivate, less to convert than to expand horizons. The full meaning of perichoresis will be explored later.

The poem begins "At about this time. . . ." The statement is intentionally vague. The company emerged, we are told, at some time between the founding of the first monasteries in the early fifth century and the founding of Monte Casino in 529, but the specific beginning of Taliessin's company cannot be dated, other than generally at some time during the reign of Arthur. It was already in existence, no doubt, before anyone became conscious of it. It was integral to the pattern of life that governed the poet's household: "a few found themselves in common" (4). Moreover, Williams's use of *this* instead of *that* places the action in the continuing present rather than in the past and invites readers to approach the poem as experience rather than history.

This company had neither vows nor rules but only a "certain pointing," the ideal of people living together in co-inherence (5). It had no name. No one knew whether its origins were to be found among the "readers" or the "grooms," intellectuals or laborers; whether it sprang from doctrine or simple toil. It was experienced as a token of love between themselves and between themselves and their Lord. It grew from the Center, grounded in the Acts of the Throne and the pacts [response] of the Themes and "lived only by conceded recollection" (13–14). The word *conceded,* meaning "accepted as true," refers primarily to Christ's death, the pattern and the power for all substitution and exchange. It also refers to the sacramental nature of Holy Communion, which is sometimes spoken of as a memorial: "Do this in remembrance of me." Williams wrote that "acts done in union with that act [his death] have a unique validity" (Essays 141). To remember or to concede is to experience it as now happening.

The company stood in relation to the Protection, divine providence, somewhat as the kingdom stood to the king, but differed in that, being neither ordered by rank nor restrained by law, they held all in common under love "when love was fate to minds adult in love" (22). The word *cult,* given emphasis by rhyming with *vult,* is used in its root meaning of adoration. The object of their devotion was the "Trinity and the Flesh-taking" (24). The doctrine of the Trinity is a symbolic statement about how man experiences God (not a definition *of* God) and of how love is described in admittedly inadequate language. It is the affirmation of love, co-inherence, as the basis of all things, below as above. The last three lines roughly translate the Three-in-One God into understandable terms: the making, the telling (manifestation), and the indwelling. The *largesse* is in itself an important image. Ridler defines it as "the giving that asks no return, and is quite independent of desert . . . none can earn it, freely given, freely received" (Supl. 39). Williams wrote: "The doctrine of the Trinity . . . the Atonement . . . the Church is a doctrine of largesse; therefore the doctrine of the individual is a doctrine of largesse. . . . To forgive and to be forgiven are the two points of holy magnificence and holy modesty; round these two centres the whole doctrine of largesse revolves" (Essays 141). Confession in the company is individual and communal. The word *mansion* carries the meaning of dwelling, echoing, no doubt, the root meaning "to remain" (27). *Session,* in the same line, means a sitting, specifically, the sitting of Jesus at the right hand of the Father after his resurrection. Together, "each in each," the words describe the indwelling of God in God and of man in God, the co-inherence.

The next three stanzas reveal the company as it operates in the kingdom, encompassing as a whole "rose-lordly Caucasia . . . maids, porters, mechanics"; the spiritualities at Almesbury, and the intellectuals – "the cells of the brain / of the king's college and council" (29, 32, 33–34). They were the "wise companions," imaging in their lives "a gay science" derived from God, patterned into the fabric of creation, and immemorially prized, however obscurely, even by heathens (36).

There were three degrees of membership of which we can speak, not because the spiritual kingdom is divisible, but, as with the Trinity, because the intellect is incapable of grasping diversity in Unity except in symbolic terms. The divisions here parallel the three levels of spiritual achievement of the Sephirotic Tree: the first representing the ordinary human sphere, the unawakened, largely unconscious; the second, the advance sphere of conscious spiritual attainment; the last, the mystic and ineffable union of man with God. Those on the first level lived with frankness of honorable exchange less because they consciously chose than because all civil polity, quite apart from the Judeo-Christian tradition, demands at least minimal recognition of co-inherence. Those in Logres accepted as conditions of citizenship "labour in the kingdom, devotion in the Church, the need / each had of other" (44–45). Indeed, only in P'o-lu was the co-inherence totally rejected.

The second order of membership is an extension of the first. Within it are those who consciously offer themselves in exchange with each other, "dying each other's life, living each other's death" (64). This goes beyond necessity or even ordinary human goodwill to embrace a willed substitution ordained for all mortal images at the time of creation. And now that those primordial images have been "botched and blotched" by the Dolorous Blow, "the Flesh-taking" has renewed from within the torn web and established and empowered again the pattern by which reconciliation can be known. The archetypal substitution is brought into focus by the rhyming of *dead* and *stead* (68). The practice of substitution and exchange, of which the largesse of the Trinity is at once the pattern and the empowerment, had long been believed and received by the company; from the cells of the household it had passed to the commons. All—"in marriage, in the priest-hood, in friendship, in all love"—remembered, in the everchanging hier-archical order, the particular substitution to which they were called (77). Wary of ostentation, they nevertheless gave and received easily, gaily, "love becoming fate to dedicate souls" (82).

The third order is restricted. Those who attain it co-inhere with each other and all with God as the Holy Trinity co-inheres. Man in this state is *restored* and made whole by the "one adored substitution" (86–87). The Virgin Mary became the supreme example of man's potential foresharing with Christ in the reconciling power of the Incarnation. She is mother of Him by whom she in turn was fathered. The few who knew "the whole charge" include Percivale, Dinadan, Dindrane, the archbishop, a mechanic here and a maid there (93). On rare occasions the poet himself catches glimp-ses of Logres as it might be if exchange "were willed and fulfilled" (96).

There follows one of the most complex passages in Williams's poetry, the summation of the poem up to this point, bringing together in one memorable image the thought, emotion, and sense of the co-inhering Trin-ity. Taliessin imagines himself standing on the high deck of a ship, perhaps the mythic ship of Solomon, and seeing, beyond Broceliande, the land of the Trinity, "a deep, strange island of granite growth" (99). It is a deep and ambiguous image: the island's durability suggests what we imagine the Trin-ity to be—the rock upon which His church is built. Granite is unyielding, inert. This rock, however, is a living growth and not inert matter. It is "thrice charged" with massive light that moves in a continuous pattern of change, "clear and golden-cream and rose tinctured," of light in darkness, of separation in oneness, of life in inertness, each of its parts at once the "Holder and the Held" (101–2). Small wonder that the eyes of the watcher alter and falter. They neither follow the rapid changes nor discern the de-tails in the pattern. Yet he realizes in the phenomena the primal law of all nature—all that lies potentially in Broceliande—rendered in an image that communicates to the limits of man's understanding the living substance of all that is "visible and invisible." It is not a rationally apprehended exposi-tion but a transcending experience. Beyond Broceliande and Carbonek, seen only in visionary image, lies the Trinity, land of perfect co-inherence, of "separateness without separation, reality without rift" (107). There the Basis, the Image, and the Gift—Father, Son, and Holy Spirit—live in a relation of perpetual exchange.

The summary word Williams uses is *perichoresis,* meaning literally "go-ing or rotating around" (106). It was first used by Damascenus to explicate the passage "I am in the Father, and the Father is in me." Later, because of the difficulty in understanding the sense in which the word was being used, it was frequently replaced by *circumincession,* the meaning of which is more immediately apparent. In itself it is an image of the co-inherent (indwelling in rotation and reciprocity) of the Trinity. The word was, no doubt, attractive to Williams because it suggested precisely those characteristics of the living granite. In its aliveness, hardness, and durability, it might well be imagined as the power to triumph over the flying figures that pursued Lamorack and Morgause.

One may ask, of course, if by using a word so technical, even esoteric, Williams might not have lost more than he gained. Many readers have indeed complained about a perceived eccentricity in Williams's diction. I think, however, that there is little pedantry or pretentiousness here. Above all, he demanded that language be accurate. Most popular talk about the Trinity is ineffectual because it is at best trite and more often meaningless. In case of those subjects of which one speaks only in images, Williams demanded that the image approximate the highest reaches of the imagination and that it be sufficiently vivid to suggest real meaning beyond its literal level. Williams's diction is integral to the mythical world in which he habitually lived, and which, I believe, he assumed, perhaps optimistically, others lived also. That world is analogous to but not identical with the contemporary one. Perhaps we should come to grips with it since it might be more enduring.

Stanzas 2 and 4 are concerned with the relation of the part to the whole, to the reassertion of the co-inherence. Stanza 5 considers the relation of the whole to the part and the return of personality after the impersonalities have passed for which Dindrane prayed in "The Departure of Dindrane." The role of the individual in the kingdom is measured within the frame of two related themes: the presence within the co-inherence of a dynamic, everchanging hierarchical order based on function or merit and governed by the laws of substitution and exchange; and the superfluity to God in his plenitude of man and his efforts.

Taliessin dreams of Dindrane, torn between his devotion to her and his duty to poetry and the kingdom, between his private love and his communal function, giving us one of the very few insights into Taliessin's intimate life. Dinadan appears and in his face Taliessin sees an analogical substitution for both Dindrane and poetry, the focus of "trifold light," a manifestation in him of the co-inherent Trinity. His momentary self-pity and regret vanish, and he accepts the truth of the taunt that if he is to save others he cannot save himself. When Dinadan refers to him as lieutenant, Taliessin protests that to claim such title exposes him to P'o-lu. The thought is emphasized in a series of rhymes: *do, to, P'o-lu, rue.* Dinadan replies that false modesty may be a vice as surely as pride. The co-inherent society is by its nature hierarchical, the various levels of order being based on either function or merit, sometimes on both—that is, a particular function that has been assigned or conceded by society (kingship, for example) or achieved by intellect and skill. The distinguishing marks of the co-inherence is that ordering of parts is never fixed. "We are not to suppose," Williams writes, "that the hierarchy of one moment is likely to be that of the next. The ranked degrees of intelligence are continually reordered. Sometimes you, and sometimes . . . I . . . shed light on the others; and it is then that you or I or that she is hierarchically ascendent, and at the next moment some other, and so onward" (Essays 127). One's position according to function may remain stable while, according to merit, it continually changes. Even the "Prime Minister must be docile to an expert scullion" (Essays 128). Taliessin is by virtue of both function and merit the master of his household. Nevertheless, God is the origin and the end of him and his slaves alike. Ultimately, the higher is caught in the lower and the lower in the higher. Any buyer of souls—and such, Dinadan says, Taliessin is—"is bought himself by his purchases" (131). Therefore, Dinadan concludes, Taliessin should take the lieutenancy "for the sake of the shyness the excellent absurdity holds" (132).

What at first seemed pride proves to be shyness. The "excellent absurdity" is that, on one level, he—not even the "lieutenant"—is master of no one. God is complete without his creation, and his sovereignty is not contingent on man's will or effort. Yet, Taliessin is superfluous to the company as he is to Dinadan and the kingdom. Even at Badon, Taliessin recalls, where he was hailed chief, the victory was won not by him alone but by the "masculine hearts" of his household charging in concert. His leadership might have fallen as readily to another. The only joy in service is that rendered as an act of giving and not of buying: it is indeed a "fetch [gift] / of grace" so to serve. "Any may be, one must" (143–45). On the Feast of Fools, indeed, when things, by an ironic reversal, are measured by a heavenly rather than earthly standard, the lowest wretch can be recognized, for the moment, as the greatest of all. The God-bearer herself is "the prime and sublime image of entire superfluity" (147). Even if she had rejected that fetch, God's plan would not have been thwarted.

Since God is all-sufficient and no man, at his best, more than an "image of peace"—a "needless" image—to those already in peace, Taliessin should, Dinadan says, take the lieutenancy and find his "comfort" in the cause. His task is to love God indirectly by loving those under his charge. Take the largesse and "think yourself the less; bless heaven" (153). So it was that Taliessin became for the "unformulated Company" its only bond of Unity beyond "the principle and the rule" (156). Unavowed to him, they nevertheless allowed the needless image of office with "joyous and high-restrained obeisance of laughter" (159).

The action of "The Queen's Servant," another poem about the Company and the spiritual co-inherence of its members, takes place on two levels. Externally the structure is simple. The first and third stanzas are an account of Taliessin's response to the Lord Kay's request that he provide from his household a girl to serve the queen, a position that carries freedom from slavery. The poet makes his choice and sends the newly freed girl off with his blessing. The middle section is more complex. The freedom granted by the external action is legal and has to do with the girl's relations within Logres. That described in the central section is internal and involves her relations within both Logres and the larger unity, the empire.

Both are presided over by Taliessin who makes the choice, signs the warrant, and seals it with his blessing. Throughout he recognizes his double role, referring to himself in the plural because he stands in place of the king who stands in place of the emperor who is "Operative Providence." On the surface his tone is light and joyous. Shuttleworth says:

> Here is Taliessin showing off his mastery of the Grand Art (which is not sanctity, but by no means excludes sanctity . . . for sanctity cannot be excluded, can it?). But the Grand Art is not belittled because it is not sanctity, however much sanctity may be considered preferable, . . . it is the way Charles and his young friends talked and walked and had their being—a background of sanctity as of poetry and Shakespeare. (Personal letter)

Williams's sense of body and soul as two modes of one being, as much a felt and lived experience as a theological conviction, made it impossible even in such a poem as this for him to speak meaningfully about either body or soul to the exclusion of the other. It is not surprising that this poem, whatever its origin or Williams's original intent, should in the course of its development take on broader and more profound significance. Nor is it inconsistent that the tone throughout remains light. Williams characteristically avoids what he called elsewhere both exterior and interior "fuss," writing always with a gay courtesy that distinguishes, he says, "the good manners of the City of God" (*Forgiveness* 71).

The theme is stated in Taliessin's charge: "now be free. / The royalties of Logres are not slavishly served" (13–14). The girl immediately challenges the possible misinterpretation that freedom and slavery are antithetical and that freedom in its fullest sense can be deserved. Not so. In spite of her faithful service, the freedom that Taliessin offers is possible only within the frame of his initial purchase. Her relation with him, master of her household, was from the beginning one of exchange, and, she says, he must continue to "hold well now to the purpose of the purchase" (21). Exchange involves mutuality; she not only receives but must also give.

Lines 21–83 detail Taliessin's role in freeing the girl personally. He, the poet, begins by evoking the spirit of Merlin, who represents duration and process, the magical (mystical) power of making. It is he who called Taliessin to be his instrument and charged him to image concretely in poetry the divine imageless. Rhyme, however, "trebles / the significance of time" by projecting the imagination beyond time to the timeless (24). Taliessin begins with Caucasia, the region in which he found the girl, although he realizes that external freedom is incomplete. She now looks disparagingly upon her old life; Taliessin, unwilling that any good be lost, describes the region as he sees it, imaginatively, in context of the whole of which it is part:

> The lambs
> that wander among roses of Caucasia are golden-lamped.
> I have seen from its blue skies a flurry of snow
> bright as a sudden irrepressible smile
> drive across a golden-fleeced landscape. (27–31)

Caucasia is the flesh, fallen but not inherently evil, marred but still beautiful to eyes that see. The imagery is encompassing. The lamb's wool signifies the useful; the rose, the beautiful, the organic; the blue skies, the clear and unclouded; the snow, the light and pure, as suddenly illuminating as an "irrepressible smile." Being insensitive to the poetry, however, she protests that she never saw such a place. Taliessin knows that there are ways by which blind eyes can be opened and made to see: by Merlin's maps, Taliessin's poetry, or by doctrine brought from Byzantium; even quicker and more effective, however, is experience. "Unclothe," he commands, asking in effect, that she cast aside timidity and return to that innocence in which she was created. "We," the poet says, "who bought you furnish you" (38). Even so, he hastens to make clear that he is not himself the Truth; he is "as truth," a type only (38). The unclothing is part of an initiation rite, a word Williams himself introduces into the poem in line 40, having anticipated it as early as lines 5–6: "one who knows / the rhythm of ceremony, also of the grand art." Once there, the word becomes inevitably a part of the poem's meaning. It is not overreading the poem, I think, to recall that in primitive Christian baptism the candidate shed his clothing, a symbol of discarding the old life, and walked naked into the water. Afterward, reclothed in white garments, symbol of new birth, he was given his first communion.

Rites, Williams insists, are the conscious evocation, the enfleshment, of myths that lie often hidden within man. Taliessin pursues: "know by Our sight the Rite that invokes Sarras / lively and lifelong" (40–42). The rite, however, is not itself Sarras. The importance of myth and ritual in the construction of social pattern is generally recognized. Joseph Campbell, for example, writes "Myths are the mental support of rites; rites, the physical enactments of myths" (35). Sacrament, the church says, is "an outward and visible sign of an inner grace." Campbell continues: "The characteristic effect of mythic themes and motifs translated into ritual, consequently, is that they link the individual to transindividual purposes and forces" (44). Williams would not have used the word *transindividual,* but rather one that linked man more specifically with other men *and* with God–in this case, the maid to Taliessin, the court, and the empire. That additional linking distinguishes the co-inherence.

Man lives both by his myths and his rites, which bring together the inner and outer life. For an Incarnationalist neither myth nor rite is complete without the other. The phrase "Our sight" refers to the imagination of the poet that, through the rite, evokes action beyond his own capacity to complete (40). At his command, the girl chooses and stands "shining-naked, / and rose-flushed . . . fair body and fair soul one organic / whole" (42–44). Thus the unity of all things is seen joyfully in the "high eirenical shire," the organic shire, of the poet's imagination. The quick clear eye, Taliessin says, will see in the rondures, especially of the naked body as in a trope of verse, the hope for the "beyond-sea meadows" (54). Thus Williams celebrates an inclusiveness often absent in sober Christian piety.

Transported by the rite, the girl stretches out her hand to catch the "crimson, centifoliae," which she flings at his feet. Under the mystic spell they stain the entire room with crimson, a reminder that all creation, including Caucasia, is capable of being redeemed and made organic:

> hued almost as the soft redeemed flesh
> hiding the flush of the rich redeemed blood
> in the land of the Trinity, where the Holy Ghost works
> creation and sanctification of flesh and blood. (88–91)

The reference in lines 75–76 to "a poet in Italy" is not immediately clear. Someone by the grace of our Lord rendering service to a beggar suggests Saint Francis. When Williams speaks of a poet in Italy, however, he most often means Dante. But neither Saint Francis nor Dante seems to fit this context. I suggest that the poet is Virgil and that Dante is the beggar, whom, after the loss of his initial vision of glory, Virgil directs from the "wood" through hell and purgatory, eventually delivering him to Beatrice on the threshold of heaven. So much poetry can do. So much has Taliessin done for this girl.

Beyond this, Taliessin cannot go since he himself is neither wizard nor saint. Startled by the girl's act of adoration, he hastens to redirect her attention. He sang, we are told, "a sweet borrowed craft from Broceliande," the source in time of all images of eternity (66). In response, the lambs shed their golden wool to clothe the girl with festive garments, useful and beautiful. The tangled curls fall with the roses and together they image the light "clear and roseal / or golden cream" (72–73).

The holy flesh, created by the Holy Spirit, is redeemed and glorified. In redemption the girl does not shed her flesh, nor in her new freedom is she relieved from servitude. Taliessin

> drew round her the old
> leathern girdle, for a bond and a quiet oath
> to gather freedom as once she gathered servitude. (93–95)

She continues to bear the marks of the old bondage as Christ retained in his resurrected body the scars of the sword and the prints of the nails. Delivered from the bonds of slavery, she became the servant of love, to remain, even in her absence, a member of the company, held by its rule of largesse and its vows of substitution and exchange:

> Let my Lord end this hour with a gift
> other than the Rite; that the Rite be certain, let
> my lord seal me to it and it to me. (103–5)

This request expresses a need for some human token to confirm the new relation into which she has entered.

Taliessin draws on a ceremony at once secular and sacred. In the manner of a Roman master freeing a slave and of a Roman bishop confirming a new convert, he strikes her lightly on the cheek, saying, "be the nothing we made you, making you something" (115). Thus her freedom is secured by inward grace, outward rite, and this further symbolic expression of human exchange. The blow, lightly struck, sounded loudly, nevertheless, to ears newly sensitized. Only the farewells remain:

He said: "Till death and after," and she: "Till death,
and so long as the whole creation has any being,
the derivation is certain, and the doom accomplished." (123–25)

The derivation is from God, and the doom, the end, is the renewed
co-inherence.

8

Beyond P'o-lu

"the feet of creation walk backward"
— "The Vision of the Empire," 131

The word *meditation* in the title of the poem "The Meditation of Mordred" is ordinarily associated with quiet thought, often as a spiritual exercise, of which "Taliessin in the Rose Garden" is an example. This poem, in ironic contrast, has as its theme the perversion of the co-inherent empire, summarized in the last line of the poem: "I will sit here alone in a kingdom of Paradise." Mordred exemplifies the Cain complex, that state of self-sufficiency that culminates always in a murderous negation of all life save one's own. The human element, the possible causes and the internal struggles that might have shaped Mordred's character and won our sympathy, are missing. He has already passed beyond Sodom, even Gomorrah, to that state where choice seems no longer possible. He has become the antithesis of human—a cynical, amoral perversion of co-inherence, depersonalized and reduced to the "nothingness" of that which existed before the Fall only as a contingency in the mind of God. He functions as a foil to the company and rounds out Williams's conception of the divine order. In order to be free, man must have the freedom to choose damnation.

The poem is also the story of the failed king. Indeed, the fate of Arthur and Mordred are interwoven, Mordred, in a sense, being the projection of Arthur's darker self, the contingency, the bastard son. Arthur, too, less openly and less ostentatiously, more hypocritically, Mordred would have said, subjected the kingdom to his own uses. He sought in Guinevere a royal consort more than a wife. Mordred, incestuously sired, carries to culmination Arthur's failures, which in him are untempered by good or nobility. We see the naked ego stripped of all largesse, an inhuman figure driven by physical lust and the urge for power: "Like son, like father; *adsum*, / said the steel trap to the wolf when the trap sprang" (31–32). *Adsum*

162

is the response of the schoolboy to the roll call: "I am here." Mordred is indeed there, a visible reminder of Arthur's wrong choices. In "Lamorack and the Queen Morgause of Orkney," we read of "The shape of a blind woman under the shape of a blind man," a blindness, however, that results inevitably from evil once it has been chosen and pursued. Arthur and Morgause failed to see that lust is really self-love, a violation of co-inherence. "She had his own face." The incest was merely the naming of one family of sin within the larger species. The deceptive power of any one sin is to be worse than it seems. There is a subtle similarity between the powerful trap and the softer predatory wolf. They are both instruments of destruction, engaged in a conflict in which the weaker is ensnared by the stronger. It pleases Mordred to think of himself as a steel trap and to depreciate Arthur as the victimized wolf.

The poem, without consistent story line, is an episodic projection of imagined events to which Mordred responds sensuously and emotionally. There is some appearance of thought. Mordred has not completely lost all use of intellect, but he has lost its good and thinks only distortedly and speciously. The narrative background implied in the poem, however, can be summarized briefly. Gawaine and Agravaine exposed Lancelot's and Guinevere's adultery and, in the fracas that followed, Lancelot, attempting to protect the queen, accidentally killed Gareth, younger brother of Gawaine and Agravaine. Partly for revenge and partly from what Williams calls "honour run mad," the brothers prevailed on the unwilling Arthur to wage war against his old friend. Arthur, leaving Mordred in charge of the kingdom, pursued Lancelot, and, seizing the opportunity, Mordred attempted to usurp the kingdom. The major theme of the poem is stated in the first section when Mordred ironically remarks that Arthur has fragmented the pope's letter demanding that he be reconciled with Lancelot. Instead, the king set "private affairs in front of public," further cutting Logres off from the empire (3). Mordred exults, "he has left to me the power of the kingdom and the glory," a cynical perversion of the lines from "The Crowning," "the kingdom and the power and the glory chimed" (4, 20). Now, at what might be called the uncrowning, Mordred seizes the power and claims for himself the kingdom and the glory.

Stanza 1 also introduces a recurring and unifying image: the trees. "The king has poled his horsemen" (1). In line 5 we learn that the poles came from the elms that Arthur has "dragged up," a verb suggesting violence. In line 6 the poles "stand immobilized round Lancelot," and in line 7 they are seen as steel points used to batter at Lancelot's defenses. In line 21 they respresent the inexhaustible living energy, the potential of all "making" in Logres, waiting to be used for the building of the kingdom and in preparation for the coming grail. Arthur, however, misuses the power, turning the trees into instruments of war, hoping, no doubt, to secure his own power. The image stands in stark contrast to the oak and the elm that in "The Last Voyage" have been lifted in the mystical Ship of Solomon to a "new ghosted power," linking Logres with Sarras. The image is extended still further in lines 23–26 where all London is seen as a forest of trees, a demented mob, throwing up arms like limbs and faces like "bare grinning leaves, a whole wood of moral wantons." Here they become images of dehumanization and of a return to the pre-Arthurian days in Logres. The perversion is felt throughout creation, human and natural. And, finally, in line 67 the image appears once again when Mordred foresees Arthur "fallen in the wood of his elms." In lines 45–64 the elms of Broceliande give way to the bamboos of P'o-lu. This extended and varied image is a structural device that helps unify the poem, the subject of which is the absence of Unity.

In Cabalistic lore there were diagrams of two trees, one before and the other after the Fall. In the Garden of Eden there were also two trees: the Tree of Life and the Tree of Knowledge of Good and Evil. Actually, the two were the same tree seen from opposing perspectives. The trees in this poem are the same as those that have appeared in other poems with the difference that these trees are viewed from the post-Fall point of view. They have trunks (stripped to immobile poles), branches (arms), and bare grinning leaves – but not fruits.

Stanzas 3 and 4 present a series of cynical contrasts. While Arthur ravages Gaul, Mordred rests on the palace roof, self-composed, confident, waiting for an opportunity to strike. "I too am a dragon," he proclaims, a Pendragon, although a bastard Pendragon (36). We recall those lines in "Bors to Elayne: on the King's Coins" that tell of little dragonlets, the coins, under whose weight house roofs "creak and break." Mordred watches the elms, intended for creative building, being turned instead into the instruments of destruction. He sees "honour mad" Gawaine and his, Mordred's, "uncanonical father" futilely battering the walls behind which Lancelot sits safe. The disgraced queen hides at Almesbury among the nuns. If he wished, he muses, he might parade her through Camelot and let the town "laugh and howl in a mania of righteousness," and he speculates cynically about what he perceives to be Camelot's double standard (15). It professes a Catholic (Christian) morality but practices a catholic (universal) mockery, an amorality. It really matters little whether one is a wittol, a passive cuckold like Arthur, or a whore like Guinevere. Either the wittol or the whore may become the excuse for war when personal power is at issue. His indictment of universal human nature includes the king, the queen, the contemptible mob, and even the pope himself. Arthur knows, Mordred says, that, if he fights and wins, the war once over, the pope will be pleased secretly if "his seal were avenged," if the ordered restoration were achieved even though by the forbidden violence.

Everything Mordred has said up to this point has been a "reasoned" self-justification. He has capacity for self-deception, claiming a prior sanction for his action, the will of the masses. They cry, he asserts, for his leadership. In line 30 the past tense ("Arthur had his importance") indicates that for him the uncrowning has effectually taken place. Mordred's time has arrived: *Adsum*. He differs from Arthur, he reasons, in that he, like the trap, is destined to dominate. Although he is a wolf, Arthur is outwitted and caught in his own snare.

Mordred refused to be enervated by his father's illusion but will pursue power with power. The word *luck* in line 37 suggests mere chance, blind and purposeless, not the "blessed luck" of events under divine protection. Mordred's world is without spiritual or moral dimension, and, for him, exchange is meaningless. Arthur, he says, depended on the grail, but he, in contrast, will prevail "without such fairy mechanism" (38). If the grail exists, which is unlikely, he vows he will send a dozen knights "to pull it in," and then he will turn it over to his cook to use as a cauldron (40). The passage is an oblique reference to the theory held by some critics that the grail is a further development of the vessels of plenty and the cauldrons of magic found in Celtic mythology—in short, that it owes its existence solely to natural processes, and not to the supernatural. Williams rejects this theory.

For Mordred, however, the presence of a magical pot is a small matter. He would be interested only if it had power to summon the "tiny-footed, slant-eyed wives" such as those who served Ala-ud-Din in P'o-lu (54). Williams apparently patterned the "small Emperor" after "Zemarchus the trader." According to Anne Scott, who gives credit to Richard Jeffery for discovering the information in the 11th edition of the *Encyclopedia Britannica*, in the last sixth century, Zemarchus led a Byzantine embassy that made a trade treaty with the Turkish khan.

Beyond the islands of Naked Man and the provinces of the Five Senses, the holy flesh lies, like Iseult's arm, "destitute, empty of glory"; beyond P'o-lu stretches another empire, where the small emperor sits among his women capriciously taking one to his bed, and, as the mood strikes, sending another to the swamps to die of thirst or to be eaten by crocodiles. As Taliessin had acknowledged his ideal in the emperor of Byzantium, Mordred finds his in that other beyond the bamboos. His prayer is that his kingdom come on Earth as it already is in P'o-lu. When Arthur has fallen, the grail been withdrawn, and Merlin returned to Broceliande, Mordred dreams, he will sit "alone in a kingdom of Paradise" (66). His end is undefeated irony.

9

Beyond Carbonek:
The Pattern in the Web

I began this study with the conviction that Williams's poetry was worthy of consideration as poetry. Throughout I have permitted it to speak for itself, presenting each poem as both an organic unit within itself and as part of a larger, coherent, skillfully executed vision of Williams's sense of what is real in human experience. The vision itself is intelligently conceived and, although expressed largely in terms of Christian theology, its scope, depth, and inclusiveness transcends sectarianism to become universal myth. It makes a statement beyond parochial limits.

It is more than just a statement, however. Expressed in a form that is emotional and sensuous as well as intellectual, it becomes poetry—the most comprehensive kind of poetry, mythical. Grounded on insights and values that are universal and timeless, it represents one effort in the twentieth century to perpetuate a continuing poetic tradition in a structure that speaks meaningfully to the contemporary reader.

I conclude with my initial conviction more firmly established in my own mind than ever, and, therefore, finish as I began by turning once again to the poetry itself. "The Prayers of the Pope," which concludes *The Region of the Summer Stars,* stands, I believe, as the consummation of Williams's thought and art. In it the clear outline of the pattern in the web is delineated most clearly and poetically.

"The Prayers of the Pope" is at once a summary, a transition, and a conclusion. It is a summary in that it gathers all the major themes of the Taliessin cycle into a co-inherent whole. It is a transition between the failed expectations for the immediate coming of the grail and the new reality that Logres-become-Britain confronted. It is a conclusion in that it says as nearly as poetry can what, I believe, Williams would have called his last words on the subject with which these two works have been concerned. The poem

166

removes the universal myth of man's redemption from the pages of history and establishes it firmly in the eternal present, coming close to communicating a sensed experience of what Williams quoted Aquinas as calling "the perfect and simultaneous possession of everlasting life."

Anne Ridler has written about the poem: "It is a most difficult poem to grasp, because it has to express, in the sequential form of poetry, happenings which require to be held simultaneously in the mind" (lxvi). Williams discusses the problem of time in *Reason and Beauty*, saying that there are three presents: the true, the specious, and the eternal. The first is the "immediate infinitely passing now"; the second, the present at any particular time "considered in relation to past and future." Of the third, he writes:

> That certainly is a different and more difficult thing, since we have not yet discovered any way of writing poetry in time which shall include all the experiences of time—"the perfect and simultaneous possession of everlasting life." But the greatest poetic experiences are of a nature which include the lesser. They do not explain them philosophically; they relate them poetically. (14)

In this poem Williams is concerned primarily with eternal time.

"The Prayers of the Pope" is composed of two kinds of material. There are those passages that are of specious time, explorations of the past and future as events flash through the pope's mind. These are the happenings that forestalled the Parousia, including the disintegration of Logres, culminating in the war between Arthur and Lancelot (stanza 3); the attack from without by barbaric hordes (stanza 4); the presence in the kingdom of "evil wizards" and the gnostics who denied the Incarnation (stanza 5); the treachery of Mordred (stanza 7); the dissolution of the company (stanza 9); the withdrawal of the grail; and, finally, the securing of the tentacles of P'o-lu (stanza 10).

The remaining sections are the pope's recollections, his identification with the events and the people involved in them, and his prayers for the redemption of time and the taking of manhood into God. These occur in the eternal present as they are offered in the Sacrament of the altar. This particular Christmas Mass signals the new epoch in the life of the church. Merlin, whose task was to prepare Logres for the grail's coming, departs after the table is destroyed and the grail is withdrawn. In place of the Parousia, we have the pope and his Mass, a continuing action in time, the mystic presence in the bread and wine, incarnationally, sacramentally, less a new creation than a reclamation and a restoration of that which was from the beginning.

In contrast to Merlin's black hair, the young pope's hair is white, not because of passing time but from the loss he suffers. As Williams states it, "The Pope (let us say) is time, losing its beauties (by deprivation or will, not by mere passing change) but affirmatively" (Ridler lxv). Merlin represents time as extension; the pope, as priest, represents time as simultaneity. His task is not the immediate apocalypse but the faithful ministering of the Sacrament, "the tri-fold Eucharist, while the world waits for the consummation of the kingdom" (10).

In the "candled shroud of dark," he prays before "the intinctured Body," both Body and Blood mystically present in the bread, exposed in the reliquary over the altar (11, 9). He speaks Virgil's new colloquial Latin, marking the transition from the old Lupercal to the new Lateran, "hastening by measure the flood of the soul in the blood," restoration of the Unity (15). The pope's *Magnificat*, like the Virgin's, praises the "total Birth intending the total Death" (16–17). Jesus was complete man and complete God, not man endued with the God-spirit at the time of his baptism, nor the all-God temporarily residing in an apparent body from which he departed before he was crucified. Nothing less could heal the breach that the Fall had affected in the Unbreachable. His death was a total loss, not of a single image nor even of all images but of the unimaged love itself. There is in creation so intricate a relation between the unimaged and the sum total of all creative acts, that body of co-inhering images, that to lose one fragment is to lose the whole. In the sense of defeated irony, of course, all the images through the process of affirmation must be lost, assumed, that is, into the unimaged so that the many are again One. For the present, however, any loss of image is loss also of substance. When the "Son of man" comes, he will bring not a hope to be realized, but Himself, the reality possessed.

Stanza 1 concludes with a refrain that is heard throughout: "Send not, send not, the rich empty away." Who then shall enter the kingdom? Not the worldly rich man who enjoys the security of possessions, but rather the spiritually rich, the "poor in spirit" who hunger and thirst after righteousness. One cannot desire fullness without first feeling emptiness; one cannot suffer loss without affirming the possibility of fullness. The prayer, then, is that those rich in a sense of need be rewarded, either because of their sense of loss or for their reach after wholeness.

The pope's losses are not merely personal, although his hair has turned white from sorrow. He stands always, in the Catholic tradition, as his people's representative before God. "It is with the intention of substituted love," Williams writes, "that all 'intercessory' prayer must be charged" (*HCD* 129). In stanza 2 the pope recalls the disintegration of Logres, fixing particularly on events that have destroyed the kingdom from within: the "bleak wars";

Gawaine's vengeance; Mordred's "whoring with fantasy"—all catalysts for events that lead to the death of Arthur, Gawaine, Mordred, and Dinadan (31). Mordred's whoring with fantasy recalls the biblical denunciation of Israel for "whoring after other gods"—Mordred's other god being himself and his sin the consummation of Arthur's incest in his own self-love. From "roaring Camelot" madness spreads to the Thames and to the governors, who, rejecting their natural Center, the emperor, choose from "among themselves, puppets of reputation, / void of communicated generation of glory," leaders who cease to be the generation of that glory that is communicated, derived and not self-generated (38–39). In line 41 the word *let* is used both in the archaic sense of hindering and in the current sense of permitting. The leaderless mob let, permitted, the Acts of the Throne to be obstructed by the infidels and the pattern of organic order to be lost. Rejecting the pattern of natural co-inherence, the rulers of Logres reaffirmed as now happening the choice of the Adam and "escaped back to the old neocromantic gnosis / of separation" (45–46).

Physical death, present everywhere in the kingdom, is the consummate expression of the separation of body from soul. Of the Crucifixion, for example, Williams wrote:

> This state of things He inexorably proposed to Himself to endure; say, rather, that from the beginning He had been Himself at bottom both the endurance and the thing endured. This had been true everywhere in all men; it was now true of Himself apart from all men; it was local and particular. The physical body which was His own means of union with matter, and was in consequence the very cause, centre, and origin of all human creation, was exposed to the complete contradiction of itself. (Essays 136)

Surely to love that contradiction is the ultimate obscenity, as perverse as erotic love for corpses. Ironically, fearing to lose themselves in others, the people of Logres delivered "one another" to reprobation—Mordred, or the kahn of the Huns, or the khalif of Asia, or, as often, a neighbor whose labor of love shamed them. The word *reprobation* conveys more than mere punishment, having also the connotation of eternal damnation. The irony is that in sentencing others they sentenced themselves also. Rejecting the city, they created their own little systems, becoming in the process "mutes or rhetoricians instead of sacred poets" (52). They perverted words and the Word. Dante assigns such to their natural place in the lake of human excrement. Williams remarks: "Flattery is precisely the unfruitful excrement of mankind; its evil is that it asserts falsely what can be asserted truly. . . . meaning is lost, accuracy is lost, and accuracy is fruitfulness. . . . The word itself is either spiritual truth or else verbal excrement" (*Beatrice* 133). The abuse of language inevitably destroys communication and distorts both inner and outer life of the kingdom.

Under the weight of such desolation, the pope prays, the burden of his petition being that a sense of loss is itself an affirmation, in fact, a "double affirmation – image and the opposite of image," the unimaged (60). The one gain, he says, is God himself, the one lack, his absence. Jesus was never more God-man than when he prayed, "Why hast thou forsaken me?" In that terrible moment he revealed himself as the self-annihilating love that is God. His statement, "It is finished," Williams says, is the real triumph of Easter: "It is at that moment that Easter began. . . . Life has known absolutely all its own contradiction. He survives; He perfectly survives. . . . His actual death becomes almost a part of His Resurrection, almost what Patmore called the death of the Divine Mother, a 'ceremony'" (Essays 136–37).

In stanza 4 the pope senses as his own all the dangers to Logres from without. The protective lines give way along the Danube and the Rhine, and the tale of peace, the coming of the grail, fades into Logres and Latetia (the old Roman name for Paris). The "Noel-song" of peace on Earth gives way to a bloody song of discord. Birth and death are indeed closely allied. We are reminded of the slaughter of the Innocents by whose deaths the baby Jesus was spared, an incident Williams justifies only because Jesus, in turn, gave his life in exchange for all babies, them and those to be.

Birth and death, the ambivalent shedding of blood in wrath and sacrifice, to destroy and to save, are inextricably interwoven. Logres returns to its original barbarism. The now bleak plains are swept by "myths bitter to bondage" (71). The "in-oneing" of all the myths in the one Myth is once again frustrated and unity is replaced by "moods infinitely multiplied" (69). Each warring chieftain claims virtue for himself and prizes his schism as a perverse grace. The barbarians storm the land, stamping into darkness cities "whose burning had lamped their path" (78). The whole passage is a description of the triumph of division, a factual account of an episode in history and a symbol of the continuing state of man since the Fall. Both the facts and the image are made vividly present and personally intense to the pope. "Where is the difference between us?" he asks. Where, indeed, is the dividing line between friend and foe? Both have their causes and their catapults, motives and means; both suffer the result of their folly, "the death of a brave beauty" (83). We, the pope and those for whom he speaks, share sin with all mankind. The saving difference is "that we declare – O Blessed, pardon affirmation! – / and they deny – O Blessed, pardon negation!" (85–86). The pope prays for the "double wealth of repentance," grace both to forgive and to accept forgiveness (90).

Tension mounts in stanza 5 as the pope meditates on the nature of evil exemplified in the "wizards, / the seers of the heathen" (92–93). Their black magic is the converse of Merlin's white magic. Their physical deformity, lack of manipulative and useful hands, signals a corresponding spiritual aberration. The words *reversed* and *accursed,* referring to the pentagram, are equally descriptive of all their nefarious powers (94). The sacred pentagram, in the hands of the wizards, has been reversed to signify perversion rather than unity, "the backward walking feet." Drawing on the powers of P'o-lu, the wizards call upon "smouldering deities whose very names were lost" (98). They uttered "half-broken and half-spoken" syllables because they were incapable of speaking the Word that was, in the beginning, with God who alone is capable of real creation. They were not without potential power, but their conjurings were limited at best to obscene and insubstantial parodies of real creation. Fallen man's obsession to create and thus control life is a continuing theme in Williams's work. Here the wizards

> called and enthralled the dead,
> the poor, long-dead, long-buried, decomposing
> shapes of humanity. . . . (106–08)

Death, Williams writes, "is an outrage, it is a necessary outrage. It is schism between those two great categories of physical and spiritual which formed the declaration in unity of one identity" (*Forgiveness* 26). Here there is no resurrection but an obscene confirmation of separation. The wizards conjure with a desecrated hazel, producing "bloodless" shapes, parodies without the Blood in which is life. They are automatons, mechanized forms in which all sense of justice and co-inherence is missing. The leaders of Logres, sensed in a portent of their own future, felt the coming cold, loss of the grail and the return to barbarism. The word *drumming,* rhyming with *coming,* and the heavily accented rhythms of the line are, no doubt, intended to suggest the drumbeat of a death march:

> from graves
> drawn by maleficent spells, but too-veritable ghosts
> before those hosts moving in a terrible twilight. (129–31)

The adjective *veritable* emphasizes that the shapes are indeed ghosts, and, being ghosts, cannot be wholly man. That "terrible twilight" falling over

Logres, settles in stanza 6 over the pope's spirit, signaling his own dark night of the soul. He experiences the ruin of the empire, its death becoming his death in all its tearing divisions, its dreadful autonomy, its self-absorption. He is the perfect example of substitution and exchange, his brain throbbing as one with "the little insane brain whimpering of pain / and its past" (137–38).

The burden of the unredeemed falls upon the pope, and he feels a fire in his body and a chill in his brain. The fixation upon the category destroys rather than defines the part's identity and splits the "themes" from the "identical glory" of the empire with which they were originally mated. "Such is death's outrage" (145–46). In the lines that immediately follow, Williams brings together in a single flash of experience the pope's offering of himself as a substitute for all Logres: "so the Pope / died in a foretasting" (146–47). He thinks first of Mordred and then beyond Mordred of the universal paradox of which he is a type: "Against the rule of the Emperor the indivisible / Empire was divided" (151–52). The division of the indivisible empire brings into clear focus a contradiction that, Williams himself believed, lay at the center of things: the conviction that all creation, intended as indivisible, is perversely divided against itself. The "Cressida experience," to which I have already referred, ceases to be personal and limited and becomes universal. Arthur *cannot* have used the kingdom for his own self-centered interests, but he has. The queen *cannot* have committed adultery with Lancelot, but she has. Pelles *cannot* still await reunion with Arthur, but he does. Logres *cannot* have become mere Britain, but it has.

Arthur and Mordred are images of every man at odds with his own nature. Mordred hungered for power and waited for opportunity. Derisively dismissing Arthur's vision of the grail, he seized the throne and allied himself with his father's old enemies. A spirit of discord engulfed the kingdom, and all Logres "burst and curst" the co-inherence (163). Mordred enhanced ("assuaged") his own image by identifying himself with the throne and setting both himself and the office against the powers of the empire, thus "begetting by the succubus of his own longing" (the fanciful creation of his own mind) the falsity and incoherence of all images (166). A succubus is a disincarnate spirit that in the form of a woman has sterile sexual intercourse with a man. Mordred's union with the succubus, an extension of Arthur's incest, produces not new life but a parody as bloodless as those corpses raised by the wizard's conjuring. The unholy union negates all images because a succubus has no substance.

The pope, in his priestly office, seeks to reconcile seemingly irreconcilable heaven and its negation, praying for the restoration of "the double inseparable wonder, / the irrevocable union" (170–71). He seeks confirmation not only of God in the image but of all images in God, who is the "term," consummation, of all images. The co-inherence is a perception of intellectual love that brings into unity worldly beauty ("the rose gardens"), theological formulations ("wardens of the divine science"), "the sacred Heart of Love," the "Flesh-taker," Jesus, Mary, and, by extension, all submissive human wills. In that union the Maker himself becomes a sharer and the making is experienced as love responding to love. Mary, "the chief of the images," was the mother of the unimaged, Jesus, but she was also His child; His mother who was her Father (177). Only through such submission of the human to the divine, and, inexplicably, of the divine to the human, can love be freed to become not merely an image or the sum of all images, but, beyond the image, wholly Itself, the unimaged. The pope countered the divided-indivisible with a vision of the Flesh-taker and God-bearer as the chief images of the co-inherence. In stanza 9 he turns to Taliessin and his household as exemplars of that union present in what remains of Logres. "Taliessin gathered his people before the battle" (187). The poet had led the charge at Mount Badon, and now, after the fading of Logres, he gathers his household for a different enterprise. He stands skeptically contemplating a new era: "the Table may end to-morrow," he says (185). Even if it survive, he knows, it will be changed. Here, however, as in the beginning, he senses urgency. He pauses, lifting "his hands to the level of his brow"–the Bright Forehead that was once young–in a symbolic gesture reminding us that he is both the visionary poet and a doer of deeds. In this stance, he declares, "We dissolve / the outer bonds" (193). His hand drops, a confirming signal of his changing role in the changing situation. He reminds them that the bonds that had existed between them were only an outward sign of their will to serve, not him, but the co-inherence. He had long acknowledged his superfluity and now willingly returns to God the "once-permitted lieutenancy" (198).

In "Taliessin at Lancelot's Mass," "that which had been Taliessin" was assumed into the greater, the Bread and the Wine of the altar where the poet rested "manacled by the web, in the web made free." Thus the lesser is at last fulfilled in the greater. The company will no longer receive the offices of the lieutenancy through Taliessin but will find them in the sacramental gifts. Taliessin's departure coincides with the withdrawal of the grail. The time for the direct transmission has passed; that of the indirect has come. "This," says a member of the household, "is the last largesse" (204). Now in a sense, each man will be a lieutenant within the ever changing hierarchy of the co-inherent body. The kingdom has failed, and barbarism seems to have triumphed, but a remnant of the faithful remains.

Even, perhaps especially, in this new society, however, the need for images, myths, and rituals continues. The company asks, once again, the privilege of recognizing the "superfluous necessity" by renewing the old bonds—only this time they realize the true relation between rite and substance. Taliessin assents, acknowledging the necessity that someone, something, be "the air in which the summer stars shine," the material means through which the divine light is transmitted (212). Air is at once a mixture of gases, which could be considered a substance, and at the same time, it is without visible properties. It partakes of and radiates the light without itself being the light's source. It is "the mode only of their placing and gracing":

> lightly each in turn and each with the other,
> and each with the king's poet . . .
> all the household exchanged the kiss of peace. (213, 215–17)

The image is not rejected. The company, no longer wholly dependent on Taliessin, pledge their love to the community, seen and unseen, visible and invisible, and within that "great cloud of witnesses" they are Taliessin's forever and he is theirs.

The pope prays for the company and for himself, "Keep thy own for thyself," an echo of Jesus' priestly prayer: "Holy Father, keep through thy own name those whom thou hast given me, that they may be one, as we are." The pope also prays for the "unknown elect," asking for security, not freedom. What "recovers / lovers in lovers is love" (231–32)—love, not lovers. Progression from being in love with someone is simply being in love. Love is both more and less than often imagined. In *The Greater Trumps,* Sybil advises Nancy to return to her lover, who at that moment is attempting to kill her father, with what is to Nancy astonishing advice: "Go and live, go and love. Get farther, get farther—now, with Henry if you can. If not—listen, Nancy—if *not,* and if you love him, then go and agonize to adore the truth of Love" (165). Paolo and Francesca loved, Williams concedes, and their formal sin was adultery, but their damnation, their poetic sin, was their shrinking from the adult love demanded of them and their "refusal of the opportunity of glory" (*Beatrice* 118). They never got beyond the first sweet tantalizing kiss. Only being an adult in love equips one to

> go into every den of magic and mutiny,
> touch the sick and the sick be healed, take
> the trick of the weak devils with peace, and speak
> at last on the coast of the land of the Trinity the tongue
> of the Holy Ghost. (233–37)

The gospel commission is positive. In love disciples are to go into dens of magic (superstition and perversion) and in mutiny, political and social, and through love cure the sick, confound the devils of division, and proclaim the Unity. This is Williams's poetic paraphrase of the words attributed to Jesus by Mark: "In my name shall they cast out devils; they shall speak with new tongues; They shall take up serpents; and if they drink any deadly thing, it shall not hurt them; they shall lay hands on the sick, and they shall recover" (16:17–18). Love is the antidote to all poisonous hate.

For this renewed vision of the earthly company united by the kiss of peace, the pope turns next to its heavenly archetype, Sarras, the land of the Trinity. Stanza 11 is an apocalyptic vision of the triumph of good over evil and the coming of Sarras. To penetrate that mystery, however, requires more than poetic imagination. Beyond Taliessin we must "proceed to Percivale," Williams said, beyond Carbonek to Jupiter. The mystical ship of Solomon, steered by a power beyond man's, carried the three lords to their destination. Taliessin, not included among the achievers, is left, like Virgil in the *Divine Comedy*, standing on heaven's threshold. Poetry cannot storm heaven.

The phrase "year and a day" in line 248 represents the same period of time as that indicated in lines 258–60. The long trance in Sarras and the ultimate triumph of Broceliande over P'o-lu are happening concurrently. The term "year and a day" is a legal one used in cases to assure that the conditions requiring a full year be unquestionably satisfied. In myth and poetry it often signifies any long period of time, sometimes suggesting extended suffering, as, for example, a term in purgatory. Here the three lords are "waiting among moving rocks and granite voices / the dawn hour of the tri-toned light" (249–50).

The language is reminiscent of the description of the Holy Trinity in "The Founding of the Company" and in the image of the perichoresis in "Taliessin in the Rose Garden." The lords await the time when "in fine" (finally) they will be drawn into the canon (brought under the rule of) the grail. It is, in short, a purgatorial period before Galahad is assumed into Sarras and Bors is returned to Logres. Line 258, "The sun outward ran a year's journey," must be read metaphorically as the time required by the sun to pass through all the houses of the zodiac and thus in its apparent revolution to complete the circle, symbol of God's universal sovereignty. The poetic image is one of interrelation and exchange within the co-inherent cosmos. Bors's mission upon his return to Britain will be to perpetuate the tradition of the grail, following in the kingdom the light of the sun and the example of Dindrane who gave herself as a substitution for another.

In the fate of the three we witness divine grace operating in relation to all humanity, which they, in their different modes, represent. In stanza 11 we see the reassertion of God's sovereignty over the cosmos with the ultimate defeat on Earth of the contingent powers of evil. The action is a reenactment of the harrowing of hell following the Crucifixion (299). The episode is especially crucial in the pope's contemplation as he faces the new era in which the church awaits the working out on Earth of that which already is in heaven. The sun ran, saw, and shuddered as the bounds of the empire gave way under the powers of P'o-lu. The tentacles of the octopods reached out in all directions, feeling, and even more disturbing, grappling under the sea, heading inward toward the very center of Broceliande. It is a situation that recalls the one so vividly expressed in a line in *Paradise Lost* that Williams often quoted: "Warring in heaven against heaven's matchless king." "A complete and obstinate futility is perfectly expressed," Williams comments; "all the future is defined in 'matchless,' all the insanity 'in heaven against heaven's . . . king'" (*RB* 15). And the tentacles

> touched and clutched,
> somewhere in the deep seas, something that invited
> holding—and they held, enfolding—and the tentacles folded
> round long, stretched limbs, like somewhat of themselves
> but harder and huger; the tentacles were touched and clutched,
> flung and were clung to, clung and were not flung off,
> brainlessly hastened and brainfully were hastened to. (268–74)

Hell, Williams says, is inaccuracy. The indefiniteness of such words as *somewhere, something,* and *somewhat* suggests the inaccurate calculations of P'o-lu, and, at the same time, the inexpressibility, the "matchlessness," of the powers against which hell warred. The tentacles were "somewhat" like the roots with which they grappled, just as evil is somewhat like the good—but totally different. The tentacles could do no more than "brainlessly" hasten toward the "brainful" resisting roots. The octopods represent those men who have lost the good not only of manipulative hands but also of intellect. The struggle, though doomed, is nevertheless tenacious. Something of its brainless sinking and slinking, touching and clutching, clinging and flinging is suggested in the internal rhyme that pulls the reader from line to line almost too rapidly for his mind to keep pace. The roots of Broceliande fasten on the tentacles in that spaceless ocean of eternity where all distance is accumulated and is at once everything and no-thing. They are hollow because they have no substance. Evil lacks ontological existence—the power from within itself—but certainly it is an existential fact. Its presence and its operation within creation, including the mind of man, is real, as Logres is discovering and as the pope vicariously experiences.

Those who say Williams ignores the reality of evil have not read him accurately. At the center of Christian thought is the Cross—the Cross and Love crucified on it. What Williams rejected was dualism, a possibility that creation owed its existence to rival creative powers. The tentacles are caught and fixed "to a regimen," held firmly within the sure grip of Broceliande where they will cling hypnotically at the tenacious roots (280). The bounds of the empire, which seemed to be breaking, will not be obliterated. The wizard and the gods of the heathens will helplessly dwindle, and even the headless emperor will sink and dissolve in the "uncoped sea":

> a crimson tincture, a formless colour, the foul
> image of the rose-gardens of Caucasia now
> losing itself, drifting in the waters, and none
> to know what was real and what unreal
> or what of sense stayed in the vagrant phosphorescence
> save the deep impassable Trinity in the land of the Trinity,
> uttering unsearchable bliss. (287–93)

In short, what seems a victory for the forces of barbarism and the defeat of the grail is only a dark, painful pause on the way toward the eventual Parousia. The headless emperor is not eradicated because he existed only as a humanly willed perversion of the emperor. He dissolved, leaving on the surface of eternity only "a crimson tincture, a formless colour" (247). Even Jesus' resurrected body bore the scars. P'o-lu's undoing was the spilled blood on Calvary. What of this apparition was real and what unreal? Only the deep impassable Trinity can really know (292). Whatever its destiny, however, it like all other things will be made eventually part of the "unsearchable bliss" that passes human understanding (233).

The entranced lords stirred—we are back at the beginning of the poem—as the "triple-toned light broke upon them" (294). They received in their own mode their destined function within the co-inherence. The roses of the world bloom and the women everywhere walk companionably in peace.

Stanza 12 is a kind of benedictus. Christ has harrowed hell and carried away "the last token" of himself; that is, he separated the real from the illusory and redeemed every token of substance. In the beginning God had spoken creation into existence, and now the Son, having stormed the center of its perversion, speaks the restoration, "qualifying" (bringing into unity) the Acts with eternity:

> That Thou only canst be, Thou only
> everywhere art; let hell also confess thee,
> bless thee, praise thee, and magnify thee for ever. (303–05)

At the beginning the pope waited; now, personal preparations completed, he passes into what Williams calls an "eternal state of contemporaneousness" (*HCD* 67) to the altar to celebrate the perpetual coming of the new birth, the continuing Incarnation. "The new life," Williams says, "might still be sequential (in the order of time) but every instant was united to the origin and complete and absolute in itself" (*HCD* 81). The Eucharist, which the pope celebrates, does not so much prolong the sacrifice in time as gather time into an eternal oneness with the sacrifice. He begins with what is doubtlessly the most difficult aspect of the co-inherence to accept, the invocation of peace upon the bodies and souls of the dead, "yoked fast to him and he to them" (308).

"The vicarious life of the kingdom," Williams asserts, "is not necessarily confined to sequence even among the human members of the kingdom. The past and the future are subject to interchange, as the present with both, the dead with the living, the living with the dead"—as, for example, in "Taliessin on the Death of Virgil" (*HCD* 130). The "magical march of the dead" was a deception because the necromancers, capable only of "vengence and the value of victory," had no power to restore Unity (310, 312). The knowledge of the separation, felt as his own by the pope, and the willing substitution of his own health—guilt, repentance, wealth (in loss) for their woe—into a "junction of communion" in the Body and Blood, became a "promulgation of sacred union" (315–16). He was, in his own degree, a repetition of the archetypal substitution on Calvary and a type of what all men must become. His prayers were effective because they were substantive. He did not only offer petitions for the dead but became himself one with the dead. Through his substance (prayer and acts) the company around him were moved to the invoked Body of the total, unimaged loss, and, by that loss, first borne by Christ and now repeated by the pope, their Unity, body and soul, was restored. Accepting their first death, they escaped the more terrible second death, permitting their corruptible bodies to disintegrate in order that they might be raised incorruptible. With that act of willed surrender, they reduced the magicians to impotency and left them hanging helpless in the air.

The light over the empire had darkened, Logres had become mere Britain, the church had begun its reconciliation with time, and the Parousia had receded to some unknown point in the future. Nevertheless, at and through the celebration of the Christmas Eucharist, consuls and lords within the empire "revive in a live hope of the Sacred City" (333).

Works Cited

Abercrombie, Lascelles. *The Epic*. London: Martin Secker, 1914.

Campbell, Joseph. *Myths to Live By*. London: Paladin Books, Granada Publishing, Ltd., 1985.

Eliot, Thomas S. *Collected Essays*. New York: Harcourt, Brace, 1932.

———. *On Poetry and Poets*. London: Faber and Faber, 1957.

Gilbert, R. A. *A. E. Waite: Magician of Many Parts*. Wellingborough, Northamptonshire: Crucible: Thorsons Publishing Group, 1987.

Jung, C. G. *Four Archetypes*. Extracted from *The Archetypes and the Collective Unconscious*, Bollingen Series Vol. 9, pt. 1 of *The Collected Works of C. G. Jung*. Trans. R. F. C. Hull. Princeton: Princeton University Press, 1969. Princeton/Bollingen Paperback Edition. 1970.

Kilby, C. S. "The Outer Dimensions of Myth." *Myth Lore* 38 (Spring 1984): 28–30.

Lewis, C. S. *Arthurian Torso: Containing the Posthumous Fragment of* The Figure of Arthur *by Charles Williams and a Commentary on the Arthurian Poems of Charles Williams*. [*AT*]. London: Oxford University Press, 1948.

McClatchey, Joe. "The Diagrammatised Glory of Charles Williams' *Taliessin through Logres*." *VII: An Anglo-American Literary Review* 2 (March 1981): 100–125.

———. "Charles Williams and the Arthurian Tradition." Marion E. Wade Lecture. Wheaton College, Wheaton, Ill., 1986.

Raine, Kathleen. *Defending Ancient Springs*. London: Oxford University Press, 1977.

Regardie, Israel. *The Golden Dawn*. Rev. ed. Vols. 1 and 2. St. Paul, Minn.: Llewellyn Publications, 1984.

Ridler, Anne, ed. *The Image of the City and Other Essays*. "Introduction," ix–lxxii; "Introductory Note to the Arthurian Essays," 163–75. London: Oxford University Press, 1958.

Supplements to *Charles Williams Society Newsletter*. [Supl.]. 1–29. London, 1977–86.

Waite, Arthur Edward. *The Hidden Church of the Holy Grail*. London: Rebman, Ltd., 1909.

Williams, Charles. *All Hallows' Eve*. London: Faber and Faber, 1945.

———. *The Descent of the Dove: A Short History of the Holy Spirit in the Church*. [*DD*]. London: Longmans, Green, 1939.

———. *Descent into Hell*. [*Descent*]. London: Faber and Faber, 1937.

———. *The English Poetic Mind*. [*EPM*]. Oxford: Clarendon Press, 1932.

———. Essays. In Ridler, Anne, ed. *The Image of the City and Other Essays*.

———. "Figure of Arthur." [FA]. In Lewis, C. S. *Arthurian Torso*.

———. *The Figure of Beatrice*. [*Beatrice*]. London: Faber and Faber, 1943.

———. *The Forgiveness of Sins*. London: G. Bles, 1942.

———. *The Greater Trumps*. London: Victor Gollancz, 1932.

———. *He Came Down from Heaven*. [*HCD*]. I Believe Series, No. 5. London: Heinemann, 1938.

———. *Heroes and Kings*. London: Sylvan Press, 1930.

———. Letters to Raymond Hunt. [Hunt]. Originals in Marion E. Wade Center, Wheaton College, Wheaton, Ill.

———. Letters to Thelma Shuttleworth. [Shuttleworth]. Originals in Bodelian Library, Oxford, England.

———. Letters to His Wife, 1939–45. [Mrs. Williams]. Originals in Marion E. Wade Center, Wheaton College, Wheaton, Ill.

———. Notes to C. S. Lewis. Notes on *Taliessin through Logres* prepared in response to questions from C. S. Lewis. [Notes]. Copy provided to author by Thelma Shuttleworth.

———. *The Place of the Lion*. London: Mundanus (V. Gollancz), 1931.

———. *Poetry at Present*. Oxford: Clarendon Press, 1932.

———. *Reason and Beauty in the Poetic Mind*. [*RB*]. Oxford: Clarendon Press, 1932.

——— *The Region of the Summer Stars*. London: PL, Editions Poetry London, Nicholson and Watson, 1944.

———. *Shadows of Ecstasy*. London: Victor Gollancz, 1948.

———. *The Story of the Aeneid*. [*Story*]. Retold by Charles Williams. London: Oxford University Press, 1936.

———. *Taliessin through Logres*. London: Oxford University Press, 1938.

———. *Thomas Cranmer of Canterbury*. London: Oxford University Press, 1936.

———. *War in Heaven*. London: Victor Gollancz, 1930.

———. *Windows of Night*. London: Oxford University Press, 1936.

———. *Witchcraft*. London: Faber and Faber, 1941.

Index

181

DATE DUE
